Criminal Justice in Islam

'This timely volume offers extremely valuable insights for anyone attempting to understand a field that has thus far been so poorly represented, and yet which governs the lives of a substantial portion of the world's population. The essays in this book represent an important contribution to ongoing debates on the topic of Islamic Jurisprudence, and should be taken as a starting point for any such discussion.'

—Awad Muhammed El-Murr, former Chief Justice of the Supreme Constitutional Court of Egypt

Criminal Justice in Islam

Judicial Procedure in the Sharīʿa

Edited by
Muhammad Abdel Haleem
Adel Omar Sherif
Kate Daniels

I.B. TAURIS
LONDON · NEW YORK

New paperback edition published in 2018 by
I.B.Tauris & Co. Ltd
London • New York
www.ibtauris.com

First published in hardback in 2003 by I.B.Tauris & Co. Ltd

ISBN: 978 1 78831 062 8
ePDF: 978 0 85771 174 8

A full CIP record for this book is available from the British Library
A full CIP record is available from the Library of Congress

Library of Congress Catalog Card Number: available

Printed and bound by CPI Group (UK) Ltd, Croydon, CR0 4YY
from camera-ready copy edited and supplied
by The Centre of Islamic Studies

Contents

Editors' Introduction vii

Part One: Generalities and Basic Principles

1 Generalities on Criminal Procedure under Islamic Sharīʿa 3
Adel Omar Sherif

2 Basic Principles of Criminal Procedure under Islamic Sharīʿa 17
Saeed Hasan Ibrahim and *Nasir bin Ibrahim Mehemeed*

3 Basic Guarantees in the Islamic Criminal Justice System 35
Gamil Muhammed Hussein

Part Two: Individual Protection, Punishments and Remedies

4 The Right to Personal Safety (*Ḥaqq al-Amn*) and the Principle of Legality in Islamic Sharīʿa 57
Mohammad Hashim Kamali

5 Compensation for Homicide in Islamic Sharīʿa 97
Muhammad Abdel Haleem

Part Three: Evidence and International Crimes

6 Confession and Other Methods of Evidence in Islamic Procedural Jurisprudence 111
Mohamed Selim El-Awa

Editors' Introduction*

From 22–23 October 1997, the Centre of Islamic Studies at the School of Oriental and African Studies, University of London, hosted a symposium on 'Criminal Procedure in Islamic Law', focusing on topics relating to the field of Islamic jurisprudence. The symposium attained even greater significance owing to legal events taking place in Saudi Arabia at that time; specifically, two British nurses had been charged with the murder of an Australian colleague, in a case that was drawing worldwide media and diplomatic attention. The prevailing topic of discussion in the media was whether a fair trial was really possible under Islamic law in general, and in the context of that case in particular. Thus, the symposium took on the challenge of addressing both this and related issues through the contributions of scholars, jurists and legal professionals from both the West and the Islamic world.

The single most important conclusion reached at the symposium was that there is a highly developed system of criminal procedure built into Islamic Sharīʿa that provides broad guarantees and protections for both the accused and the victims of crimes. Its contributors highlighted the fact that misperceptions about Islamic Sharīʿa, and the protections and guarantees provided thereunder, are due in no small part to the coincidence of two factors. First is the marginalization of the Islamic world by mainstream western scholarship on account of its 'otherness', its perceived treatment of women, and its unwitting connection with anti-western extremist elements in societies around the globe. Second is a lack of transparency surrounding the field, brought about by a lack of serious texts on the Sharīʿa, and by the daunting complexities inherent in the practical application of a theocratic criminal system.

*The editors wish to thank Ian Edge of SOAS for his help and support given in planning the symposium on which this book is based.

Yet, through the presentations given at this symposium, clear light was shed on criminal procedure in Islamic law and its relationship to modern criminal legislation in the Arab world, along with discussions on principles of legality; evidentiary weight and burdens of proof; sentencing; the role and nature of the judiciary in Islam; comparative analyses with more widely-known western models; and the practical application of Islamic law in newly emerging Islamic states. This book aims to extend that effort by bringing together the work of these contributors in one volume, thereby making a valuable addition to the field of Islamic studies.

Although this volume was first published in 2003, in today's unstable world it is more timely and necessary than ever. The individual essays that comprise this book have been included without substantial editorial interference, so as to preserve their unique perspectives and to demonstrate the diversity of thought in the field. Furthermore, at a time when an apparent 'struggle' between the West and Islam underpins western views of Islam, it is important that an academic work such as this be available, in order to demonstrate that Islam has very well-developed concepts of justice, along with a clear and accountable system for enforcing law and order and the will of God in the daily lives of all members of society.

The ways in which the global media have so quickly dismissed the Islamic legal system also indicates that there is a genuine need for scholarship of this kind. Rather than view this book solely as a treatise on Islamic law, the reader is also invited to engage in what is now a highly relevant and timely debate, and to contemplate issues that warrant so much more than media sound bites can provide.

London 2018

Part One

Generalities and Basic Principles

1

Generalities on Criminal Procedure under Islamic Sharīʿa

Adel Omar Sherif

Criminal procedure under Islamic Sharīʿa is a theme of much interest to scholars and researchers worldwide, particularly since it touches on and relates to various basic human rights and freedoms. This introductory essay will focus on those general rules of Islamic Sharīʿa which concern criminal procedure, which will include, *inter alia*, the bases of the Islamic justice system and the various procedural processes before, during and following the accusation and trial stages for criminal offences.[1]

As a preliminary remark, when dealing with criminal procedure under Islamic Sharīʿa within the contemporary context, two important considerations should be taken into account. First, if we are to compare criminal procedure in Islam to criminal procedure in modern legal systems, one must recognize the fact that, while studies on criminal procedure in contemporary legal systems have witnessed noticeable progress and are now fully structured, studies on criminal procedure under the Sharīʿa have not been developed accordingly.[2] It is, therefore, inequitable to compare criminal procedure in Islam to that of modern legal systems. What is fair, however, is to compare the main features and basic foundations.

A second consideration is that, in terms of its nature and history, Islamic Sharīʿa is an extremely complex subject, the discussion of which could fill many volumes. Thus, it is not easy to present succinct discussions of topics relating to the Sharīʿa. The brevity of this chapter, therefore, should not be taken as an indication that the Sharīʿa is in any way a simple concept or system; indeed, although the Sharīʿa is commonly referred to as 'Islamic law', even by Muslims, it is not only a legal system – as that term is generally understood – but rather a code based on religious principles designed to regulate the conduct of all Muslims in all aspects of life. This includes social, commercial, domestic, criminal and political affairs, as well as devotional practices.[3] By keeping these simple facts in mind, the content and nature of criminal procedure in Islam will be best understood.

The Initiation and Termination of Criminal Proceedings

Among the first topics to attract attention when studying criminal procedure in Islam are the initiation and termination of the proceedings, the definition of the persons and institutions involved, and the nature of the process itself.

Prosecutors

Under Islamic Sharī'a, there are no 'prosecutors' as that word is now understood. The criminal investigation process is interrelated with the trial itself, as investigations are considered a judicial process rather than an executive one (as in the contemporary French legal system). This means that the judge, who is entitled to dispose of the case, carries out the investigation.[4] Although the nature of the Islamic State allows for other officials – such as the *ṣāḥib al-shurṭa* (Police Commissioner) and the *muḥtasib* ('Religious Police')[5] – to play a part in initiating and carrying out investigations, their findings are scrutinized by the judge before a final decision on the accusation is reached. Prosecutorial investigation, then, is totally within the control of the judge.

Abbreviated Proceedings

It is agreed among Islamic jurists that criminal procedures under Islamic Sharī'a should be handled with simplicity, justice, and in the most expeditious way. Hence, abbreviated proceedings, in general, do not contradict the Sharī'a for as long as the proceedings used do not affect the fairness and credibility of the trial.

The Guilty Plea

The concept of a guilty plea is known in Islam. A guilty plea under Islamic Sharī'a has almost the same definition as that used in modern legal systems; it is defined as being the 'formal admission before a judge of having committed the criminal acts charged, which a defendant may make if he or she does so intelligently and voluntarily'. The accused may make such a plea only after being fully advised of his or her rights before the judge. A guilty plea is as binding as a conviction after a trial on the merits. It has the same effect in law as a guilty verdict, and hence warrants the imposition of the punishment prescribed by the Sharī'a.

Plea Bargaining

The concept of plea bargaining is not known in the Sharī'a. The reason for this is that the punishments prescribed for *ḥudūd* (set penalty) crimes, *qiṣāṣ* (just retaliation, or parity of punishment) crimes, and *diya* (compensation) crimes are fixed rigidly in the Qur'an and the *sunna* (*ḥadīth*, or sayings and actions of the Prophet), and cannot be altered. Even for *ta'zīr* (discretionary penalty) crimes, history reveals that this practice has never been applied. However, it should be mentioned that repentance (*tawba*) shown in the cases of some *ḥudūd* crimes might release the accused from being punished under certain circumstances.[6]

Initiating and Terminating Criminal Proceedings

Under the Sharī'a, both the executive and individuals play a role in initiating and terminating criminal proceedings depending on the nature of the crime being prosecuted, which, in turn, depends on the nature of the right infringed.

Categories of Rights

In Islam, all rights are viewed as bestowed by God (*Allah*), and may be divided into two categories: 'Rights of God' and 'Rights of Worshippers'. Whether a right falls within the former, rather than the latter, category depends on the extent to which that right is related to the public interests of society. Rights granted in the public interest are considered Rights of God, while rights bestowed to protect private interests are deemed Rights of Worshippers.[7]

Crime Definition

The distinction between Rights of God and Rights of Worshippers is reflected in criminal justice under Islamic Sharī'a, in that crimes in general are defined as acts that injure either the Rights of God or the Rights of Worshippers, or both. A crime results from an infringement of a Right of God, or a Right of Worshippers, or both at the same time.

Categories of Crimes

In Islamic jurisprudence crimes may be placed into many categories. An important categorization of crimes is one founded on the nature of the violated right.[8] Crimes affecting the Rights of God are set forth in the doctrinal provisions of either the Qur'an or the *sunna*. These are known as *ḥudūd* crimes, and also carry punishments set forth in the Qur'an or *sunna*. Some *ḥudūd* crimes are agreed upon (adultery, libellous accusations of adultery, theft and highway robbery), while there is disagreement over whether other crimes (apostasy, consumption of alcoholic drinks and attempts to overthrow the government by force) rise to the level of *ḥudūd* crimes.

Crimes affecting the Rights of Worshippers include acts that affect a person's life and safety, such as murder, manslaughter, beating and wounding. These crimes are generally referred to according to the punishment warranted by the circumstances surrounding the prohibited act. If parity of punishment (*qiṣāṣ*) is warranted, the crime is known as a *qiṣāṣ* crime. If compensation (*diya*) is appropriate, the crime is known as a *diya* crime.[9]

In addition to *ḥudūd*, *qiṣāṣ* and *diya* crimes, there are also *ta'zīr* crimes, which affect either the Rights of God or the Rights of Worshippers, or both. Some *ta'zīr* crimes are specified in the Qur'an or *sunna*, such as charging interest (*ribā*), bribery and slander. The caliph is empowered to define other *ta'zīr* crimes where necessary, in response to the evolving needs of society. Whether specified in the Qur'an or *sunna* or otherwise, the caliph is to determine the proper punishment for all *ta'zīr* crimes. The main difference between the crimes provided for in the Qur'an and *sunna* on the one hand, and the crimes to be established by the ruler on the other, is that crimes falling within the former category are perpetually prohibited, while acts belonging to the latter category may be subject to decriminalization.

In the absence of a caliph and an Islamic State (in the historical sense), those criminal laws enacted by the governing bodies of contemporary Islamic countries would perhaps constitute the equivalent of the category of *ta'zīr* crimes, specified in neither the Qur'an nor *sunna*.[10]

The Importance of the Distinction between Different Rights

The distinction between the Rights of God and the Rights of Worshippers is important in the initiation and termination of criminal proceedings under Islamic Sharī'a. Criminal cases relating to the Rights of God, be they *ḥudūd* or *ta'zīr*, may be initiated only by the caliph or his designated representative. Today, the government concerned (and its agencies) may be seen to take on that role in any given Islamic country. Thus, it may be said that, under the Sharī'a, the government concerned – hereinafter referred to as 'the state', in keeping with contemporary terminology – has the exclusive power to initiate criminal procedures in all such cases (i.e., it has the power that is reserved for the caliph). Beyond submitting their grievance to the state, victims are not involved in this process. In contrast, criminal procedures in cases involving the Rights of Worshippers, be they *qiṣāṣ*, *diya* or *ta'zīr* crimes, are not to be initiated under the Sharī'a without the prior request or consent of the injured individual.

As to the termination of criminal procedures, cases involving the Rights of God cannot be terminated, nor can the defendant be pardoned, either by the victim or the state (previously the caliph). When the case involves the Rights of Worshippers, the injured person (but not the state) can either terminate the proceedings, or release the accused from the punishment set by the judge. However, for crimes affecting both the Rights of God as well as the Rights of Worshippers, this forgiveness by the victim only implicates the proceedings to the extent that they relate to his or her personal rights; it does not preclude the state from going forward with the proceedings, since they relate to a Right of God.[11]

Officials Initiating Criminal Proceedings

To a certain extent, the state is involved in the initiation of criminal proceedings. Islamic Sharīʿa provides that the official acting on behalf of the state may be either an official of the executive or an official of the judiciary, depending on the circumstances of the case. Those having the power to initiate criminal proceedings for the state include the executive (in lieu of the caliph), judges, the *ṣāḥib al-shurṭa* and the *muḥtasib.*[12]

Protection of the Rights of the Accused/Suspect

It should be noted that the terms 'accused' and 'suspect' are often one and the same under Islamic Sharīʿa, because of the occasional overlapping of the investigation and trial proceedings. Nonetheless, the Sharīʿa recognizes the importance of protecting the rights of the accused/suspect,[13] indeed, numerous basic rights of the accused/suspect are guaranteed thereunder. For instance, the Sharīʿa recognizes the right of an accused/suspect to defend him or herself against any accusation, either by proving that the evidence cited is invalid, or by providing evidence to the contrary, including the testimony of witnesses. In addition, the right to be informed of the crime for which one is being investigated or charged is regarded as a fundamental right deriving from the right to defend oneself.

As to the right to legal aid, it is noted that in the early days of the Islamic State, there was no perceived need for professional legal advice for the accused/suspect, since court sessions were attended by legal scholars and experts, who actively assisted the judge in deciding the case according to the Sharīʿa. However, there is no provision in the Qur'an or *sunna* that precludes the accused/suspect from seeking the assistance of counsel during the investigation or trial, and such assistance was eventually viewed as helping him or her to prepare an effective defence, and was thus routinely allowed. Hence, although there is no explicit right to counsel under the Sharīʿa, such a right would be entirely consistent with its underlying general principles of fairness and justice.

In addition, the Sharīʿa adheres to the principle that no crime or punishment can be inflicted except by virtue of affirmative legislation, and in fact it was one of the first legal systems to do so. It also recognizes that the accused/suspect is innocent until proven guilty, and that guilt has to be established beyond reasonable doubt. The accused/suspect has the right to remain silent, and any confession taken under force is invalid; he or she also has the right to retract any earlier confession.

Moreover, the Sharīʿa provides for a number of other procedural and substantive rights which guarantee a fair trial in its modern sense, such as the right to have an independent and impartial judge decide the merits of the charge made against the accused, the right to equal protection of the law, the right to a public trial, and the right to obtain a judgement within a reasonable time. In fact, it is fair to say that all of those rights now recognized for the accused/suspect in contemporary legal systems can be seen as being subsumed within the basic rights recognized by the Sharīʿa, and are thus not incompatible with its aim to achieve fairness and justice in society.[14]

Access of the Accused to Evidence while Preparing for Trial

Under Islamic Sharīʿa, the accused/suspect has the right to confront the evidence against him or her, including that presented by the victim. Therefore, the accused/suspect has the right to be informed about the particulars of the indictment and its supporting materials, and must be allowed the opportunity to refute them by all legal means. This right is always preserved for the accused/suspect, and can be asserted by him or her or by his or her counsel, either before the commencement of trial, or while it is in progress.[15]

Illegally Obtained Evidence

Obtaining evidence illegally is not consistent with the Sharīʿa.[16] Various verses in the Qur'an and *sunna* honour human beings and prohibit any infringement upon their personal life. This means that evidence must be built upon truth and obtained through legal means, otherwise this would violate the privacy rights protected by the Sharīʿa. As such, it can be argued that the use of illegally obtained evidence is not permissible under Islamic Sharīʿa. By this analysis, searching the accused/suspect or his or her premises or correspondence, or listening to his or her conversations without proper cause, would render the process illegal, and would even permit the injured to seek compensation for damages.

In short, illegally obtained evidence should not be considered: individual rights and freedoms must not be sacrificed in a Machiavellian way, merely to prove the commission of a prohibited act by someone. Benefits gained from a Machiavellian approach neither justify, nor compensate for, the injuries resulting from that sacrifice of the most basic of human rights.

The Role of the Victim

The victim plays an important role under Islamic Sharī'a.[17] As we have already seen, crimes involving the Rights of Worshippers are not to be initiated without the request or consent of the victim, who also has control over termination of the procedures (for so long as a Right of God is not involved). In order for the victim to sustain his or her allegations, he or she must testify and present any collaborating evidence, as well as respond to any attempt by the defendant to refute his or her testimony and evidence. The role of the victim in giving evidence with regard to crimes involving Rights of God is similar. Though criminal procedures in such cases are initiated by the state, the victim is required to give whatever legal evidence he or she has, and to provide the supporting materials.

Whenever a victim feels that he or she requires protection, he or she can explain this to the judge who, within his discretionary powers, will then decide upon the necessity of such protection, and whether it can be granted without infringing upon the rights of the accused.

The Examination of Witnesses

Examination of witnesses in the Sharī'a is adversarial. Revealing the truth and achieving justice are its essence and, to that end, adversarial examination (including cross-examination) of witnesses is allowed. Nevertheless, the judge still plays a role in directing and exercising the investigation, as in the Inquisitorial System. In this way, the Islamic system differs from the contemporary application of the Adversarial System, wherein the judge acts solely as an independent magistrate, and plays no prosecutorial role.

The identity of the prosecution witnesses may generally not be concealed from the accused/suspect and his or her counsel, as the accused/suspect must have the opportunity to review all evidence in preparing his or her defence. Otherwise, trials would have no credibility in the eyes of the public. Lastly, although witness protection programmes did not develop under Islamic Sharī'a, the judge, as mentioned earlier, will always retain the power to grant witnesses whatever protection is needed. Written testimony, in the form of affidavits, is permissible, but generally the witness must be available for examination at trial, in order to give the accused the opportunity to effectively confront all witnesses against him or her.

The Remedy for Unlawful Detention

Detention affects the right to free movement; the Sharī'a defines detention as 'preventing an individual from dealing with others, in any manner that would lead to his or her being harmed'. When detention occurs, the rights of the person detained must be protected.[18] The state (previously the caliph) is responsible for providing the food, clothing, health care and all other facilities required, to ensure that the person detained retains his or her rights as a human being.

Under Islamic Sharī'a, freedom of movement cannot be restricted without a legally valid reason. If a person believes he or she is being detained unlawfully, he or she can seek an order from the judge to be released, which the judge will grant if warranted. In addition, unlawful detention, as well as any unlawful judgement, entitles the injured to receive compensation. It is the duty of the government – in the absence of a caliph – to preserve the correct implementation of the Sharī'a. The state and its officials are not beyond liability, whenever and wherever an unlawful act occurs, and their participation in such an act renders them liable for damages. Although Islamic jurists agree that the state is responsible for unlawful detention, they are divided over whether payment of compensation for the unlawful act should be made from the official's own money, or from the public treasury.[19]

Trial in the Absence of the Accused

As a general rule, trial in the absence of the accused is not permitted under Islamic Sharī'a. Islamic jurists agree that a person cannot be subject to a judicial ruling unless he or she attends the court session, either personally or through somebody representing him as an agent (such as counsel). This follows from the rule that a judge cannot dispose of a case in favour of one party before listening to the other party (or parties). Trials conducted in the absence of the accused or his agents are invalid.

The accused/suspect must also be involved at the investigation stage, and must be allowed the opportunity to refute any evidence submitted against him or her. If procedures are commenced in the absence of the accused, they will be deemed invalid and, at that time, the official who initiated the procedures (should he wish to go forward) must reveal the evidence to the accused, and allow him or her to discuss, challenge or refute it.

Finality of Rulings

Generally, once the ruling is rendered, it becomes final and cannot be appealed against or reconsidered. Since judicial rulings in the Sharī'a are generally final, the possibilities of vacating a judgement are very rare. A judgement cannot be appealed (there are no appellate courts), but any judge may declare a judgement void if he finds it in contradiction with a provision of the Qur'an or *sunna*. A challenge on these grounds can be made by anyone. A judge who renders a judgement may also revisit it of his own accord, in the belief that it may violate the Qur'an or *sunna*.[20]

Limits of Application

If it is proved that a ruling was rendered in violation of any provision of the Qur'an or *sunna*, then it will be declared void, and a new trial must take place. The new trial may be conducted by the judge who rendered the illegal ruling, for as long as there is no reason to prevent him from hearing the case. In the event of a judge excusing himself, another judge who is competent to hear the case will handle the trial.

As to the application of Islamic Sharīʿa within criminal procedure in modern Arab states, there are doubts as to the reality of this application. This may be explained by the fact that criminal procedure in most of the modern Arab world is not in fact derived from Islamic Sharīʿa. To take Egypt as just one example, the misunderstanding prevails in western societies that, since Egypt is considered an 'Islamic' state, its legislation – including that setting forth criminal procedure – is based on Islamic Sharīʿa.[21] In fact, the comprehensive application of Sharīʿa law in Egypt, its neighbours and other countries who witnessed the spread of Islam in the seventh century CE, occurred during a limited period of time. It was confined to the period between the arrival of Islam and the late nineteenth century CE, when new codes, derived mainly from European codes, began to be introduced to the Ottoman Empire and its affiliated Arab countries. After this, the application of the Sharīʿa declined dramatically. Today, legislation in most Arab countries, including Egypt, is not generally drawn from the Sharīʿa, but is rather grounded in those European codes. For instance, the civil and criminal codes now applied in Egypt are derived basically from French codes.[22] It is difficult to ascertain with certainty – given the complexity of Islamic Sharīʿa – which countries in the Arab world, if any, derive all their legislation from the Sharīʿa, although Saudi Arabia is generally believed to be the only Islamic country to attempt to do so.

That said, it must be pointed out that there has recently been a tendency in those Arab countries with codes derived from European codes to adopt legislation that is compatible with the requirements of Islamic law, a trend motivated by a respect for religious tradition as well as the call by certain Islamic movements for an Islamic State based on Islamic Sharīʿa.[23] This move by governments to accommodate Islam appears to be supported by a great proportion of the populations of these countries, wherein the vast majority are Muslims.[24]

Despite this trend, and despite the fact that the constitutions of Islamic countries ensure their religious nature, recent moves to accommodate religion have not yet resulted in a noticeable change to the systems of government and the practices of public authorities in these countries, which remain essentially secular. This presents a conflict between state and religion in Islamic countries, which these countries are now attempting to address in various ways. The prevailing impression today is that this conflict will gradually disappear, as governmental action is brought into line with the Sharīʿa. In any event, given the current circumstances, it would be a mistake to assume that the criminal codes of Egypt and most Arab countries have been dictated by the tenets of Islamic Sharīʿa.[25] Some countries, such as Saudi Arabia, do apply Sharīʿa, but do not have consolidated criminal codes that lend themselves to being studied easily.

Another factor affecting the application of the Sharīʿa within criminal procedure in modern Arab states is that it dictates only a few specific criminal procedural rules, leaving the remainder to be developed according to general principles. Islamic Sharīʿa does not provide for a particular framework for criminal procedures and judicial processes, it merely lays down the guiding principles and objectives without attempting to address the details. This is because it was meant to develop and evolve according to the changing needs of the people and their different circumstances. The details of the system – including the procedures to be used in the criminal justice system – are to be determined by Muslims as circumstances dictate, within the broader, basic principles of the Sharīʿa.

The continued application of Islamic Sharīʿa in those countries that witnessed the spread of Islam suggests that a system of criminal procedure must have developed in the Islamic State. Unfortunately, however, the replacement of the Sharīʿa with western codes led to a decline in studies of the procedural rules of that system to the point that virtually no comprehensive, contemporary studies exist that attempt to identify those procedural rules that are compatible with the Sharīʿa. Many jurists have written individually on different aspects of the Sharīʿa and criminal law, but these studies have been somewhat selective, and fall short of constituting a comprehensive analysis of the procedural rules of the Sharīʿa. Given the absence of such material from which to draw, any attempt to ascertain those criminal procedures that are compatible with the general principles of the Sharīʿa – as I have endeavoured to do in this essay – is inherently difficult, and is sure to meet with disagreement in some quarters.

The Building Blocks for Criminal Procedure under Islamic Sharīʿa

Notwithstanding the lack of contemporary studies on criminal procedure under the Sharīʿa, the broad principles of justice, equality, fairness and honesty are beyond dispute. These principles can be said to be the 'building blocks' for criminal procedure under the Sharīʿa. Moreover, given these guiding principles, I think it fair to surmise that, from the beginning of the Islamic State, the Sharīʿa has recognized the many substantive as well as procedural rules now universally required in order to guarantee the protection of human rights and the dignity of individuals subjected to criminal procedure. These include – to mention but a few – the rules of equality, the presumption of innocence and the right to a fair trial, the notion that crimes and punishments should be imposed only by virtue of criminal legislation, and that criminal provisions should not be applied retroactively.[26] In short, I see no conflict between contemporary standards of criminal procedure and Islamic Sharīʿa, and submit that the latter led the way in this area.

Separation of the Judiciary from Other State Powers under Islamic Sharīʿa

The principle of the separation of powers, now viewed as a key element in modern states, did not develop under Islam. This was because the Prophet Muḥammad exercised judicial, legislative and executive powers himself, which gave rise to the tradition of these powers being exercised by the ruler of Islam (which, after the Prophet's death, was the caliph). As for judicial power, under the Prophet – and after his death, under the ruling caliphs – some of this power was delegated to local governors (known as *wulāh*) and specialized judges (*quḍāh*), with these authorities being required to administer justice in compliance with Islamic law. As the Islamic State expanded into various countries, the caliph had to rely on local officials to apply the Sharīʿa throughout the State. This, however, did not affect the caliph's right to review their actions. Therefore, in Islam, the caliph – or the supreme ruler of Islam – is to be the centre of power, and judges and other officials are to derive their respective powers through delegation from him.

Of course, today, there is no 'Islamic State' like that which existed fourteen hundred years ago, but rather a number of nation-states with Muslim majorities that refer to themselves as 'Islamic' states. In addition, technically, there is no caliph today (in the sense that there is no one person who has been appointed by Muslims around the world to be their supreme leader in all aspects of life). When one talks about Islamic Sharīʿa, then, it is necessary to try to adapt its tenets to the geopolitical circumstances that exist today, rather than speak simply of its literal teachings, or how it was applied in the past. With respect to the question of the separation of powers, I submit that such a separation is not inconsistent with the Sharīʿa, though others may disagree on this point.

Notes

[1] Arabic jurisprudence on criminal procedure is rich, and many distinguished Egyptian jurists in the modern era have produced volumes on this topic. I have consulted many of these works while preparing this essay, and have depended heavily on those whose essential goal is to simplify the whole topic of criminal procedure in Islamic law. These include, but are not limited to, the works of Muḥammad Abū Zahra, *al-Jarīma wa'l-'Uqūba fī Fiqh al-Islām*, 2 Vols (Cairo, 1998); 'Abd al-Qādir 'Awda, *al-Tashrī' al-Jinā'ī al-Islāmī Muqāran bi'l-Qānūn al-Waḍ'ī*, 2 Vols (Cairo, 1984)

[2] This should not undermine the general fact that the existing legal and codificatory tendency in the Arab world since the nineteenth century has been increasingly in support of western and in particular European models, rather than Islamic ones. Nonetheless, some changes have taken place during the last few decades, when Arab countries recognized that returning to Islamic Sharī'a was a proper policy option that would better serve their needs and meet the will of the vast majority of their peoples. Egypt, a leading Islamic country in the Arab world, has gone through such an experience; for details on historical developments, see Adel Omar Sherif, 'An overview of the Egyptian judicial system and its history', in *The Yearbook of Islamic and Middle Eastern Law*, V, 1998-9 (The Hague, 2000), p 10

[3] There are writers in the West who believe that the Sharī'a in its traditional form provides an extreme example of a legal science divorced from historical considerations, a view that is not greatly appreciated in the Islamic world. For details, see N. J. Coulson, 'Introduction', in*A History of Islamic Law*(Edinburgh, 1964)

[4] It should be noted that, historically, the caliph was the centre of power in Islam, and it was he who determined the jurisdiction and competence of judges and other officials throughout the Islamic State. As a result, he had the power to assign officials to conduct investigations as he commanded.

[5] For more details on these two important positions in the Islamic State and the distinctive elements between them, see Sihām Muṣṭafā Abū Zayd, *al-Ḥisba fī Miṣr al-Islāmiyya: Min al-Fatḥ al-'Arabī ilā Nihāyat al-'Aṣr al-Mamlūkī* (Cairo, 1986), p 235

[6] For details, see Muḥammad Salīm al-'Awwā, *Fī Uṣūl al-Niẓām al-Jinā'ī al-Islāmī*, 2nd ed (Cairo, 1983), p 109

[7] The distinction between Rights of God and Rights of Worshippers is one of many jurisprudential methods for defining crimes in Islam. Islamic jurists, in addition, adopt other criteria. Among elements to be taken into account in this regard are criminal intent, the degree of harm, the time of the crime's commission and the surrounding circumstances. See 'Awda: *al-Tashrī' al-Jinā'ī al-Islāmī*, I, pp 78; 109

[8] On this classification, see Abū Zahra: *al-Jarīma wa'l-'Uqūba*, I, p 42

[9] *Diya* is not 'blood money', as it is normally translated, and is better translated as 'compensation'. This is an example 'of how translating Islamic terminology has been responsible for the traditional, bad image of Islam in the West. It should also be remembered that compensation is an option, because both parties, heirs and murderer, must agree to it. The option of compensation is constructive and fair, and can be seen to obviate the criticism levelled against capital punishment, namely that it might be proved later to have been inflicted on an innocent party.' See Muhammad

Abdel Haleem, 'Compensation for homicide in Islamic Sharī'a, chapter five of this volume.

[10] The ruler's power and that of judges to establish *ta'zīr* crimes is not absolute. They are restricted by the basic principles and commands of Islam in general, namely requirements of proportionality between crime and punishment and the circumstances of the accused. See al-'Awwā: *Uṣūl*, pp 125; 286

[11] It is said with regard to the punishment of the crime that both *qiṣāṣ* and *ta'zīr* crimes are not *ḥudūd* crimes. This is because *ḥudūd* crimes affect only the Rights of God, while *qiṣāṣ* crimes affect only the Rights of Worshippers. In addition, punishments for *ta'zīr* crimes are determined by the ruler, and are not fixed by God. See Abū Zahra: *al-Jarīma wa'l-'Uqūba*, I, p 43

[12] For further information on the relationship between the judiciary, *ḥisba* and *shurṭa*, see Abū Zayd: *al-Ḥisba fī Miṣr al-Islāmiyya*, pp 217-39

[13] See Awad Muhammad Awad's article, 'The rights of the accused under Islamic criminal procedure', in M. Cherif Bassiouni (ed), *The Islamic Criminal Justice System* (London, 1982), pp 91-109

[14] On the Islamic concept of fair trial, see Awad Muḥammed El-Murr, 'Human rights in the constitutional systems of Egypt and other Islamic countries: international and comparative standards', in Kevin Boyle and Adel Omar Sherif (eds), *Human Rights and Democracy: The Role of the Supreme Constitutional Court of Egypt* (The Hague, 1996), p 181

[15] A detailed study on evidence in Islamic Sharī'a can be found in Shaykh Aḥmad Ibrāhīm Ibrāhīm's *Ṭuruq al-Qaḍā' fi'l-Sharī'a al-Islāmiyya* (Cairo, 1928)

[16] On methods of evidence and their legitimacy in Islamic Sharī'a in general, see Shaykh Aḥmad Ibrāhīm Ibrāhīm, *Ṭuruq al-Ithbāt fi'l- Sharī'a al-Islāmiyya* (Cairo, 1985)

[17] On the role of parties in evidence and judicial process, see Ibrāhīm: *Ṭuruq al-Qaḍā'*, p 16

[18] On protecting the dignity of the accused, see 'Abd al-Ḥakīm Ḥasan al-'Alī, *al-Ḥurriyyāt al-'Āmma fi'l-Fikr wa'l-Niẓām al-Siyāsī fi'l-Islām* (Cairo, 1983), p 367

[19] Existing constitutions in Islamic and Arab countries do provide for many guarantees against arbitrary arrest and detention. El-Murr: 'Human rights in the constitutional systems of Egypt', p 175

[20] For more details, see 'Ādil 'Umar Shanf, *al-Qaḍā' fi'l-Islām* (Cairo, 1985), p 21

[21] For a brief examination of the way criminal procedure is regulated in Egyptian law, see Adel Omar Sherif, 'Egypt's report', in *The Prosecutor of a Permanent International Criminal Court*, ed Louise Arbour, Albin Eser, Kai Ambos and Andrew Sanders (Freiburg im Breisgau, 2000), p 291

[22] For further details, see Sherif: 'An overview'

[23] As a result, today many Arab constitutions stipulate explicitly that Islamic Sharī'a is a source or is the main source of legislation. In Egypt, for instance, the 1971 Constitution provides in Article 2 that Islamic Sharī'a principles are the main sources of legislation.

[24] On Islamic Sharī'a in the constitutional texts of Arab countries, see Nathan J. Brown and Adel Omar Sherif, 'Inscribing the Islamic Sharī'a in Arab constitutional law', presented to the Symposium on Legal Systems in the Arab World, Centre for Contemporary Arab Studies, School of Foreign Services at Georgetown University, Washington DC, April 2001

[25] For an in-depth discussion of the development of the codification movement in modern Egypt, see 'Abd al-Ḥalīm al-Jundī's *Naḥw Taqnīn Jadīd li'l-Mu'āmalāt wa 'Uqūbāt fi'l-Fiqh al-Islāmī* (Cairo, 1973), p 76

---

[26] Many writers on criminal law appreciate the jurisdictional and jurisprudential bases of Islamic criminal law and affirm that this law solves confrontations between various legal systems, while presenting one exclusive legal system. See Farhad Malekian, *The Concept of Islamic International Criminal Law*(London, 1994), p 11

2

Basic Principles of Criminal Procedure under Islamic Sharīʿa

This chapter comprises two sections on criminal procedure in Islamic law: the first deals with the limits of a judge's power and discretion within the criminal context, while the second discusses some general concepts within the areas of crime and punishment. Inevitably, some overlaps or repetition occur, since this is a work which seeks to reconcile free and far-reaching discussion with faithfulness to the authors' original contributions.

I: Judicial Powers in Criminal Cases

Saeed Hasan Ibrahim

The powers of a judge in criminal cases differ according to the criminal policies held by an individual criminal system, although every system seeks to deliver justice through its administration. Judicial power in the Islamic criminal system varies according to its categories of crimes, and the characteristics of each category. Crimes in this system are defined as:

> ...legal prohibitions that are prescribed by God and carry definitive legal deterrents [*ḥudūd*] or other punishments. In the case of an accusation, a state of purification is required by religious dictates, and, when proved and found correct, a state of execution is obligated by the legal commandments.[1]

This has several implications. First, an act is considered a crime only through prohibition by the law-giver, with all the attendant details. Second, a punishment can take effect only with the permission of the law-giver. For an act prohibited by Islamic Sharīʿa, the punishment prescribed is either a *ḥadd* (a punishment definitively prescribed by Divine Law), or a punishment such as the law has prescribed for perpetration of such prohibited acts, whether in the form of a deed or 'abandoning'. Further, that which concerns criminal proceedings – namely, the means – are in the field of legal policy, because they relate to forms and styles rather than objective, proven facts. In this way, they should be left to the specialized authorities to tackle, in the light of the changing circumstances. Finally, it is incumbent upon a government to establish this criminal system in a situation of accusation or acquittal after the presenting of evidence, and to apply the prescribed judgement as an obligation by law. In the case of an acquittal, a government does not have the right to change or retract the judgement.

Powers of the Judge in the Field of Criminology

In the field of criminology, the powers of a judge depend on the description of the acts that attract accusation, and whether or not perpetration of such acts falls under the definition of a crime delineated in the various categories of crimes. Other factors include whether this is a crime for which there is a *ḥadd*, or whether it is a crime requiring only reproof or reprimand.

Categories of Crimes

For us to understand the judicial powers of a judge in the Islamic criminal system, it is essential to explain the categories of crimes, as well as the characteristics of each category. Crimes in this system fall into three categories: crimes of *ḥudūd* (fixed prescribed penalties) and *qiṣāṣ* (retaliation), crimes affecting the Rights of God, and crimes affecting the Rights of Worshippers.

Crimes of *ḥudūd* may be defined as 'prohibitions ordained by Divine Law [Sharīʿa], from which we are restrained by God with punishments decreed by Him; they form an obligation to God'.[2] The degree of punishment is fixed and decreed by legal texts, the Qur'an and the *sunna* of the Prophet. It consists in retaliation in all forms, because punishment by retaliation is fixed by divine decree, except where it is not possible to determine its amount, as in the case of certain wounds. Many of the jurists support this, and use the word *ḥadd* for all crimes that carry punishments that are fixed and decreed by legal texts, and whose assessment is not left to the discretion of either the authorities or an authorized body, a view supported by this author. There are many others, however, who use the term *ḥadd* solely for punishments that are purely or mostly an obligation to God. As such, retaliation is not termed a *ḥadd*, because in it the rights of God's worshippers are dominant.[3]

Crimes affecting the Rights of God are those that endanger higher values and welfare, and which are prescribed by the Qur'an, which ordains that one's life should be based upon them. Their real damage affects the community as a whole, and the benefit of the imposition of their penalties is returned to the whole of the community. These crimes are: apostasy; the drinking of wine; adultery; false accusation of fornication or slander against women; minor theft; major theft (plundering and highway robbery); and insurrection against a lawful Muslim authority. The jurists are agreed that perpetration of these acts constitutes a crime that must be punished, although there is some disagreement over whether some of these crimes fall within the category of crimes of *ḥudūd*, such as revolt, drinking and apostasy.[4]

Crimes affecting the Rights of Worshippers include aggression against a person's life, e.g. murder, or the causing of harm to the organs of a person's body (e.g. injury to teeth, eyes and ears), be it deliberate or accidental. This applies to the rights of both society and individuals simultaneously. The rights in this category are assigned to near relatives of the victim of the crime, in the case of a crime against a person's life, or the aggrieved party in person, in the case of injury to organs. There are five such crimes affecting the Rights of Worshippers: deliberate murder; quasi-deliberate murder; deliberate injury to organs; accidental murder; and accidental injury to organs.

Powers of the Judge in *ḥudūd* and *Qiṣāṣ* Crimes

The powers of the judge in *ḥudūd* and *qiṣāṣ* crimes are subject to the characteristics of each category of crime, and whether these affect rights due to God or to other individuals. In the case of crimes of *ḥudūd*, when the crime has been established, it is mandatory for the judge to award the punishment decreed for such a crime, without diminishing or adding to it. No judge has the power to replace the decreed punishment with another, nor can he prevent the implementation of the punishment. The powers of a judge in the case of crimes of *ḥudūd* are defined by the limits imposed by the punishment decreed for the crime; a judge serves only to pronounce the judgement.

In crimes of *qiṣāṣ*, the judicial powers of the judge are limited to the implementation of the decreed penalty, once the crime against the accused has been proven. When retaliation is the punishment and the aggrieved party foregoes his or her right to retaliation, or when the enforcement of the decree is not feasible for legal reasons, the judge must order *diya* (compensation), if the aggrieved has not forgiven the accused. If he does forgive the accused, however, the judge may award some other punishment as a reprimand to safeguard the interests of the community.

In crimes of *ḥudūd*, there is absolutely no room for any amnesty or intercession, whether from the aggrieved party or the head of state; nor does the judge have the power to award this to anyone. Should he do so, it will be null and void and will have no effect on either the crime or its punishment. In crimes of *qiṣāṣ*, however, pardon is allowed, and when retaliation is forgiven it does have an impact: the aggrieved should give pardon in return for *diya*, and even has the right to forego *diya*. When the aggrieved forgives or foregoes *diya*, the culprit will be forgiven.

The head of state has no power in his own right to relieve punishment in crimes of retaliation, because the right to pardon in cases of this category of crimes rests with the victim of the crime or his legal guardian. Yet, if the aggrieved is incapable or has no guardians, then the head of state, i.e. the judge, shall be his guardian, according to the legal principle that the ruler is the guardian for a person who has no other guardian. In such a situation, it is permissible for the head of state or judge to grant pardon in his capacity as a guardian of the victim of the crime, but the pardon must be given freely, and can be given in no other capacity.

Extenuating circumstances have no effect whatsoever on crimes of *ḥudūd*, *qiṣāṣ* and *diya*; in all such cases, the decreed penalty must be implemented, whatever the culprit's circumstances.[5]

Crimes of *Ta'zīr*

A *ta'zīr* crime is one whose 'punishment is not decreed, and is an obligation to God or Man in all cases of disobedience for which there is no specified *ḥadd* or atonement'.[6] In the Islamic penal system, *ta'zīr* crimes have wider scope and range than crimes of *ḥudūd* and *qiṣāṣ*. *Ta'zīr* represents the flexible part of this system, and is governed by a number of principles and general rules associated with the objectives of the Sharī'a, and safeguards against anything that may threaten them. These objectives are the protection of religion, life, reason, race and property, as supported by textual evidence in the Qur'an and *sunna*. This system has been so formed, it would appear, to allow the criminal system to work harmoniously with fresh conditions in terms of time, place and people.

For some crimes (sins) in this category – such as usury, bribes, breach of faith and fraud – certain laws are prescribed, while leaving the rest to be decided in the light of general principles and rules from the words of God, e.g. 'and the reward of an evil is an evil like thereof' (Q.42:40), and the principle of 'no harming and no reciprocation of harm'. Indeed, these principles and rules become legally desirable if the interests of the community are bound to them.

Types of Ta'zīr *Punishment*

Ta'zīr punishments vary according to the nature of the crime or sin. The concerned authorities determine the type and degree of punishment needed to implement justice, so different punishments may be awarded for one crime, depending on the different circumstances surrounding the crime and the culprit.

A *ta'zīr* punishment can begin with a word of reprimand by the judge, and can extend to capital punishment in the case of more serious crimes, such as spying for the enemy. Indeed, the jurists have explained that the smallest reprimand consists in a stern look by the ruler (i.e. the judge) at the sinner, or for the judge to say to him words such as: 'I have heard such and such a thing about you', when the sin is a minor offence and the sinner comes from a noble and respectable family for whom even such a reprimand is sufficient to restrain them from offence. The most severe *ta'zīr* punishment is death, when the offence is a serious one and the need to deter people demands such harshness.[7]

Powers of the Judge in *Ta'zīr* Crimes

Muslim jurists have discussed the punitive powers of the judge in crimes of *ta'zīr* in the light of the Qur'anic text and the *sunna*. They say that *ta'zīr* is 'entrusted to the opinion of the ruler to decide in the light of the conditions of the people and crime rate among them'.[8] This means that *ta'zīr* punishments are laid down and their amount decided by the specific relevant authorities, and that the powers of the judge are limited to awarding the punishment to the culprit who actually commits a *ta'zīr* crime. The Sharī'a gives the judge the power of assessment in choosing a penalty that is appropriate for a culprit, taking into account his personality, previous character and social conditions, which is more effective as a warning and deterrent against committing a crime. The judge must also take into account the effect of the crime on society at large; therefore, he will award the culprit a punishment after taking into consideration all of the above circumstances, selecting the most suitable of the various prescribed penalties. With him also rests the power to stop the implementation of a penalty, thus he has the power to choose and assess, but not to rule and dominate.

There is, apparently, a contradiction here between this legislative power – given to the ruler or the specific state authorities – and the rule which says that the power to prohibit (*taḥrīm*) or the power to permit (*taḥlīl*) which judges exercise rests only with God in the sight of Islam. This is an incorrect assumption, however, and no 'contradiction' can be said to exist. This is because detailed laws are not provided in either the Qur'an or *sunna*, nor are these presumed to provide for all aspects of human life, at all times and under all circumstances. Indeed, Qur'anic laws are limited, and are delineated in the *sunna* for the detailed organization of a few, select issues whose legal position suffers no change with changes in circumstances and times.

Besides these limited number of commandments, there are also some general rules and principles therein on which detailed commandments suitable for the various conditions and times in which Muslims live are based. It follows that Muslims are given the right to stipulate whatever they may wish outside the areas covered by the Qur'an and *sunna*, in order to safeguard their multi-lateral interests, provided this does not conflict with general textual law and its antecedent general rules. These legal stipulations will, in fact, be based on those texts that make it incumbent upon the community to realize good and refrain from evil, and those that affirm the right to *ijtihād* (the exercise of independent judgement). The jurists recognize this right for the community – or specific agency in the state – under the name of *al-siyāsa al-shar'iyya*, or the administration of justice according to the Sharī'a, which is the name given to the commandments and regulations by which the affairs of the community are arranged through its government, legislation, judiciary and all other executive and administrative agencies, and through its foreign relations that bind it to other nations.[9]

The jurists concede that *al-siyāsa al-shar'iyya* means nothing more than the legality of framing laws within the interests of the welfare of the community, in areas where nothing is prescribed in the Qur'an or *sunna*. When these laws are in the criminal field – such as incriminating actions and prescribing penalties for them – they are in the realm of *ta'zīr*, and are based on its principles and general rules.[10] Both logic and reason tell us that no individual nor any penal system in any age can envisage all the crimes and penalties that could ever take place, in view of changes in situations and circumstances, nor can any individual or penal system anticipate what might happen in the future.

Powers of the Judge in Establishing Evidence in Criminal Cases

Establishing criminal evidence is immensely important in Islamic law, being the legitimate means by which a judge is helped to reach a judgement and establish justice among the people. Before passing a judgement, the judge examines, scrutinizes and verifies the proof, in order to arrive at the truth. The establishment of proof is defined as 'establishing the argument before the judiciary by means prescribed by the Sharī'a to attest the truth or incident from which other actions flow'.[11]

The basic methods of establishing evidence in the Islamic criminal system are testimony, confession and circumstantial evidence; some jurists also include the knowledge of the judge in the means of establishing evidence as part of criminal material. Testimony is the normal method for establishing the perpetration of a crime, indeed, most crimes are established through testimony, which was originally that of two just Muslim males, who witness that they have direct information.[12] As to confession, a man should confess against himself that he did what is deemed criminal. This is in addition to circumstances related to the events concerning the crime, or the circumstances of the lawsuit and the judgement of the judge, based on his knowledge of the conflict.

With regard to the judge, the crime is an event that happened in the past, and to know about it with certainty is possible under just two circumstances: that he witnessed the incident personally, or that he obtained access to the facts concerning the event through successive evidence or the reports of a group of people for whom it would be impossible to collude in telling a lie. Both of these are highly unlikely to be investigated, however, and if we were to make the proof dependent on these conclusive matters, many rights would be lost, justice in society would be perverted, and chaos would spread. That is why the Sharīʿa has chosen to rely on likely proof without any certain knowledge, even when it appears on the surface that this could involve risk and error in the application of Qur'anic legal texts to factual conditions, and in the giving of rulings in accordance with them.

The judicial decision in the Sharīʿa rests basically on presumed (*ẓannī*) proof, while observing extreme caution and circumspection. The most desirable situation would be for it to be based on conclusive proof, if found, whereupon the Sharīʿa allows the judge to base his judgement on the testimony of just witnesses and the confession of the accused, despite the possibility of witnesses giving false testimony or being untruthful concerning that to which they were witness, and the possibility of the confessor giving false confession.

Powers of the Judge in Evaluating Evidence

On the powers of the judge in evaluating evidence, two trends are found in Islamic penal thought. The first trend is represented by the majority of the jurists, who view the judge as strictly bound in his choice and number of methods of evaluation, in the light of what is found in the legal texts. The judge must operate within these methods; he cannot violate or go beyond them. Likewise, the parties in the case are bound to these fixed methods, and can prove their rights only by their use. The case must be established via strictly fixed means, so that the properties, lives and souls of people are not exposed to loss or damage at the hands of unfair judges, who base their judgements on people's status and flimsy circumstances. Were the means of asserting and proving a case not defined and limited, this would encourage false claimants to transgress the rights of others, causing anarchy, disorder and injustice.

The second trend is represented by Ibn Taymiyya, Ibn al-Qayyim and others, who take the view that any and every possible means of making the truth clear and convincing to the judge may be used. Similarly, they argue that these methods should neither be limited in number nor strictly confined, and that the judge has the freedom to convince himself by any argument presented to him, while the parties involved are free to use any argument in order to establish their rights.[13]

In this regard, Ibn Taymiyya says:

> The Qur'an does not mention two [male] witnesses, or a man and two women, under the methods of judgement by which a ruler [judge] reaches a verdict. It mentions two kinds of proof, under the methods by which man can safeguard his rights [...] and that by which rights are protected is one thing and that by which the ruler gives a ruling is another. Indeed, the methods of judgement are wider than two [male] witnesses or a man and two women.[14]

Related to the question of the judge's power to evaluate evidence is his freedom to be convinced by these proofs, to thoroughly evaluate the strengths of each argument and arrange them in order, until he reaches the stage where he is convinced of the soundness of the incidence under consideration. The judge can then pass a verdict of either innocence or conviction, provided that he ensures that this freedom to evaluate and be convinced by the arguments does not extend to arbitrary decisions that might violate any given rights.

Powers of the Judge in Interpreting Penal Texts

Related to the judge's freedom to evaluate and judge the strength of the arguments is his authority to interpret and elaborate on the penal texts. As the judge applies the penal texts to material conditions, he has the right to explain these texts if he finds in them any vagueness, unclear arguments, or contradictions in their statements. The jurists and the legal specialists have laid down a system and rules that should be followed while interpreting the texts and commandments derived from them; some of these rules are philological, while others are legislative in nature.

It is the duty of the judge to use these rules in understanding the texts, and to gain knowledge about their purposes, and that which is included in them. These rules will also help him in understanding those texts whose application is mandatory, and the extent of his powers in interpreting, acting on or invalidating the texts. If the judge is a city-dweller he may apply these rules extensively, and may rely on analogy, convention, justice and any other such consideration, while interpreting the texts and applying them to the situation before him. He has no power to create a crime or punishment by way of analogy, convention or discretion, even if the case before him is objectionable in the eyes of noble and distinguished people. A judge dealing with penal cases has no power to act in open violation of a clear text, whatever the conditions or considerations.[15]

It is also the duty of the judge to bear in mind, under all circumstances, two major principles of the Sharī'a, namely, that the *ḥudūd* should be repealed in the case of doubt, and that it is better for a ruler to err in granting forgiveness than to err in punishment. These two principles are given in the *ḥadīth*, one of which says:

> Repeal the *ḥudūd* punishments from Muslims as far as you can, so if there is a way out, leave him alone, for it is better for a ruler to make a mistake in forgiving someone rather than in punishing him.[16]

Despite the weakness in the *ḥadīth* found on this subject, Imām Shawkānī cites other *ḥadīth* narrated through a chain of authorities and statements of the Companions of the Prophet, and says:

> But as to this subject, the position is well known: though in it there is some weakness, it strengthens what we have mentioned, and thereafter it is a valid ground for arguing the legality of repealing the *ḥudūd* by possible doubts, rather than unspecified doubt.

Doubt is a state which the perpetrator of a crime finds himself in or is subject to when he may have had some excuse for perpetrating the crime, or is deemed as having such an excuse. In such cases, the *ḥadd* is removed from him.[17] Some of the jurists consider the rule of repealing the *ḥudūd* on account of doubt a legal rule rather than one based on a text, and reject the *ḥadīth* concerned because of the weakness in its chain of authorities. Even if we admit this, a majority of jurists still take the former view, making it an integral part of the Islamic penal system, and presenting it in a detailed manner in the books of *fiqh* of the various schools. That is why some jurists have noted that, in the absence of doubt, the basic rule is the consensus of the jurists on establishing a *ḥadd* in a specific form. They take this as proof of non-existence of doubt in that form, and for so long as there is no doubt, there is consensus on establishing the *ḥadd* in that state.[18]

This exemplifies the rule that 'doubt favours the accused' in man-made laws. Even if doubt is not elaborated in detail, it is, in our view, a specific text just like the changing, man-made law. If we intend not to apply this text – or this rule, according to those who do not consider it a text – to the practical situation, we must study the situation further, for doubt is a kind of flaw in perception that adversely affects certainty. This requires a study of doubt and an understanding of its ingredients, which can be done only through contemplation and investigation. Thus, it is found at times that doubt is itself an object – that is, an issue – while it may be in the mind of the speaker or may concern some extraneous matter. This division results from investigation and contemplation and, in the eyes of the jurists, becomes a basis. No one is prevented from speaking against it, because as yet it has not been fully investigated, but so far no one has challenged it.

Depending on the strength or weakness of the doubt, it does have an impact on the judge's verdict. If it is strong, the actions of the culprit in that condition cannot be termed a crime, and so the penalty is removed from him. But, if it is weak, the judge exercises extreme caution, although the act as such continues to be deemed a crime. Furthermore, the punishment of *ḥadd* is removed on account of it, and is replaced with a lesser *taʿzīr* punishment. Without any restriction, this principle may also be applied to the lesser crimes of *taʿzīr*, as this rule seeks to achieve justice and render support to the accused. Every accused person stands in need of an objective consideration of his or her case, whether s/he is accused of a *ḥudūd* or *taʿzīr* crime.

The second principle, which states that it is preferable to err in forgiving than to err in punishment, flows from the rule of repealing the *ḥudūd* by doubt, and requires further explanation and elaboration. No judgement against the accused can be passed unless the judge is absolutely certain and it is conclusively proven that the accused has perpetrated that crime. If there is any doubt, then the accused must be granted pardon and released, because his acquittal in a state of doubt is better for the community and nearer to justice than the punishing of an innocent person when the allegation against him is not proven beyond doubt. This is so because the Sharīʿa does not intend to cause hardship for people; rather it aspires to give them life in the widest possible sense. To punish a person mistakenly is often difficult, and at times impossible, to rectify.

Knowledge of the Judge as a Means of Proof in Penal Law

By the 'knowledge' of the judge here is meant his witnessing of the incident of a case, such as adultery or theft. Also at question is a judge's personal experience of a similar incident: can he formulate his judgement based on such knowledge, or add his testimony to that of others in order to make up the required number of witnesses? And can his knowledge be treated as one of the means of proof in penal cases?

The majority of jurists take the view that the judge should refrain from making decisions on the basis of his knowledge, lest he become a party and a judge in the case at the same time. It is, however, permissible that, if the judge has witnessed an incidence of crime and there are others with him in this, then he may complete the required number of witnesses by giving his testimony. If, for instance, there are three witnesses in a case of adultery and he adds his testimony, he will complete the required number of witnesses. In such a case, he should not sit as a judge but should appear as a witness; if he remains a judge, then his testimony cannot be considered complementary, perfecting the testimony of the other three witnesses.[19]

Imām Shāfi'ī, however, holds the view that a judge may pass a judgement based on his knowledge. Those who support this view argue that, since it is permissible for a judge to give a judgement based on the testimonies of witnesses and their statements based on their presumptions, and if it is permissible for him to judge on the basis of what he hears or sees, then what he knows for certain must be preferable.[20]

The Ẓāhirī school is unique in its view regarding the power of the judge to formulate a verdict based on his own knowledge. It makes it incumbent upon him in cases of murder, retaliation, loss of property, *ḥudūd* and adultery, irrespective of whether such knowledge relates to the period prior to or after which his authority took effect. Based on his knowledge, his judgement is seen to be more valid, because it represents certainty of truth over and above confession and proof. Ẓāhirī jurists supports this argument with the Qur'anic verse: 'O you who believe, stand forth firmly for justice, as witnesses to God' (Q.4:135). They also refer to the statement of the Prophet, who said: 'Whoever among you sees an evil should try to change it by hand, and if he cannot do that, then by word of mouth.' This, they claim, suggests that it is the duty of a judge to do justice, and that it is not justice to leave the injustice of an unjust person without attempting to change it. Furthermore, it is correct to suppose that it is the duty of a judge to change by hand any evil that he comes to know, and to render to every person having a right his due, except if he is unjust.[21]

Those who deny the judge the right to decide on the basis of his knowledge use the Ẓāhirī argument to support their view. The best that has been said regarding the plea of the rejecters and deniers, in response to those who hold it permissible, is by Ibn al-Qayyim:

> If it were the case that there was a time when an equitable judgement was one formed on the basis of a judge's knowledge and awareness, the judges of today should be prevented from doing the same. Moreover, even if one were speaking of the eminent Shurayḥ, the Kufan judge, Ka'b ibn Siwār, or al-Ḥasan al-Baṣrī, the same criterion would apply. The Master of Judges (peace and blessings of God be upon him) knew things about the hypocrites which would make lawful their blood and assets, yet he did not use his knowledge of that to rule against them, even though he was free from any reprehension in the eyes of God, His angels and the believers, lest it be said 'Muḥammad is murdering his companions.' He who reflects upon Islamic law and the way it incorporates general interests and

> blocks certain means [to evil] would appreciate the correct opinion in this respect.[22]

It appears to this author that to prevent a judge from passing a judgement on the basis of his knowledge is most appropriate, in order to prevent the making of decisions according to personal desire or greed, and in order to secure the rights of people, especially during periods of weak religious and moral conditions. This also prevents bad opinions and accusations against judges, a lack of trust in judges by the people, and the corrupting of social life in general. The judge may, however, use his knowledge while assessing the arguments, and may convince himself of their veracity, co-ordinating with them and benefiting from other sources. In this way, he can satisfy himself that the judgement is supported by other means in accordance with his knowledge.

Thus, it would appear that, according to the preponderant schools of jurists, Islamic Sharī'a entrusts the judge to decide, in the light of what is before him, when validity is proven, whether by evidence or any other means. Similarly, the Sharī'a does not permit the judge to consider testimony when it becomes clear to him from other sources that what the testimony was given for did not take place. For instance, if four witnesses bear witness against a woman in a case of adultery, but it then becomes apparent that she is still a virgin, it is not permissible to say that, since the prescribed number of witnesses were present, it is mandatory to pass judgement against her. On this point there is consensus among the jurists.

It is also the duty of the judge to assess the arguments offered before him in a lawsuit in the light of its circumstances and the situation in which it occurred. In no case should he pass judgement except when he is convinced that the evidence produced before him proves the case. This cannot be rejected by the plea that the Islamic juristic schools are agreed on affirmation of the evidence by two male witnesses, or a man and two women. This method of affirmation of evidence has been mentioned in the Qur'an with regard to legal matters and not material cases that affirm or disprove in penal cases. The Qur'an has mentioned the testimony of two male witnesses, or of a man and two women, to affirm inscribed debts and in matters of divorce. A legal measure is aided by other auxiliaries, by the recording of the testimony and witnesses to it, taking into account any future questions or doubts concerning its proof or denial. In a material case, however, especially one constituting a punishable crime, its perpetrator would, naturally, be extremely cautious to ensure that the crime is not proven, or that he is not accused of it. Indeed, he would hide it from people, and it cannot be imagined that any sane person would commit a crime in the presence of just witnesses who could bear witness against him and affirm the crime's incidence. For this reason, logic demands that there be wider room for the affirmation of a material case in favour of the accused, or such as should negate the accusation against him, by allowing him to use all means that could lead to certainty or near certainty.

The Sharī'a is strict and uncompromising in the affirming of crimes, and exercises great care in following the rule of repealing punishments in cases of doubt. Yet, it is not severe when it comes to methods of proving the non-perpetration of crimes, and does not specify any method to prove the inaccuracy of the testimony or the witnesses, or to reject whatever they bore witness to.[23] As to the specific arguments for affirmation, the Sharī'a allows reliance on other arguments and methods, provided they are strong in their bearing upon the affirmation of the incidents in a conclusive or near-conclusive manner. In conclusion, the goal of the Sharī'a in adopting specific arguments or latitude for the judge in taking other arguments into account is consideration for the rights of people and helping the accused.

II: Criminal Justice in Islamic Sharī'a: Concepts and Precepts

Nasir bin Ibrahim Mehemeed

Criminal justice in Islamic Sharī'a has its origin in divine revelation, and its judiciary has certain peculiar characteristics and distinguishing marks that set it apart from all man-made laws. This is because it comes from the Creator of humans and the universe, who has revealed it for their benefit and made it suitable to their life conditions and situations.

Among the most important characteristics of criminal justice in Islamic law are its absolute integrity; its judicious simplicity, free of all complications and formalism; its remoteness from domination, superiority and deification; its prohibition of whatever is acquired through injustice and fraud; its freedom for all parties in a case to defend their rights without fear or obstacle; its emphasis on the best behaviour of judges, and on their fearing God and guarding themselves against punishment in the hereafter, while preserving correct mediation between themselves and witnesses of the parties, trustees, guardians and their helpers; and its tendency to enhance and complement secondary Islamic laws based on the revelation.

Definitions of *Jināya* (Crime) and '*Uqūba* (Punishment)

When we examine the philological meaning of *jināya* (perpetration of a crime), we see that it is derived from the verb *janā* (to commit a crime, to sin). It is defined as a crime or a sin which, if committed, makes retaliation mandatory for its perpetrator and incurs punishment in this world and in the hereafter. Thus, when it is said '*janā 'alā nafsih wa 'alā ahlih*' ('he perpetrated a crime against himself and his family'), such an evil is termed *jināya*.[24] Technically, a *jināya* is an aggression against a person or his rights, making retaliation or some other punishment mandatory.[25]

Philologically, the word '*uqūba* (punishment) is a noun derived from the verb '*āqaba* (to punish). It is used when a person incurs a punishment as a result of the sin that he has committed.[26] Technically, the word '*uqūba* is used to define the restrictions placed by God in order to restrain men from doing what He has forbidden and to leave what He has asked them to leave.[27] It is said to be a part of what is prescribed for the benefit of the community against disobeying the commandments of the law-giver.[28]

Categories of Crimes and their Forms

The crimes that carry prescribed punishment may be divided into several types. The first are crimes against body and limbs, e.g. murder and wounds; then there are crimes against the modesty of women, e.g. adultery and fornication; then there are crimes against property. Whatever is taken by robbery is termed highway robbery when it cannot be interpreted otherwise; under certain pretexts, it is called insurrection. If an item is taken secretly from a protected place, it is theft, and if it is taken by force by one who holds a high position or power, it is termed usurpation. Other crimes include crimes against one's honour or defamation, known as *qadhf*, which includes the slandering of innocent women, and crimes of aggression that make lawful the partaking of certain foods and drinks, such as wine, which the Sharī'a has prohibited.[29] For these crimes the Sharī'a has prescribed appropriate penalties that help ensure against their violation.

Forms of Punishment

The judge in Islamic Sharī'a enjoys vast discretionary powers in fixing *ta'zīr* penalties, their amount, and their enforcement in such a manner that will help restrain the culprit from the crime. This power does not extend absolutely, and is by no means free of constraints or restrictions. Rather, it is constrained by the appropriate laws concerning this punishment and its suitability to the crime, the culprit and society, and the extent of the prevalence of crime in this society. It is a capability that gives a judge freedom within the framework of consideration of general welfare.

Of those specific punishments meant to deter the culprit and prevent crime are the following: imprisonment; banishment and exile from the place of the crime and the city in which it was perpetrated; death; reprimand and rebuke; threat; boycott; publicizing of the crime perpetrated; financial punishment, by the seizing or destroying of wealth or assets; and flogging – often the subject of much controversy. In fact, flogging is one of the punishments prescribed in the Qur'an, *sunna* and through consensus of opinion (*ijmāʿ*). As the Qur'an says: 'Give a hundred lashes each to the adulterer and the adulteress' (Q.24:2). It is also reported by Abū Ḥurayra that a man who had drunk wine was brought to the Prophet, who said: 'Beat him.' Abū Ḥurayra adds: 'So some of us beat him with hands and others with their clothes.'[30] Further, it may be argued that there has been a practical consensus on flogging as a punishment with regard to *ḥudūd* and *taʿzīr* crimes since the time of the first prophet, since all earlier revealed Sharīʿa both approve of and prescribe this punishment.

It should be emphasized here that, when enforcing this punishment, the condition of the person to be flogged must be taken into due consideration, as must the number of lashes and the nature of the crime or sin committed. It must also be understood that the punishment of flogging is constrained by certain conditions and specific methods. What is portrayed in this regard by the international media is often untruthful and misleading, the purpose being – it would seem – to portray Islam and its laws in a negative light.

The punishment of flogging is prescribed for some *ḥudūd* crimes, and also for some other *taʿzīr* crimes carrying lesser punishments. There are several benefits in applying this punishment for crimes as prescribed, such as ease of enforcement while simultaneously achieving the objective of warning and prevention. Then there is the physical effect of this punishment on the one who is flogged, which directly encourages him to desist from crime, now and in the future. In addition, this punishment contains a psychological pain far greater than any physical pain, which again serves as a deterrent. What is more, this punishment is at times sufficient to replace other punishments, such as imprisonment, which frequently brings criminals into contact with one another and provides opportunities for them to learn each other's criminal ways. Other benefits include the fact that the punishment of flogging can be awarded in cases of all minor and major crimes, depending on the seriousness of the offence, and that the punishment is limited only to the perpetrator of the crime. In this way, it affects none other than him, unlike punishments such as imprisonment, the harm of which extends to the prisoner's family and children, and also represents a waste of the community's resources.

The Purpose of Criminal Punishments in Islamic Sharīʿa

A punishment is a necessary remedy for treating a crime. Its purpose is not vengeance against the culprit; rather, its purpose is to protect society from the aggressions of transgressors and to purify their souls and put a stop to transgression and crime. Thus, in Islam, punishment is a mercy for man, whether he is obedient or disobedient; it is a necessary requisite of divine justice; it seeks to prevent crime before its incidence and is a warning against its repetition. It thereby has a simultaneously preventive as well as curative role.

It is belief in this purpose that impels us to submit to whatever penalties Islamic Sharīʿa has prescribed for the various categories of crimes. In all cases, the crimes described therein are measured with a divine balance of justice, so that punishments are harsh where necessary and lenient where appropriate. There is thereafter no room for attributing harshness to this system, for no matter how strong, criminal punishments in Islamic Sharīʿa are ultimately merciful.

The punishments prescribed in Islamic Sharīʿa and their appropriateness in deterring crime in all times and political climates are also clear. They are prescribed in the interests of society from various aspects. As stated, punishment is a mercy for man whether obedient or disobedient; it is a mercy for the obedient since it includes protecting him from the power of evil and transgression, helping him in obedience and preventing him from disobedience, and saving him from the harm of the crime. It is also a mercy for the disobedient since it restrains him from the pursuit of crime, removes the corruption resulting from his disobedience, and arrests his criminal tendency. Therefore, it is not correct to regard punishment as if it were a form of revenge against the culprit; in fact, it should be seen as a reward for his actions, and a betterment of his condition. The punishment as such is not the object, but is merely a measure taken in response to a genuine need.

The prescription of punishment is also a necessary requisite of justice, and God is just in all that He has commanded. But justice cannot be achieved without punishing the culprit, for if he is left unpunished, it will damage the interests of society and will be detrimental to the culprit. Furthermore, punishment is an effective deterrent: the fact that it is prescribed and people know that a crime will be punished is generally sufficient to deter them from crime. Lastly, punishment lightens the psychological ills that afflict the victim of a crime, be it an individual or a society.

The Implementation of Punishments

After a ruling has been given by the judge awarding the prescribed punishment, the enforcement of this judgement is mandatory. For, unless implemented fully, its requisites and supportive securities cannot be realized. A special department is responsible for the enforcement of the punishment pronounced against the culprit; alternatively a representative of the ruler, who is responsible for the implementation of the commandments, is delegated authority in this respect. The rules laid down by Islamic Sharīʿa for the enforcement of a punishment must be observed during its implementation; this applies to the punishment itself, the one who is to be punished, and the place of the punishment. In short, the punishment should be administered as prescribed, and there should be no addition to or retraction from it, nor any obstruction or difficulty in its enforcement.

The condition and capacity of the person to be punished should also be taken into account, and if his condition is not conducive to the infliction of the prescribed punishment, the matter should be referred back to the judge who passed the sentence, so that the case may be reviewed. This will determine any change in the enforcement of the punishment, or in the method of its implementation. It will also take into consideration the possibility that the punishment might be increased from what was originally determined. As to the place of punishment, we should consider that the texts call for particular punishments to be accompanied by publicity. If publicity is not required, however, then the punishment may be implemented without it.

To close, the implementation of punishment in Islamic Sharīʿa is based on the principles of moderation and compassion, and is viewed as a means of preventing crime and protecting the dignity of man. This is achieved by attempting to cleanse the culprit's life of all traces of criminality, and by preventing him from lapsing back into criminal ways. Thus, from the Islamic legal standpoint, punishment, though painful, is in full conformity with the dictates of balanced reason. The pain felt on its implementation is seen to be like that caused by a surgeon's knife to the body of a patient, its aim being to restore health and provide a cure.

Notes

[1] ʿAlī ibn Muḥammad al-Māwardī, *Kitāb al-Aḥkām al-Sulṭāniyya* (Cairo, 1986), p 219

[2] ʿAlāʾ al-Dīn al-Kasānī, *Badāʾiʿ al-Ṣanāʾiʿ fī Tartīb al-Sharāʾiʿ*, VII, 2nd ed (Beirut, 1982), pp 33; 56

[3] See, for instance, Ibn Rushd's *Bidāyat al-Mujtahid wa Nihāyat al-Muqtaṣid*, II (Cairo, n.d.), pp 394-5

[4] See Muḥammad Salīm al-ʿAwwā, *Fī Uṣūl al-Niẓām al-Jināʾī al-Islāmī*, 2nd ed (Cairo, 1983), pp 125-70

[5] Al-Kasānī: *Badāʾiʿ al-Ṣanāʾiʿ* p 249; Abū Isḥāq Ibrāhīm ibn ʿAlī al-Shīrāzī, *al-Muhadhdhab fī Fiqh al-Imām Shāfiʿī*, II (Cairo, n.d.), p 212; and Muḥammad al-Khaṭīb al-Sharbīnī, *Mughnī al-Muḥtāj ilā Maʿrifat Maʿānial-Minhāj*, IX (Cairo, n.d.), p 472

[6] Shams al-Dīn Muḥammad al-Sarakhsī, *al-Mabsūṭ*, IX (Cairo, 1906), p 36

[7] Ibn ʿÂbidīn, *Ḥāshiyat Radd al-Muḥtār ʿalā Durr al-Mukhtār*, III (Damascus, 1421 AH), p 179; al-Māwardī: *Kitāb al-Aḥkām*, p 237, and Abū ʿAbd Allāh Muḥammad ibn Abī Bakr ibn Qayyim al-Jawziyya, *al-Ṭuruq al-Ḥukmiyya fiʾl-Siyāsa al-Sharʿiyya* (Cairo, 1953), pp 117-19

[8] Ibn ʿÂbidīn: *Ḥāshiya*, III, pp 182-5, and the statements of the jurists of all successive schools, disagreement among them being limited and mostly verbal. See also al-Shīrāzī: *al-Muhadhdhab*, II, p 306

[9] ʿAbd al-Raḥmān Tāj, *al-Siyāsa al-Sharʿiyya* (Cairo, 1953), pp 7–8

[10] Al-ʿAwwā: *Uṣūl*, pp 292-3

[11] Al-Majlis al-A'lā li'l-Shu'ūn al-Islāmiyya, *Mawsū'at al-Fiqh al-Islāmī*, (Cairo, n.d.), p 2136
[12] Al-Sharbīnī: *al-Mughnī*, IX, p 158
[13] Ibn al-Qayyim: *al-Ṭuruq al-Ḥukmiyya*, p 28
[14] Ibn al-Qayyim: *al-Ṭuruq al-Ḥukmiyya*, p 97
[15] 'Abd al-Qādir 'Awda, *al-Tashrī' al-Jinā'ī al-Islāmī Muqāran bi'l-Qānūn al-Waḍ'ī*, I (Cairo, 1984), p 207
[16] Al-Tirmidhī, *Sunan al-Tirmidhī*, IV (Beirut, 197-?), K. al-Ḥudūd, p 25, *ḥadīth* no 1424
[17] Muḥammad Abū Zahra, *al-Jarīma wa'l-'Uqūba fī Fiqh al-Islām*, I (Cairo, 1998), p 199
[18] Abū Zahra: *al-Jarīma wa'l-'Uqūba*, I, p 199
[19] Al-Kasānī: *Badā'i' al-Ṣanā'i'* VII, p 52; Muḥammad ibn 'Abd al-Bāqī al-Zurqānī, *Sharḥ al-Zurqānī 'alā Muwaṭṭa' al-Imām Mālik*, VII (n.p., 1936), p 150; al-Shīrāzī: *al-Muhadhdhab*, II, p 320; and al-Sharbīnī: *al-Mughnī*, X, p 191
[20] Al- Shīrāzī: *al-Muhadhdhab*, II, p 320
[21] Abū Muḥammad 'Alī ibn Aḥmad ibn Ḥazm, *al-Muḥallā*, IX (Cairo, 1347), p 427
[22] Ibn al-Qayyim: *al-Ṭuruq al-Ḥukmiyya*, pp 231-2
[23] Al-'Awwā: *Uṣūl*, p 293
[24] Ibn Manẓūr, *Lisān al-'Arab*, II (Cairo, 1308 AH), pp 392-3
[25] Manṣūr ibn Yūnus Idrīs al-Buḥūtī, *Kashshāf al-Qinā' 'an Matn al-Iqnā'*, V (Beirut, 1982), p 503
[26] Ibn Manẓūr: *Lisān al-'Arab*, II p 110
[27] Al-Māwardī: *Kitāb al-Aḥkām*, p 221
[28] 'Awda: *al-Tashrī' al-Jinā'ī*, I, p 617
[29] Ibn Rushd: *Bidāyat al-Mujtahid*, II, pp 394-5
[30] Al-Bukhārī, Ṣaḥīḥ *al-Bukhārī*, XII (Cairo, 1296 AH), p 66

3

Basic Guarantees in the Islamic Criminal Justice System

Gamil Muhammed Hussein

Islamic law, or Sharīʿa, recognizes all of the basic guarantees contained within the most developed systems of criminal justice today. Indeed, the principle of legality, the presumption of innocence and the inherent dignity of the individual – with all that these entail – are basic and general principles and guarantees which were recognized in the Islamic criminal justice system under Sharīʿa long before any modern criminal justice system. Islamic Sharīʿa proscribes arbitrary arrest or detention, coercion (duress), spying and other forms of unlawful interference in the private life of the individual. Sharīʿa also recognizes the right to a fair and speedy trial before a competent, independent and impartial judge or court, and the right to a judicial review before a higher court. Furthermore, all defence rights are recognized under Sharīʿa law. The Islamic criminal justice system also recognizes the right to compensation for unlawful criminal procedures and/or any miscarriage of justice. As such, this chapter will focus on the basic guarantees in criminal justice under Islamic Sharīʿa.

The Principle of Legality within the Islamic Criminal Justice System

In legal terms, the principle of legality is represented in the two postulates *nullum crimen sine lege*, or no crime without law, and *nulla poena sine lege*, or no punishment without law. The purpose of these two postulates is to protect individuals from the abuse of power by authorities, thereby leading to the loss of life, liberty or property. They also protect against governmental repression and suppression of the political, economic, social and other rights of the individual or of any group of individuals. The objectives of the postulates of the principle of legality can be achieved only if prior notice of the requirements of law and the consequences of its violation are declared legally, the knowledge of which is made available to all.

The principle of legality has been designated one of the most basic principles of human rights within all civilized systems of law, including international law. It is not our purpose here to study the application of this principle, along with its postulates, in various domestic or international legal systems, but rather to refer to such application in relation to various issues pertaining to the Islamic criminal justice system.[1] We may suggest, however, that the principle of legality has not been applied as stringently as may have been expected in any positive system of law.

The principle of legality, with its two stricter postulates, is recognized and established under Islamic Sharīʿa. The principle finds its origins in the two most basic sources of the Sharīʿa, namely the Qur'an and the *sunna*. The Qur'an – the single most important, most basic and most fundamental source of the Sharīʿa – contains a good number of verses which are very clearly indicative of what is now known as the principle of legality with its two postulates. For example, the Qur'an stipulates:

> *Who receiveth guidance, Receiveth it for his own benefit: Who goeth astray doth so to his own loss: No bearer of burdens can bear the burden of another: Nor would We visit with Our Wrath until We had sent an apostle* [*to give warning*]. (Q.17:15)

In addition, it states:

> *Nor was thy Lord the one to destroy a population until He had sent to its Centre an apostle rehearsing to them Our Signs; nor are We going to destroy a population except when its members practise iniquity.* (Q.28:59)

Moreover, the Qur'an reads in part:

> *God forgives what is past: For repetition God will exact from him the penalty. For God is Exalted, and Lord of Retribution.* (Q.5:95)

Furthermore, it declares:

> *Say to the Unbelievers, If* [*now*] *they desist, their past would be forgiven them; But if they persist, the punishment of those before them is already* [*a matter of warning for them*]. (Q.8:38)

Q.4:22-3 proscribes certain conduct and activities and warns those who commit such conduct or activities of great punishment, although its two verses declare that such punishment will not apply retroactively. Q.4:23 reads:

Except for what is past; for God is Oft-forgiving, Most Merciful.

The Prophet Muḥammad declared that Islam proscribed and criminalized blood offences and usury and that punishment would apply, but he also declared that such punishment would not apply retroactively. Those who committed such crimes before these offences were proscribed were forgiven, provided they did not repeat the commission of any of the said offences.[2]

Thus, it would appear that the two most important and fundamental sources of Islamic Sharīʿa, the Qur'an and the *sunna*, have adopted the precepts of the principle of legality. To be more specific, one must also examine how Islamic Sharīʿa applies the precepts or postulates of what is now known as the principle of legality. Islamic Sharīʿa classifies various criminal offences according to the corresponding punishment for each offence, giving three main categories: *ḥudūd* offences, *qiṣāṣ* offences and *taʿzīr* offences. *Ḥudūd* and *qiṣāṣ* offences represent the strictest and most stringent application of the principle of legality, with its postulates or precepts, that have ever existed in human history. *Taʿzīr* offences represent the application of a somewhat more flexible formula of the principle of legality, which is similar to the application of the principle in other, modern systems of law.

Ḥudūd *Offences*

Ḥudūd offences under Islamic Sharīʿa[3] are crimes against God or against the essential system and basic foundations of the Islamic State, or against the interests of society as a whole. Punishments for such crimes are determined by God in the Qur'an or by the Prophet in the *sunna*. *Ḥudūd* crimes, once proven before the judge, are not and cannot be subject to forgiveness or pardon; punishment must be imposed upon criminals who are proven guilty of committing such crimes. Descriptions of *ḥudūd* crimes follow.

(a) Adultery

Adultery as a crime is proscribed by the Qur'an:

Nor come nigh to adultery: For it is a shameful [deed] and an evil, opening the road [to other evils]. (Q.17:32)

Punishment for adultery is also determined in the Qur'an, which states:

The woman and the man guilty of adultery or fornication, – Flog each of them with a hundred stripes: Let not compassion move you in their case, in a matter prescribed by God, if ye believe in God and the Last Day: And let a party of the Believers witness their punishment. (Q.24:2)

Another, added punishment is imposed by the *sunna*, being the exiling of the person guilty of adultery or fornication for a year. If the person guilty of the said crime is married to another person, however, then the punishment which must be imposed is the stoning of the guilty person to death, as decreed by the *sunna*.[4]

The reasons for these severe punishments are to protect the family, which is the basic unit of society; to guard against mistrust, which threatens the family; to prevent diseases; to prevent the mixing of blood relationships; and to prevent the introducing of members into the family who are not the product of a marriage relationship between the father and mother. In addition, adultery or fornication affects the rules of transfer of private property by way of succession, inheritance and will. Moreover, it leads to the opening of the path to other infinite and unforeseeable evils.

In order to apply the above severe punishments, the establishment of guilt must be proven beyond doubt. This is almost impossible to satisfy, since Islamic law requires that four male, adult, trustworthy witnesses must testify that they saw the two partners committing the act of adultery, and that the man's organ was inside the woman.[5] The presentation of this form of proof has not once occurred in the history of the application of the Sharī'a. Another means of establishing the guilt of the person in respect of adultery or fornication is his or her own confession, which he or she should willingly and freely present to the judge.[6]

(b) Launching a False Charge against a Chaste Person

This crime, known as *qadhf*, is proscribed by the Qur'an and the *sunna*:

Those who slander chaste, indiscreet but believing women, are cursed in this life and in the Hereafter: For them is a grievous Penalty. On the Day when their tongues, their hands, and their feet will bear witness against them as to their actions, on that Day God will pay them back [*all*] *their just dues, and they will realize that God is the* [*very*] *Truth, that makes all things manifest.* (Q.24: 23-5)

In addition, the same *sūra* proclaims:

And those who launch a charge against chaste women, and produce not four witnesses [*to support their allegations*], *– Flog them with eighty stripes; and*

> *reject their evidence ever after: for such men are wicked transgressors* ... (Q.24:4)

The *sunna* also proscribes slander or launching false charges against chaste persons.[7] Thus, the Qur'an and the *sunna* proclaim that slandering or launching false charges against chaste women is a crime punishable both in this world and the next. It should be mentioned, however, that various Muslim schools of law have interpreted the relevant Qur'anic and *sunna* texts to cover the launching of false charges against both chaste women *and* men, in accordance with the rule of equality.[8] It should also be added here that the crime of *qadhf* covers only those cases where a person launches a charge that a chaste person has committed adultery, and where the person launching the charge fails to produce four male adult witnesses to prove his charge before the judge.[9]

The purpose of proscribing and criminalizing slander is to protect the integrity and good reputation of persons in society, and to prevent the launching of false charges against various individuals. The protection of the family and of the whole of society is yet another intended objective.

(c) Drinking Alcohol

The drinking of wine and other intoxicating materials was proscribed gradually under Islamic Sharī'a. The Qur'an first proscribed being drunk during prayer times:

> *O ye who believe! Approach not prayers with a mind befogged* [*or while you are drunk*], *until ye can understand All that ye say* ... (Q.4:43)

The text of the Qur'an later provides another degree of proscription:

> *They ask thee concerning wine and gambling. Say: 'In them is great sin, and some profit, for men; but the sin is greater than the profit.'* (Q.2:219)

After, absolute and total proscription is imposed:

> *O ye who believe! Intoxicants and gambling,* [*dedication of*] *stones, and* [*divination by*] *arrows, are an abomination, of Satan's handiwork: Eschew such* [*abomination*], *That ye may prosper.*
>
> *Satan's plan is* [*but*] *to excite enmity and hatred between you, with intoxicants and gambling, and hinder you from the remembrance of God, and from prayer: Will ye not then abstain?*

> *Obey God and obey the Apostle, and beware [of evil]: If ye turn back, know ye that it is Our Apostle's duty to proclaim [the Message] in the clearest manner.* (Q.5:90-2)

In addition, the Prophet Muḥammad proclaimed: 'Every intoxicating matter [every intoxicant] is proscribed and prohibited.'[10] He also declared: 'Any thing much of which intoxicates, the little of it is prohibited.'[11] Thus, both the Qur'an and the *sunna* proscribe drinking, and consider intoxicants an abomination of Satan's handiwork.

Punishment for this crime is determined by the *sunna* of the Prophet, by the practice of his Companions, and by the various schools of Islamic Sharīʿa. Depending on the school of law adopted by the ruler, the punishment that must apply is the flogging of the person who commits the crime with forty to eighty stripes.[12] Protecting the human mind, preventing enmity and hatred between members of the community, preventing all other crimes and offences which can be committed by the person who is drunk, and achieving prosperity and avoiding all other evils, are the reasons for proscribing and criminalizing the drinking of wine and all other intoxicating substances.

(d) Theft

Theft is proscribed and criminalized in both the Qur'an and the *sunna*. The Qur'an stipulates:

> *As to the thief, male or female, cut off his or her hands: A punishment by way of example, from God, for their crime: And God is Exalted in Power.*
> *But if the thief repent after his crime, and amend his conduct, God turneth to him in forgiveness; for God is Oft-forgiving, Most Merciful.* (Q.5:38-9)

The practice of the Prophet condemned theft as a crime, and showed the implementation of the Qur'anic verses quoted above.[13]

Protecting private property and the right to ownership is a basic right of every person under the Sharīʿa, which considers any form of aggression against property or ownership a serious threat to society and to the social order of the state. Therefore, it is necessary to consider theft a serious crime, which warrants serious punishment, as stipulated in the Qur'an.

(e) Ḥirāba

Ḥirāba, or waging war against God and his Apostle and making or spreading corruption on earth, is another serious *ḥudūd* crime under Islamic Sharīʿa. The Qur'an states:

The punishment of those who wage war against God and His Apostle, and strive with might and main for mischief through the land is: execution, or crucifixion, or the cutting off of hands and feet from opposite sides, or exile from the land: That is their disgrace in this world, and a heavy punishment is theirs in the Hereafter;

Except for those who repent before they fall into your power: In that case, know that God is Oft-forgiving, Most Merciful. (Q.5:33-4)

The *sunna* of the Prophet and prevailing views in Islamic schools of the Sharīʿa designate certain criminal acts as falling within the definition of this crime, among them: a person going out to violently and/or coercively take the money of another person or persons, which leads to frightening that person or persons; the criminal cannot take the money and does not kill any person; a person going out to violently and/or coercively take the money of another person or persons; the criminal takes the money but does not kill any person; a person going out to violently and/or coercively take the money of another person or persons; the criminal cannot take the money but he kills the person; or a person going out to violently and/or coercively take the money of another person or persons; the criminal kills the person and takes the money.

Contemporary scholars of Islamic Sharīʿa adopt the view that terrorism is included under the crime of *ḥirāba*, or waging war against God and his Apostle and making or spreading corruption on earth. Punishment for any of such criminal acts is execution, crucifixion, the cutting off of hands and feet from opposite sides, or exile from the land.[14]

(f) Unjustified and Violent Disobedience to the Muslim Ruler in the Islamic State

The Qur'an contains a number of verses dealing with this crime:

If two parties among the Believers fall into a quarrel [*fight each other*], *make ye peace between them: but if one of them transgresses beyond bounds against the other, then fight ye* [*all*] *against the one that transgresses until it complies with the Command of God. But if it complies, then make peace between them with justice, and be fair: for God loves those who are fair* [*and just*].

The Believers are but a single Brotherhood: So make peace and reconciliation between your two [*contending*] *brothers; and fear God, that ye may receive Mercy.* (Q.49:9-10)

In addition, the Qur'an states:

O ye who believe! Obey God, and obey the Apostle, and those charged with authority among you. If ye differ in anything among yourselves, refer it to God

> *and His Apostle, if ye do believe in God and the Last Day: That is best, and most suitable for final determination.* (Q.4:59)

Furthermore, the *sunna* includes a good number of sayings to the effect that Muslims must not revolt or use force against their Muslim rulers; that renegades are considered the enemies of the Muslim community; and that punishment for those who renege and use force against the Muslim community is death.[15] It should be stressed, however, that Islamic schools of Sharī'a require the existence of three elements: violating the *imām* or the Muslim ruler and making efforts to remove him from office; the use of force or violence against the *imām* or the Muslim ruler; and the existence of the criminal intent or *mens rea.* Thus, the person who violates the *imām* and uses force or violence against him to oust him from office, must know that he is violating the law and that he is wilfully using force or violence to achieve this result.[16] The purpose of criminalizing unjustified and violent disobedience to the *imām* or Muslim ruler and the use of force to oust him is to protect the existence, unity, continuity and progress of the Muslim *umma.*

(g) Turning Back from the Muslim Faith

Turning back from the Muslim faith (*ridda*) is discussed in the Qur'an, which reads in part:

> *And if any of you turn back from their faith and die in unbelief, their works will bear no fruit in this life and in the Hereafter; they will be companions of the Fire and will abide therein.* (Q.2:217)

Equally, the Prophet proclaimed: 'Kill whoever turns back from his faith.'

In order for this crime to exist, however, a person must knowingly and wilfully commit an act, abstain from committing an act, or make a pronouncement which has the effect of making him/her turn back from the Islamic faith. But, if the person commits an act, abstains from committing an act, or makes the pronouncement without willing or knowing the effect of turning back from the Islamic faith, he/she will not be considered to have committed this crime.[17]

The punishment for this crime, in this life, is death.[18] The purposes behind this severe punishment for those who change their Islamic faith or turn back from their faith are to protect the Muslim *umma* from discord, spying, disrespect and mockery. Under the Sharī'a, Islam is a religion, a nationality and a state; adherents of Islam are members of the Islamic State and the Muslim *umma,* and enjoy Muslim 'nationality'. Thus, to turn back from the Islamic faith in an open way is tantamount to waging war against

God, the Apostle, and the Muslim state or *umma.* Therefore, severe punishment is required to defend the *umma* against this serious crime.

Qiṣāṣ *Offences*

Qiṣāṣ (retaliation) and *diya* (compensation) crimes are the second category under Islamic Sharī'a where the principle of legality is fully and strictly observed. The Qur'an includes a number of verses concerning such crimes, for example:

> *O ye who believe! The law of equality* [*retaliation*] *is prescribed to you in cases of murder: The free for the free, the slave for the slave, the woman for the woman. But if any remission is made by the brother of the slain, then grant any reasonable demand, and compensate him with handsome gratitude. This is a concession and a mercy from your Lord. After this whoever exceeds the limits shall be in grave penalty.*
>
> *In the Law of Equality* [*Retaliation*] *there is saving of Life to you, O ye men of understanding; that ye may restrain yourselves.* (Q.2:178-9)

In addition, the Qur'an states:

> *Nor take life – which God has made sacred – except for just cause. And if anyone is slain wrongfully, We have given his heir authority* [*to demand* qiṣāṣ *or to forgive*]*: But let him not exceed bounds in the matter of taking life; for he is helped by the Lord* [*or, he shall become victorious*]. (Q.17:33)

Moreover, it proclaims:

> *We ordained therein* [*the Torah, or the Law revealed to Moses*] *for them; 'Life for Life, eye for eye, nose for nose, ear for ear, tooth for tooth, and wounds equal for equal.' But if any one remits the retaliation by way of charity, it is an act of atonement for himself. And if any fail to judge by what God hath revealed, they are the unjust* [*wrongdoers*]. (Q.5:45)

Furthermore, the Qur'an sets out the general rule concerning the Law of Equality or Retaliation (*qiṣāṣ*); stating:

> *The prohibited month for the prohibited month, – and so for all things prohibited, – there is the law of equality. If then any one transgresses the prohibition against you, transgress ye likewise against him. But fear God, and know that God is with those who restrain themselves.* (Q.2:194)

The Qur'an also deals with unintentional murder, stipulating:

Never should a Believer kill a Believer; but [if it so happens] by mistake, [compensation is due]: If one [so] kills a Believer, it is ordained that he should free a believing slave, and pay compensation to the deceased's family, unless they remit it freely. If the deceased belonged to a people at war with you, and he was a believer, the freeing of a believing slave [is enough]. If he belonged to a people with whom ye have a treaty of mutual alliance, compensation should be paid to his family, and a believing slave be freed. For those who find this beyond their means, [is prescribed] a fast for two months running: By way of repentance to God: for God hath all knowledge and all wisdom. (Q.4:92)

Meanwhile, the same *sūra* deals with intentional murder, declaring:

If a man kills a Believer intentionally, his recompense is Hell, to abide therein [for ever]: and the wrath and the curse of God are upon him, and a dreadful penalty is prepared for him. (Q.4:93)

Qiṣāṣ crimes include intentional murder; semi-intentional murder; unintentional murder or murder by mistake; intentional cutting off of limbs; and unintentional wounding and unintentional cutting off of limbs. The Qur'an determines punishments to be applied according to the law of equality or retaliation (*qiṣāṣ*) and/or cases of compensation (*diya*). The *sunna* of the Prophet also spells out detailed cases of *qiṣāṣ* and *diya*.[19] Thus, it seems clear that the principle of legality has been strictly followed insofar as *qiṣāṣ* crimes are concerned.[20]

Ta'zīr *Offences*

Ta'zīr crimes are offences which do not fit the definitions of *ḥudūd* or *qiṣāṣ* offences under the Sharī'a. They also include offences which fit the definition of *qiṣāṣ* offences, but in cases where the victim, or his next of kin among his blood relatives, selects to remit the retaliation, or to remit both the retaliation and compensation.[21] In cases of such remission, the legislative body or the judge may decide to apply a lighter sentence, in order to protect the interests of society and prevent the repetition of such offences.[22] Protection of society at large; protection of the legitimate interests of the individual; protection of the state and its values and interests; and protection against serious violations of Islamic law, are the general and basic criteria which limit the authority of the ruler or the legislative body in defining *ta'zīr* crimes, and in determining corresponding punishments. The same criteria govern the authority of the judge in selecting the sentence to be applied.[23]

Thus, it is evident that the principle of legality is followed with regard to *taʿzīr* offences, inasmuch as this principle is followed in most modern positive legal systems, which entrust the judge with wide discretionary powers concerning the selection of sentences to be applied. Examples of *taʿzīr* offences include bribery, embezzlement, defamation and slander (including false charges of committing adultery, which, as we have seen, is a *ḥudūd* crime), libel, lying under oath, contempt of court, violations of law or regulations, and a host of other offences as may be defined by the competent authority.

The Principle of Non-Retroactivity

The principle of non-retroactivity of criminal laws is a natural result of the principle of legality. The Islamic criminal justice system under Islamic Sharīʿa adopted and applied the principle of non-retroactivity of criminal laws long before this was known in modern positive legal systems, and the Qur'an itself is the origin and basic source of this principle. Q.17:15, Q.28:59, Q.5:95, Q.8:38 and Q.4:22-3 are all examples of Qur'anic verses adopting and applying what is now known as the principle of non-retroactivity, insofar as matters of proscription and criminalisation are concerned. The *sunna* also emphasizes the application of this principle.[24]

The Presumption of Innocence under Islamic Sharīʿa

A basic norm of Islamic Sharīʿa is that man is innocent and pure. The innocence and purity of man constitute original and fundamental precepts upon which Islamic Sharīʿa and the Islamic faith itself are built. God has created man innocent and pure, and man must protect his innocence and purity. Every person is under an obligation to believe in the innocence and purity of every other person, and to treat him accordingly. Thus, every person is presumed to act righteously and properly unless it is proved otherwise. A person has the right and liberty to act as he pleases and to exercise any activity, except if such an action or activity is proscribed under the Sharīʿa. And, as we have seen, the Sharīʿa accepts and applies the principle of legality with its strict postulates, and therefore crimes and punishments are exceptions. Lastly, a person is innocent unless proven guilty by a competent judge or court, in accordance with the proper rules of evidence and due process of law under Islamic Sharīʿa.[25]

The presumption of innocence under Islamic Sharīʿa has a number of aspects. Firstly, *ḥudūd* punishments must be averted by suspicions or doubts. This constitutes another basic tenet of Islamic Sharīʿa, and is based on the Prophet's saying: 'Avert *ḥudūd* punishments by suspicions or doubts and if the accused has a way out, release him. It is better for the *imām* to pardon erroneously than to punish erroneously',[26] and his saying: 'Avoid killing

Muslims as you can.'[27] This means that a punishment cannot be applied unless the criminal guilt of the accused can be truly proven and established. Any suspicion or doubt, which may weaken the truthfulness and/or validity of evidence of criminality or guilt, must lead to the averting of punishments. Suspicions and doubts leading to the averting of punishments can be classified into four main categories: suspicions or doubts concerning proscription and criminalization, and the evidence related thereto; suspicions or doubts concerning the criminal intent or *mens rea*, and the ignorance thereof; suspicions or doubts concerning the evidence of the commission of the crime or the material element of the crime; or suspicions or doubts concerning the application of criminal laws to the details of the facts of the situation. Muslim jurists agree that all such rules are applicable to all types of crimes under the Sharīʿa, and to *ḥudūd* and *qiṣāṣ* cases in particular, which are considered the most serious under Islamic law.[28]

A second aspect to the presumption of innocence is that erroneous pardon is better than erroneous punishment, which is also a basic tenet of the Sharīʿa. As we have already quoted, the Prophet said that 'it is better for the *imām* to pardon erroneously than to punish erroneously',[29] which suggests that criminal guilt must be proven beyond any doubt, and that the slightest suspicion or doubt that the accused has not committed the crime must lead to the averting of the punishment.

A third aspect is that the rules of evidence and due process of law must be properly and strictly followed within the Islamic criminal justice system. This is one of the most basic and fundamental tenets of the Sharīʿa, and of the Islamic criminal justice system itself. Islamic Sharīʿa has specified detailed rules of evidence for each crime, particularly *ḥudūd* and *qiṣāṣ* crimes. Such rules must be properly and strictly followed, in order to prove and establish the criminal guilt of the accused, and must remain legally valid, sound and conclusive throughout all stages of the criminal proceedings and the execution of the sentence. If, at any stage of the trial proceedings, or during the execution of the sentence, any doubt arises as to the credibility, validity, soundness or conclusiveness of the evidence, the accused must be declared innocent and released, even if he has been convicted and sentenced, and even if the execution of the sentence, after a final and definitive judgment, has begun to take place.[30]

To give an example, the establishment of guilt for the crime of adultery requires the existence of four male, adult, trustworthy Muslim witnesses, who must testify before the judge or court that they saw the two persons commit adultery, and that they saw the man's organ inside the woman. But if they testify that they saw the man's organ inside the woman without describing this act as adultery under Islamic law, the evidence would be neither valid nor conclusive, for there would be a doubt, however remote, that adultery was indeed committed. Rather, there could be some other form of legal or semi-legal relationship between the man and woman, which would warrant the existence of suspicion or doubt that their act was not adultery, and that it may have been an incomplete marriage or some other legitimate relationship. Furthermore, if three witnesses testify to the act of adultery and the details of the crime (as illustrated above), and the fourth witness so testifies but does not use clear and conclusive words, the criminal guilt of the accused cannot be established. Similarly, if the fourth witness testifies that he heard but did not see the two persons commit the crime with its details, this would again be insufficient to establish the criminal guilt of the accused. Moreover, should any of the witnesses elect to deny, change or modify his testimony at any stage of the trial proceedings, or at any time thereafter before the completion of the execution of the sentence, the accused must be released and declared innocent, and the final and definitive judgment convicting and sentencing him must be annulled and vacated. Furthermore, in all such cases, witnesses must be punished for slander, as one of the *ḥudūd* crimes.

If, however, four adult, male, trustworthy Muslim witnesses testify that the man and the woman did indeed commit adultery and describe the details of the crime, but a number of trustworthy women testify that the accused woman was still a virgin, then the two persons must be declared innocent and released. In addition, if technical, medical or forensic evidence reveals or demonstrates that any of the two accused persons is incapable of having sexual relations, then the two persons must be declared innocent and released. Furthermore, the four witnesses must specify the time and place of the act of adultery. If any difference or conflict, however slight, arises between their testimonies as to the time or place of the crime or any surrounding circumstances, the evidence will not be deemed valid or conclusive, and the accused must be declared innocent and released.[31]

The only other means of proving adultery is the confession of the person committing the crime, which must be presented in a court of law of his or her own free will, and must remain valid and conclusive until the complete execution of the sentence. But, if the person elects to deny his or her confession at any stage, even be it during the execution of the sentence, he or she must be freed, and the sentence must be terminated or discontinued.[32]

Likewise, every other *ḥudūd* or *qiṣāṣ* crime must be proven in accordance with strictly specified rules of evidence. Furthermore, correct procedures must be strictly followed, otherwise the criminal guilt of the accused cannot be properly proven and established. Similar rules are also applicable to *taʿzīr* crimes.[33] As such, correct and strict procedures must be followed throughout all stages of the criminal procedure, and due process of law must be followed properly under Sharīʿa rules concerning the Islamic criminal justice system. Any violation of such rules, however slight, makes the evidence of criminal guilt insufficient and, therefore, the accused must be declared innocent and freed.

Consequences of the Presumption of Innocence

The principle of legality and the presumption of innocence are intertwined and inseparable, as each of the two principles is the basis and result of the other. These two principles must co-exist as the most basic foundation of any just and fair criminal justice system. The four most significant consequences of the recognition of the presumption of innocence as the basic foundation of the Islamic criminal justice system, some of which are also consequences of the principle of legality, are that, first, the accused is presumed innocent, therefore his dignity and his personal freedom and safety must be respected, preserved and protected throughout all stages of the criminal procedure, until a final and definitive judgement establishing his guilt and sentence is issued by the competent court. Second, that due process of law and full respect for the rules of evidence and correct criminal procedures must be observed throughout all stages of the criminal procedure, as stated above. Third, that the accused is not required to prove his innocence, but has the right to refute the evidence presented against him and to defend himself using all legal and technical means available. He also has the right to use legal and technical experts to refute the evidence against him, and to defend himself. In addition, he has the right to the assistance of the court, insofar as matters of his defence are concerned. Fourth, any suspicion or doubt must by interpreted in favour of the accused, i.e. the accused must be given the benefit of the doubt. As stated before, suspicions, however great, are insufficient and incapable of proving or establishing the criminal guilt of the accused. Thus, such guilt must be properly and correctly proven and established, beyond any doubt whatsoever.

The Inherent Dignity of the Human Being

As we have seen, God has created man innocent and pure, and has dignified him. The Qur'an reads:

> *We have honoured the sons of Adam; provided them with transport on land and sea; given them for sustenance things good and pure; and conferred on them special favours, above a great part of Our Creation.* (Q.17:70)

In addition, the Qur'an provides:

> *Behold, the Lord said to the angels: 'I am about to create man from clay: When I have fashioned him [in due proportion] and breathed into him of My spirit, fall ye down in obeisance unto him.' So the angels prostrated themselves, all of*

them together. Not so Iblīs: he was haughty, and became one of those who reject Faith. [*God*] *said: 'O, Iblīs! What prevents thee from prostrating thyself to one whom I have created with My hands? Art thou haughty? Or art thou one of the high ones?'* (Q.38:71-5)

Many other verses in the Qur'an show that God has honoured and dignified man, that man has been created innocent and pure, and that the honour, dignity, innocence and purity of every man must be fully respected and observed by every other man. Thus, arbitrary or capricious arrest or detention is proscribed under the Sharī'a.[34] Similarly, all types of coercion or duress and torture are proscribed and produce no legal effects.[35] Spying and other forms of unlawful interference in the private life of the individual are absolutely prohibited.[36] Criminal procedures which violate any such rules are of no legal value or effect. Those who violate such rules in fact commit crimes under Islamic Sharī'a, and are as such criminally liable.[37]

The Right to a Fair and Speedy Trial and Other Defence Rights

Under the Sharī'a, the accused has the right to a fair and speedy trial before a competent, independent and impartial judge or court, and the right to a judicial review before a higher court. The accused also has all other defence rights, since justice is the foundation of governance in Islam. As the Qur'an proclaims:

God commands justice, the doing of good, and liberality to kith and kin, and He forbids all shameful deeds, and injustice and rebellion: He instructs you that ye may receive admonition. (Q.16:90)

Thus, God commands justice and forbids injustice and rebellion.

As we see from the Qur'an, the Prophet was also ordered to judge justly:

But say: 'I believe in the Book which God has sent down; and I am commanded to judge justly between you. (Q.42:15)

Believers, too, are ordered to judge justly, as the Qur'an ordains:

O ye who believe! Stand out firmly for God, as witnesses to fair dealing, and let not the hatred of others make you swerve to wrong and depart from justice. Be just [*and judge justly*]*: that is next to piety: and fear God. For God is well-acquainted with all that ye do.* (Q.5:8)

Moreover, the Qur'an reads:

> *God doth command you to render back your Trusts to those to whom they are due; and when ye judge between man and man, that ye judge with justice: Verily how excellent is the teaching which He giveth you! For God is He Who heareth and seeth all things.* (Q.4:58)

Numerous books and studies have been written on Islamic justice and the judiciary in Islam. Fair trials and correct and proper judicial procedures have also been subject to extensive studies under Islamic Sharīʿa. Among the other rights of the accused we find:

(a) Defence Rights
This includes the right to refute the evidence presented against him/her and the right to present contrary evidence, the right to be heard, and the right to full equality in treatment with the accuser or opponent before the court or judge. The *sunna* ensures all these rights, as stipulated in the sayings of the Prophet. Equally, the accused may defend himself or herself, or may select experts and lawyers to defend him or her.

(b) The Right to Use an Attorney or Lawyer
Although classical Islamic Sharīʿa did not specifically include any express provision which obliges the court to avail the accused of the right to use a lawyer, essentials of a fair and just trial under Islamic law cannot be satisfied in any modern society without ensuring the right of the accused to use a lawyer or attorney of his or her own choice. Contemporary writers on Islamic Sharīʿa recognize the right to use a lawyer or attorney as one of the most basic rights of the accused in any criminal proceedings.[38]

(c) The Right to be Silent, and the Right Not to be a Witness Against Oneself
The accused has the full right to speak freely without any coercion or pressure whatsoever. Further, he has the full right to be silent and not to speak, while it is proscribed to force any accused to speak or present any information which he or she does not wish to present.[39] Any confession, obtained out of duress or coercion of any type, is of no legal value or effect, and has no legal validity whatsoever. Obtaining confession under duress or coercion, or any type of illegal pressure, is in fact a crime under Islamic Sharīʿa.[40]

The Right to Compensation for Unlawful Criminal Procedure
Under Islamic Sharīʿa, judges are responsible for any serious mistakes or wrongdoing. If the judge commits serious mistakes, rules unjustly or commits a miscarriage of justice, he may be dismissed from office, punished, and held

responsible for any injury or damage he causes, and must pay just compensation for any such injury or damage.[41]

Under the Sharīʿa, the judge has full authority over all criminal procedures; therefore, he bears full responsibility for any serious or unwarranted mistake or wrongdoing. In addition, if any person in charge of any criminal procedure, such as executing arrests or executing sentences, exceeds his authority and causes damage or injury to the person subject to execution in excess of what is necessarily required to properly execute the ordered arrest or sentence, that person would be responsible for a *qiṣāṣ* crime, as has been stated earlier, or may become liable to pay compensation, if the victim so accepts.[42]

Concluding Remarks

This short paper has shown that the fundamentals of the Sharīʿa recognize the most basic norms and guarantees provided for in any criminal justice system in today's world. Thus, the principle of legality with its two postulates of no crime without law and no punishment without law; the principle of non-retroactivity of criminal law; the presumption of innocence; due process of law and no punishment without proper and correct legal procedures; the respect for the inherent dignity of the human person and the full respect of the honour and dignity of the accused throughout all the criminal procedures; the right to a fair and speedy trial; all other defence rights; the right to use an attorney or lawyer; the right to remain silent and the right not to be a witness against oneself; the right to compensation for unlawful criminal procedures and any miscarriage of justice; and other fundamental rights relating to criminal proceedings, are all recognized and guaranteed under Islamic Sharīʿa. Any violation of such rights leads to the declaration of the innocence of the accused and his or her release. In addition, any serious violation of such rights and guarantees must result in the dismissal of the person committing the serious violation, and the payment of a just compensation if the victim of such violation or his or her family so demands or accepts. Serious violations may also result in a *qiṣāṣ* crime, which in turn requires a *qiṣāṣ* punishment.

Notes

[1] For a general review of the principle of legality in international law and in various other major criminal justice systems, see M. Cherif Bassiouni, *The Law of the International Criminal Tribunal for the Former Yugoslavia*(New York, 1996), pp 265-91
[2] These rules were included in the address given by the Prophet Muḥammad in his last pilgrimage (*ḥajj al-wadāʿ*), as recorded by the narrators of the *ḥadīth* and *sunna*.
[3] For a full list of *ḥudūd* offences, see Muḥammad Abū Zahra, *al-Jarīma wa'l-ʿUqūba fī Fiqh al-Islām*, 2 Vols (Cairo, 1998); ʿAbd al-Qādir ʿAwda, *al-Tashrīʿ al-Jināʾī al-Islāmī Muqāranan bi'l-Qānūn al-Waḍʿī*, 2 Vols (Cairo, 1984); al-Sayyid Sābiq, *Fiqh al-Sunna*, II (Jeddah, 1985), pp 260-371
[4] ʿAwda: *al-Tashrīʿ al-Jināʾī*, II, p 379
[5] ʿAwda: *al-Tashrīʿ al-Jināʾī*, II, pp 350; 395; Abū Zahra: *al-Jarīma wa'l-ʿUqūba*, II, p 241
[6] ʿAwda: *al-Tashrīʿ al-Jināʾī*, II, p 432
[7] ʿAwda: *al-Tashrīʿ al-Jināʾī*, II, p 461
[8] ʿAwda: *al-Tashrīʿ al-Jināʾī*, II, p 461
[9] ʿAwda: *al-Tashrīʿ al-Jināʾī*, II, pp 388; 480; 488
[10] ʿAwda: *al-Tashrīʿ al-Jināʾī*, II, p 498
[11] ʿAwda: *al-Tashrīʿ al-Jināʾī*, II, p 498
[12] ʿAwda: *al-Tashrīʿ al-Jināʾī*, II, p 505
[13] ʿAwda: *al-Tashrīʿ al-Jināʾī*, II, p 515
[14] For a detailed study of this crime, See ʿAwda: *al-Tashrīʿ al-Jināʾī*, II, p 638; Abū Zahra: *al-Jarīma wa'l-ʿUqūba*, II, p 151; Sābiq: *Fiqh al-Sunna*, II, p 151
[15] ʿAwda: *al-Tashrīʿ al-Jināʾī*, II, p 671
[16] ʿAwda: *al-Tashrīʿ al-Jināʾī*, II, p 674
[17] ʿAwda: *al-Tashrīʿ al-Jināʾī*, II, pp 707; 719
[18] ʿAwda: *al-Tashrīʿ al-Jināʾī*, II, p 720
[19] ʿAwda: *al-Tashrīʿ al-Jināʾī*, II, pp 260-92
[20] ʿAwda: *al-Tashrīʿ al-Jināʾī*, II. For further details of *qiṣāṣ* crimes and punishments, see Sābiq: *Fiqh al-Sunna*, II, pp 372-404
[21] ʿAwda: *al-Tashrīʿ al-Jināʾī*, II, pp 260-92
[22] For details of *taʿzīr* crimes and punishments, see Abū Zahra: *al-Jarīma wa'l-ʿUqūba*, I, pp 195-204; Maḥmūd Shaltūt, *al-Islām: ʿAqīda wa Sharīʿa* (Cairo, 1989), pp 291-4
[23] See note 22
[24] See Qur'anic verses given in the text.
[25] See note 2
[26] For detailed studies of the presumption of innocence, see*The Accused and His Rights Under Islamic Sharīʿa*, published by The Arab Center for Security Studies and Training (ACSST) (1986), specifically Jaʿfar al-Faḍlī, 'The original principle under Islamic Sharīʿa is the innocence of the accused', pp 189-99; ʿAbd al-Majīd Maṭlūb, 'The original principle is the innocence of the accused', pp 201-42; Muḥammad al-ʿAwwā, 'The original principle is the innocence of the accused', pp 243-65; and ʿAbdullāh al-Manīʿa, 'The theory of the innocence of the accused until proven guilty', pp 276-82
[27] Maṭlūb: 'The original principle', p 222
[28]. Maṭlūb: 'The original principle', p 222
[29] See references given in note 26
[30] Maṭlūb: 'The original principle', p 222
[32] Abū Zahra: *al-Jarīma wa'l-ʿUqūba*, II, p 240
[33] Abū Zahra: *al-Jarīma wa'l-ʿUqūba*, II, p 245

[34] Abū Zahra: *al-Jarīma wa'l-'Uqūba*, II, p 240
[35] See Taha al-Alwani, 'The rights of the accused during the investigation stage', in *The Accused and His Rights Under Islamic Sharī'a*, pp 15-50
[36] See al-Alwani: 'The rights of the accused', p 42; Bandar al-Suwaylim, *al-Muttaham: Mu'āmalātuh wa Ḥuqūquh fi'l-Fiqh al-Islāmī* (Riyadh, 1987), pp 80-122; Abū Zahra: *al-Jarīma wa'l-'Uqūba*, I, p 528
[31] Abū Zahra: *al-Jarīma wa'l-'Uqūba*, II, p 240
[37] Al-Alwani: 'The rights of the accused', p 32; see also the Qur'anic verses and sayings of the Prophet referred to by the same author, pp 33-5
[38] Al-Alwani: 'The rights of the accused', p 35
[39] Al-Alwani: 'The rights of the accused', p 36; al-Suwaylim: *al-Muttaham*, pp 289; 337
[40] Al-Alwani: 'The rights of the accused', p 38
[41] Al-Alwani: 'The rights of the accused', p 41
[42] Al-Alwani: 'The rights of the accused', p 41

Part Two

Individual Protection, Punishments and Remedies

4

The Right to Personal Safety (*Ḥaqq al-Amn*) and the Principle of Legality in Islamic Sharīʿa

Mohammad Hashim Kamali

Criminal procedure is generally predicated on the twin but contrasting objectives of either tending to due process or the control of crime. Due process focuses on providing the accused with various protections, so as to minimize the possibility of unjust or arbitrary criminal convictions. It also seeks to facilitate an efficient administration of justice, which promotes objectivity and coherence in trial proceedings. Crime control, by contrast, emphasizes a broader social interest in crime detection and prevention, and limits procedural protections for the accused, so as to ensure an efficient prosecution and conviction of the guilty.[1]

Islamic criminal procedure also faces this dilemma, and seeks to strike a fair balance between the interests of the accused and those of society. Specific procedural safeguards are occasionally prescribed by the Qur'an or the *sunna*, but have generally been left to the discretion of the ruler. Under the doctrine of *siyāsa sharʿiyya*, or Sharīʿa-oriented policy, the ruler is authorized to take measures and devise procedures that are in harmony with the goals and objectives of the Sharīʿa, and to secure public interest as best as possible. Simple and direct detection and trial procedures that were deemed adequate for earlier times may not be sufficient for more complex societies, where progress in various fields has also opened new avenues for more sophisticated levels of criminality and abuse. The integrity of a procedural system under these circumstances is tested by its openness to refinement and growth. Since procedural matters in the Islamic system of justice are open to considerations of public policy and justice under *siyāsa sharʿiyya*, the process remains in principle open to further development and reform.

This essay is presented in seven sections, beginning with a preliminary discussion of the definition and scope of *ḥaqq al-amn* (the right to personal safety), followed in section two by an enquiry into the source evidence of the Qur'an and *sunna*, and the early precedent of the Pious Caliphs on this subject. Sharīʿa, while section four addresses the twin concepts of accusation (*tuhma*) and suspicion (*ẓann*). These lead the discussion, in the fifth section, to arrest and detention, and the debate that has arisen among the *'ulamā'* over the basic permissibility of preventive detention. The sixth section enquires into the permissibility or otherwise of physically beating the accused, in certain types of accusations, during interrogation. The last section discusses the right to counsel.

The larger part of this work consists of a presentation of the Sharīʿa evidence as the author has found in the sources consulted. On certain issues, where the evidence remains somewhat less than conclusive, and on matters over which the *'ulamā'* are themselves in disagreement, the author has advanced a certain perspective that is reflective of his own understanding of the source evidence.

Definition and Scope of *Ḥaqq al-Amn*

The individual's right to personal safety may be defined as his right to live a peaceful life without fear of aggression, unlawful arrest, detention and punishment: the assurance, in other words, that his personal safety is inviolable, and shall not be compromised nor subjected to coercion and abuse except under the law.[2] Some writers have expanded the scope of this right to include not only the personal safety of the individual, but also his property and honour. Thus, according to an alternative definition, 'the right to safety' (*ḥaqq al-amn*) means the safety of the person, his property and honour against aggression, humiliation and torture by other individuals or the state.[3] Another writer has simply described *ḥaqq al-amn* as the inner assurance of the individual and absence of fear on his part over his personal safety.[4] Notwithstanding the likelihood that aggression against the personal property and honour of the individual implies aggression against his person, but since personal property and honour are subjects for which the law takes separate measures, it is preferable perhaps to confine the scope of *ḥaqq al-amn* here to aggression against the person of the individual in the sense of physical aggression, unlawful detention and violation of his right to due process. The right to due process relates, in turn, to the principle of the rule of law, also known as the principle of legality, which contemplates the legal regime that regulates investigation and trial procedures, and protects the individual against the abuse of coercive power.

Evidence in the Qur'an and *Sunna*

The rules of Sharīʿa pertaining to the right to safety proceed from the Qur'anic affirmation of the dignity of man and its recognition of ***homo sapiens*** as the prize creation of God, who must therefore be treated with dignity and justice. The Qur'an is replete with warnings against tyranny and persecution, which occur in no less than 299 places in the text, just as it is emphatic on the value of justice and fair treatment for everyone, without discrimination.[5] Rights and liberties in Islam are therefore seen as a manifestation of the dignity of man, which is in turn an expression of the divine grace that God Most High has bestowed on the human race. The Qur'an thus proclaims:

> *And surely We have honoured the progeny of Adam; We carry them in the land and the sea; We provided them with good things and excelled them over most of those whom We have created.* (Q.17:70)

The reference to the dignity of man in this verse (*āya*) is substantiated by the rank he is given over most of God's creatures, as well as by the affirmation of his freedom of movement to traverse the land and sea in order to utilize the earth's resources. Other manifestations of human dignity in the Qur'an are found in references to the physical and spiritual attributes of man, and the divine affirmations that 'We created man in the best of forms' (Q.95:4); that 'I breathed into him of my spirit' (Q.38:72) and that God endowed him with a spiritual rank above the angels (see Q.2:34). More specifically, the Qur'an entitles the individual to safety against aggression, when it declares in the broadest of terms that 'there shall be no hostility except against the aggressors' (Q.2:193). The text thus proscribes hostility (*ʿudwān*) of all kinds against those who have not committed acts of aggression, and permits acts of hostility only against the aggressors (*ẓālimūn*). Aggression is recognized as the only ground that validates recourse to hostile action against the individual. The text, in other words, validates the use of force for defensive purposes, both in individual circumstances and in matters pertaining to war and peace. The Qur'an further specifies that a hostile response to aggression must not exceed the limits of reciprocity and justice:

> *Whoever is aggressive toward you then your response must be proportionate to the aggression that was inflicted upon you* [*in the first place*]. *And fear God, for God is with those who are conscious of His presence.* (Q.2:194)

> *Whoever forgives and makes peace, God will reward him for it. Verily God loves not the transgressors* [ẓālimīn]. (Q.42:4)

Meanwhile, violation of the limits set by God, or a deliberate disregard of the rule of law, is equated with *ẓulm* (transgression, wrongdoing), as the Qur'an declares:

> *Those who transgress the limits that God has laid down are indeed the transgressors.* (Q.2:229)

The Qur'an thus envisages an orderly life in the community, which is observant of the rule of law and the limits of just and peaceful behaviour. Unlike the image that is often portrayed of the Sharī'a as one of eagerness to punish, there is considerable support in the Qur'an for leniency, forgiveness, and compassion – so much so that this outlook is an integral part of the Sharī'a and of government under the rule of law. There is no question over the resolute attitude that the Sharī'a takes toward lawlessness and transgression, yet this attitude is often tempered with its opposite pull on the side of compassion and understanding of the offender, and the causes that led him to deviant behaviour. The Qur'an thus declares:

> *Whoever repents after his wrongdoing* [ẓulm], *and reforms himself, God will turn to him* [*with mercy*], *surely God is Forgiving, Merciful.* (Q.5:39)

The law entitles the victim of *ẓulm* to defend himself, as the Qur'an proclaims:

> *And whoever defends himself after having been oppressed, he is not to be blamed.* (Q.42:41)

The victim of the aggression is, in turn, advised in the following terms:

> *And if you decide to punish, then punish with the like of that with which you were afflicted. But if you show patience, it is certainly best for those who remain patient.* (Q.16:126)

The Qur'anic rule of reciprocity and equivalence in the use of force should, in other words, be tempered by one's dedication to the right cause, patience and self-restraint. Thus, the Qur'an not only recommends patience in the sense of not insisting on reprisal, but also recommends that one should not be rash in the enforcement of penalties, and allow time and opportunity for forgiveness, reconciliation and reform.

The *sunna* of the Prophet is also emphatic on the inviolability of the personal right to safety, as declared in the following *ḥadīth*: 'All that belongs to a Muslim is forbidden to his fellow Muslim – his blood, his honour and his property.'[6] This *ḥadīth* begins with a general reference to all of the basic rights of the individual (the word 'Muslim' in this *ḥadīth* can be substituted for human being), and declares them all to be sacrosanct; it then specifies three of these, namely life, property and honour, as being the most important. The general reference of this *ḥadīth* to 'all that belongs to a Muslim', when read together with the universal Qur'anic affirmation of the dignity of man, serve to show that the Sharī'a takes an affirmative stand on all of the basic rights of man, specified or unspecified. Any right or liberty that is deemed complementary to human dignity is therefore protected and upheld. The substance of the above *ḥadīth* is endorsed in another, which declares: 'Muslims are brethren; none may commit acts of aggression against his brother nor humiliate and degrade him. One who helps his brother in need, God will help him in his own moment of need.'[7] According to yet another *ḥadīth*, 'The back [or flesh] of a believer is safe [against aggression] unless it be for a right or a transgression of God's limit.'[8]

Protecting the individual against physical aggression, annoyance, intimidation and espionage is the explicit theme of a large number of *ḥadīths*, a perusal of which leaves one in no doubt that the attitude conveyed by them is not merely a matter of conformity to rules, but one which partakes in the integrity of the believer's commitment to the faith. To quote one example: 'Do not annoy [*la tu'dhū*] the Muslims, nor defame them, and do not expose their nakedness. For one who exposes the nakedness of his Muslim brother, God will expose his own nakedness.'[9]According to another: 'It is not permissible for a Muslim to intimidate another Muslim',[10] while the same message has been more emphatically conveyed in another *ḥadīth*: 'Do not intimidate a Muslim, for intimidating a Muslim is one of the gravest of all transgressions [*ẓulm 'aẓīm*].[11] In yet another: 'God will punish in the hereafter those who afflict others with torture in this life.'[12]

The provisions of the Qur'an and *ḥadīth* on the right to safety apply equally to all individuals, regardless of the religious, economic or social status of the individual. The Prophet has declared to this effect that 'men are equal like the teeth of a comb. No Arab individual is superior to a non-Arab except in piety.'[13] The law must therefore be applied equally to all individuals alike. To emphasize this point, the Prophet stated in a *ḥadīth* that even if his own daughter Fāṭima were to commit theft, she would be treated as any other offender and subjected to the prescribed punishment.[14]

From his reading of the source evidence, 'Abd al-Wahhāb Khallāf has drawn the conclusion that

> ...all the evidence that is found in the Book of God and the *sunna* of His Messenger to others is premised on the inviolability of the right on the prohibition of hostility, oppression [*ẓulm*], harm and

> annoyance to personal safety [*ḥaqq al-amn*], and the safe conduct of all human beings against all forms of aggression and abuse.[15]

Violating the individual's right to safety is, in other words, prohibited (*ḥarām*), and the right to safety is in principle a right which is not amenable to derogation and compromise.

It is reported that the Caliph 'Umar ibn al-Khaṭṭāb instituted a policy of meeting with his officials during the *ḥajj* season. On one such occasion, the Caliph addressed his officials and asked them to avoid insult, humiliation, physical abuse and misappropriation of people's property at all times. The Caliph then pledged that he would personally see to it that violators were retaliated against. The Governor of Egypt, 'Amr ibn al-'Āṣ, who was present when the Caliph issued this directive, then asked whether the Caliph would retaliate in instances where government officials disciplined (*addaba*) members of the public. To this the Caliph replied, 'By Him in whose hand the life of 'Umar reposes, I shall indeed retaliate, for I have seen the Messenger of God subject even himself to retaliation.'[16]

Anas ibn Mālik has reported another incident that also involved 'Amr ibn al-'Āṣ:

> It is thus stated that Muḥammad ibn 'Amr, the son of the Governor of Egypt, 'Amr ibn al-'Āṣ, had lashed an Egyptian, apparently for no reason other than that he blocked him from seeing his horse racing. The man then complained to the Caliph and the Caliph summoned both the Governor and his son, and then ordered that the victim may retaliate by lashing the culprit – which he did. The Caliph then asked the man to lash the Governor, for 'you would not have been struck were it not for the fact that he was the Governor's son.' The man said, 'I have lashed the one who lashed me.' The Caliph then said, 'I would not have intervened had you in fact lashed the Governor.' The Caliph then turned to the Governor and said, 'Since when did you enslave the people while their mothers gave them birth as free individuals?'[17]

The recognition in Sharī'a of life as one of the five essential values (*al-ḍarūriyyāt al-khamsa*) is a recognition simultaneously of the right of every individual to personal security and the right to live an honourable life. The Sharī'a recognizes this as one of its overriding values, alongside other such values, as the immunity of one's right to practise one's faith, to own property, to have a family, and the right to the protection of one's intellect. In its positive sense, this last right means the right to seek knowledge and, in its negative sense, it means the right to protection against corrupt influences, such as drug abuse. All measures that protect and promote these values are consequently upheld by the Sharī'a.[18]

The right to personal safety applies equally to pre-trial procedures involving criminal investigation and collection of evidence against the accused. The latter is, in principle, entitled to safe conduct, especially when s/he is not notorious for criminality and corruption. The accused may neither be exposed to pressure, nor persecuted in order to incriminate him - or herself. Should there be a confession by the accused, it must be free and voluntary, as any amount of pressure and coercion that mars the integrity of a confession is likely to lead to the suspension of punishment. This is the requirement of the *ḥadīth* which categorically declares: 'Drop the prescribed penalties in all cases of doubt'.[19] A confession that is obtained through pressure tactics is doubtful and fails to serve its purpose. The Caliph 'Umar refused to give credit to confession made under fear, and went on record to say that 'a man would not be secure when he is in pain, frightened or imprisoned in order to make a confession and incriminate himself'.[20] The law enforcement officer, the head of state and judge are generally advised not to be eager in the enforcement of penalties. This is the purport of the remainder of the above *ḥadīth*, which reads: 'Drop the prescribed penalties [*ḥudūd*] whenever you can. When you can find a way out for a Muslim, then clear his way. For if the *imām* errs, it is better that he err on the side of leniency than on the side of punishment.'[21]

Abū Yūsuf, Chief Justice of the 'Abbāsid state under Hārūn al-Rashīd, wrote that when a person is accused of the crime of theft or any other crime, he may 'neither be beaten nor promised anything nor intimidated in order to illicit a confession from him'. Abū Yūsuf added that anyone who confesses to an offence, including murder and theft, under compulsion 'is not liable to the prescribed punishment and his confession shall be devoid of effect'.[22] It is also reported that during the time of the Companions, someone by the name of Ṭariq, who was accused of kidnapping a man from Syria, was beaten until he confessed. 'Abd Allāh ibn 'Umar, who adjudicated the case, ruled that 'no punishment may be applied as the confession was made after the accused was beaten'. Ibn 'Umar also added that people may not be arrested merely on the basis of a mere accusation, and no claim of theft or murder should be admitted unless it is supported by upright witnesses or a confession that is free of threat and intimidation. Ibn 'Umar added further that it was unlawful to imprison a man on the grounds of mere suspicion, since the Prophet refused to arrest people on the basis of suspicion alone. However, it is proper that the claimant and defendant be brought together before the court. If there is evidence, the claim should be adjudicated, otherwise the defendant should be released or asked to give a surety.[23] 'The judge has no powers', wrote

Māwardī, 'to detain anyone unless it is for violation of a right that is clearly established'.[24]

Abū Yūsuf also wrote that the state must ensure that prisoners are not in dire need, and that it must assign to the needy men and women among them a monthly payment sufficient for their food, besides providing them with clothing in summer and winter and, in the event of death, their funeral expenses. Prisoners are also entitled to safe and fair treatment that precludes punishment and torture. The precedent for this, Abū Yūsuf added, was set by the Pious Caliphs, especially the fourth Caliph, 'Alī ibn Abī Ṭālib, who entitled prisoners to allowances from the public treasury unless they were affluent, in which case he would spend on them of their own property.[25] Abū Yūsuf has also quoted in this connection the Caliph 'Umar ibn 'Abd al-'Azīz's letter, which he sent to his officials, advising them to ensure that

> ...one of the Muslims in their prisons is restricted to the extent that he cannot stand upright to perform his prayer, and that no one is restricted so much so as to be unable to sleep at night, except for those who are wanted for murder. They should all be given charitable donations that would improve their basic food and the variety of the food they eat.[26]

We turn next to an examination of the principle of legality and the extent of its application in Islamic law.

The Principle of Legality

This principle means basically that no one may be incriminated or punished without a legal text which specifically defines the crime and the punishment in question. It also means that the judge may not punish anyone on the basis of his own wishes, without lawful evidence and proof. Even then, the legal text that is applied must have been in existence at the time the offence was committed. The law may not, in other words, be retroactively enforced. It also means that only the offender and no one else must be held responsible for his deeds. The requirement of due process in interrogation and trial is also designed to ensure that the accused is protected against the abuse of coercive power. The principle of legality is thus essentially concerned with the limitation of the power of the state, and its operation acquires special significance in the area of criminal law.[27]

Islamic constitutional theory is explicit on the principle of the limitation of the power of the state under the rule of law. The Islamic state is, accordingly, bound to administer and uphold the Sharī'a.[28] Further, there is no place in Islam for arbitrary rule by a single individual or a group; the basis of all decisions and actions in an Islamic polity should not be individual whim and caprice, but the Sharīʿa.[29] The *ʿulamāʾ* have unanimously held that the head of state and government officials are accountable for their conduct like everyone else, and that they are equally bound by the decisions of the courts of justice. In response to the question as to how the decision of a *qāḍī*, who is an employee of the *imām*, can bind the *imām*, it is stated that the judge discharges his duty not as an employee of the *imām*, but as a representative of the community whose task it is to implement the Sharīʿa. There is consequently no recognition in Sharīʿa of special privileges for anyone. Equality before the law and before the courts of justice is clearly recognized for all citizens alike.[30] This is once again indicative of the high priority that Islam accords to the rule of law, since it frees the citizen of the duty to obey political authority if the latter itself violates the law. This is the clear message of the *ḥadīth* which declares: 'There is no obedience in transgression; obedience is in lawful conduct only.'[31] According to another *ḥadīth*: 'There is no obedience to man in disobedience of the Creator.'[32]

Based on the unequivocal authority provided in a number of similar *ḥadīth*s, Māwardī has drawn the conclusion that 'Islam confers on every citizen the right to refuse to commit a crime, should any government or administrator order him to do so'.[33] Mahmassānī has concurred with Ibn Khaldūn to the effect that the sovereignty of an Islamic state is restricted in so far as the state in Islamic law is under obligation to comply with the Sharīʿa. Hence, when the state issues a command that violates the Sharīʿa, the citizen is no longer under duty to obey it.[34]

The Sharīʿa safeguards the life, honour and liberty of the citizen by laying down a set of principles designed to ensure due process in the administration of justice. Included in these is the presumption of original non-liability (*barāʾa al-dhimma al-aṣliyya*), which simply presumes that no one is guilty of a crime unless the contrary is proved through lawful evidence.[35] The presumption of innocence is not overruled by mere accusation, which is not devoid of doubt, and doubt does not negate certainty. The certainty here is the prior innocence of the accused. The principle of legality also entitles the accused to defend himself, and to attend his own trial. This is established in a *ḥadīth* in which the Prophet is reported to have advised ʿAlī ibn Abī Ṭālib upon the latter's departure as judge to the Yemen: 'When the litigant presents himself before you, do not pass a judgement unless you hear the other party in the same way as you hear the first.'[36] In a similar vein, Islamic law does not permit the judge to sentence a person in his absence. The defendant must, in other words, be present in the court or be represented by an authorized person.[37] There is some disagreement among the Ḥanafīs and Shāfiʿīs as to whether accusation by itself can weaken the force of the original principle of non-liability: the Ḥanafīs maintain that it does, but the Shāfiʿīs hold that a mere claim or accusation does not affect the original absence of liability, or innocence, of the accused. It is important, as al-Saleh has rightly noted, that the presumption of innocence is strictly upheld, as the accused will otherwise be faced with the onerous, if not impossible, task of proving that he did not commit the crime.[38]

Anyone, be it the individual or the state, who accuses a person of an offence must prove it beyond reasonable doubt.[39] The burden of proof lies on the plaintiff, a principle derived from the following *ḥadīth*: 'The burden of proof is on him who makes the claim, whereas the oath is on him who denies.'[40] The plaintiff, in other words, may ask the court to put the defendant on oath if the latter denies the claim. If the claimant is required to prove his allegation, then it would follow that, until such proof is forthcoming, the defendant is presumed to be innocent. This is also upheld in another *ḥadīth*, which provides: 'If men are to be granted what they claim, some will claim the lives and properties of others. The burden of proof is on the claimant, and an oath is incumbent on him who denies.'[41] According to Ibn Qayyim, if the claimant supports his claim by evidence, the court will adjudicate in his favour, otherwise the last word is that of the defendant and the court shall credit what he says, provided he take a solemn oath to affirm that he is telling the truth.[42]

Punishment is not executed unless there is proof to establish the guilt, and hearsay evidence is not admissible in the execution of penalties. Ibn Taymiyya wrote that there was at the time of the Prophet a woman in Medina who had a reputation for debauchery, and the Prophet said, concerning her: 'If I were to stone anyone without evidence, I would have stoned this woman.'[43] Ibn Taymiyya also quoted on the same page a statement of the Caliph 'Umar, to the effect that no one may be punished on the basis of suspicion and mistrust. Al-Qarāfī and Ibn Farḥūn have specified that proof (*thubūt*) is evidence that is sound and free of doubt and loopholes, has met all its proper conditions, and is focused on a definite result. Ibn Qayyim has observed that offenders are not punished without proof, and proof comes either from the offender when s/he makes a confession, or what might amount to a confession, or else it is provided independently. In both cases, the proof must be sound, free of doubt and clear of espionage.[44]

Confession in crimes, but not in civil disputes, can be withdrawn even after the sentence has been passed or during its execution. Once a confession is so withdrawn, particularly in the prescribed *ḥadd* offences, the punishment may not be carried out, for withdrawal in this manner gives rise to doubt (*shubha*), which would in turn obstruct the enforcement of punishment.[45] For a confession to be valid, the confessor must also be in full possession of his faculties. Confession must, in addition, be true in that it does not seek to conceal the truth in order to protect another person or group of persons, and when the cause and underlying intention of a mendacious confession is known to the judge, he is under duty to reject it.[46] A valid confession needs to be specific and categorical. If it is ambiguous to the extent that it requires interpretation, it is not admissible. Hence, it is not enough for someone to say 'I committed adultery', or, 'one of us committed theft.' Both statements are vague, as they fail to provide relevant details and do not, therefore, amount to valid proof.[47]

Judicial decisions must be based on apparent truth, which is substantiated by valid evidence. The hidden truth, should there be any, is considered a matter between the individual and his Creator, and it lies beyond the immediate concern of the court. In al-Sha'rānī's phrase, 'God Most High has ordered us to settle disputes among people on the basis of visible proof, and leave the rest to the Day of Judgement.'[48] This conclusion is supported by the following *ḥadīth*, in which the Prophet is reported to have said:

> I am but a human being. When you bring a dispute to me, some of you may be more eloquent in stating their case than others. I may consequently adjudicate on the basis of what I hear. If I adjudicate in favour of someone over something that belongs to his brother, let him not take it. For it would be like taking a piece of fire.[49]

The Prophet has, in other words, confirmed that he adjudicated disputes only on the basis of evidence that was presented to him.

Evidence must be allowed to be given in an atmosphere of impartiality. It is a generally agreed-upon rule of the Sharī'a law of evidence that the judge must avoid inculcating the witnesses, but should instead hear what they have to say.[50] The Qur'an demands impartiality in the administration of justice; the witnesses, judge and enforcement authorities are accordingly required to

> *...stand firmly for justice as witnesses to God, even if it be against yourselves, your parents or your relatives, and whether it be* [*against*] *the rich or poor, for God can best protect both. Follow not the lust [of your hearts] lest it detract you from the course of justice.* (Q.4:135)

Evidently, this undiluted Qur'anic emphasis on impartiality in the administration of justice means that investigation and trial procedures must, from beginning to end, be impartial and objective.

The Qur'anic guideline with reference to sentencing is that it proscribes excess in retaliation and punishments that are out of line with the offence itself. We note once again the following Qur'anic directive, which is addressed to all parties in judicial disputes, including the enforcement authorities and the state:

> *Whoever is aggressive toward you, then your response must be proportionate to the pain that was inflicted on you.* (Q.2:194)

The Qur'an further lays down the principle that no one may be accused or punished for an offence committed by another person:

> *Everyone is accountable for his own deeds, and no soul shall bear the burden of another.* (Q.6:164)[51]

This is reiterated in a *ḥadīth* to the effect that 'no person may be incriminated for a crime committed by another person'.[52] The Qur'an further provides in an address to the Prophet:

> *We revealed to you the scripture with the truth that you may judge between people by that which God has shown to you, and be not thou a pleader for the treacherous.* (Q.4:105)

This *āya* was revealed concerning a dispute between a Muslim and a Jew. In this incident, the Muslim, Ibn Ubayraq, had stolen a coat of mail and, having hidden it in the house of a Jew, later accused the latter of the theft; he was supported in his false accusation by his tribe. The Prophet cleared the Jew of the charge but Ibn Ubayraq fled and renounced Islam. The following two *āyāt* were also revealed concerning the same case:

> *Whoever commits a sin only makes himself liable for it ... and whoever commits a delinquency and then throws the blame thereof upon the innocent has burdened himself with falsehood and a flagrant crime.* (Q.4:11-12)[53]

This Qur'anic principle marked a departure from the ancient Arab excesses in retaliation and revenge. The Arabs sometimes doubled the penalty or claimed more than one life in retaliation. They often demanded exaggerated sums in *diya* (blood money or compensation), and held the whole tribe responsible for the crime of one of its members.[54] A well-known exception to this principle is the case of *'āqila*, which is a pre-Islamic Arabian custom that was subsequently adopted by the *sunna* and consensus (*ijmā'*), and required the kinsmen of the offender to pay the blood money in unintentional homicide. According to al-Awza'ī and Dāwūd al-Ẓāhirī, the offender himself does not participate with his *'āqila* in the payment of *diya*, but he does according to Abū Ḥanīfa and Mālik; according to al-Shāfi'ī, he participates only if the *'āqila* is unable to pay the *diya*. We learn that during the time of 'Umar, the *'āqila* included colleagues at work (*ahl al-dīwān*).[55] This has led Maḥmūd Shaltūt to observe that the proper purpose of *'āqila* is co-operation and help in respect of an unintended crime. It is not meant to transfer the responsibility of the offender to another person, which is why the *'āqila* is not required to participate in the *diya* of a deliberate crime.[56]

Muslim jurists have formulated a number of legal maxims which complement the principle of legality in the Sharī'a. One of these provides that 'the conduct of reasonable men (or the dictate of reason) alone is of no consequence without the support of a legal text'. This obviously means that no conduct can be declared forbidden (*ḥarām*) on grounds of reason or by the action of reasonable men alone, and that a legal text is necessary to render the conduct in question an offence. No one, therefore, should be deemed a violator because of committing or omitting an act which is not forbidden by clear provisions of the law.[57] The substance of this principle is also upheld in another legal maxim, which declares that 'permissibility is the original norm' (*al-aṣl fi'l-ashyā' al-ibāḥa*).[58] The majority of *'ulamā'* have thus reached the conclusion that all things are permissible unless the law has declared them otherwise. Consequently, no one may be accused of an offence in the absence of a legal text.

The third legal maxim under discussion provides that 'no one bears any obligation unless he is capable of understanding the law which imposes it; nor may any one be required to act in a certain manner unless he is capable of knowing the nature of the act he is required to do or avoid doing'.[59] This principle indicates that the law which creates an obligation or an offence can only be addressed to a competent person who is capable of understanding it, and that it is only possible for him to comply with the law when he knows of it. To make the knowledge of the law possible for the citizen, the legal text must be published and made accessible to all. Consequently no crime is committed until the text which creates it has been publicly announced and brought to the knowledge of the people.[60] These conclusions are supported by several passages in the Qur'an; to quote a few:

> *We do not punish until we have sent a messenger [to give warning].* (Q.17:15)

> *Nor was thy Lord the one to destroy a population until He had sent in its midst as messenger rehearsing to them Our signs.* (Q.28:59)

People are thus accountable for their deeds on the basis of the message and scripture that is conveyed to them. The principle contained in these Qur'anic passages is that, without prior warning, scripture and guidance, there shall be no punishment. Thus, according to 'Awda, 'in the absence of a clear text which may require affirmative action or abandonment of a particular conduct, the perpetrator or abandoner incurs no responsibility and no punishment can be imposed'.[61] Anyone who looks into the Sharī'a, 'Awda adds, will find that there is a clear text for every punishable offence, although the approach may differ with regard to the types of offences, as we shall presently explain.[62] Commenting on the same Qur'anic passages, Khallāf writes, and this is the majority position, that a person who has lived in complete isolation so that no message, law or guidance has been communicated to him is non-*compos mentis* (*ghayr mukallaf*). Such a person could not therefore be rewarded for his good deeds, nor could he be punished for his evil conduct and crime, for it is a prerequisite of responsibility (*taklīf*) that the law be communicated to its proper audience.[63]

There is evidence in the Qur'an to the effect that punishment must not be applied retroactively:

> *Say to the unbelievers that if they desist [from unbelief], what they have done in the past would be forgiven.* (Q.8:38)

Elsewhere in the Qur'an, it is provided with reference to pre-Islamic marital practices:

> *And marry not those women whom your fathers married, except for what has already passed.* (Q.4:22)

Abū Zahra draws the conclusion from these *āyāt* that the Qur'an forbids applying the penal law of Islam for offences that were committed prior to the advent of Islam. This would, in principle, establish the non-retroactivity of penalties under the Sharī'a.[64] The substance of these *āyāt* is again confirmed in the following *ḥadīth*: when 'Amr ibn al-'Āṣ embraced Islam, he pledged allegiance to the Prophet and asked if he would be held accountable for his previous transgressions. To this the Prophet replied, 'Did you not know, O 'Amr, that Islam obliterates that which took place preceding it?'[65] Nor did the Prophet question Abu Sufyān and his wife for their previous conduct, or the man who had killed his uncle, Ḥamza, even though his death caused him deep sorrow. The only exception to this principle to be noted is that the new law has a retroactive effect when it is in favour of the accused.[66]

The Sharī'a does not advocate a rigid approach in its implementation of the principle of the rule of law. Broadly speaking, the Sharī'a employs three different methods for implementing the principle of legality in criminal law. In the case of serious crimes which pose a major threat to society, the Sharī'a specifies both the offence and the punishment –the punishment so specified may fall under the *ḥudūd*, just retaliation (*qiṣāṣ*) and *diya*. For offences which pose a relatively lesser threat to public safety, the Sharī'a does not specify the penalty, but defines the offence and provides only general guidelines about the punishment. These are the *ta'zīr* offences, where the Sharī'a specifies the conduct but empowers the judge to select the type and amount of punishment he deems most suitable, from a range of approved penalties. *Ta'zīr* offences consist primarily of conduct which the Sharī'a has defined as transgression (*ma'ṣiya*). It is not for the judge to define the offence; he can only specify punishment for a certain conduct, the criminality of which has already been determined by a legal text (*naṣṣ*).

While discussing the common misconception that the judge has a free hand in dealing with *ta'zīr* offences, 'Awda points out that the Sharī'a imposes certain restrictions on the powers of the judge. It is, consequently, a mistake to say that *ta'zīr* offences are not regulated by the *naṣṣ*, or to suggest that the judge is at liberty to determine both the crime and its punishment. The judge must first of all determine whether the conduct is a *ma'ṣiya*, according to the clear text of the Sharī'a. The offence must then be proved through lawful evidence. The judge selects only that type of punishment which the Sharī'a has validated. 'Awda goes on to illustrate the foregoing by referring to a number of *ta'zīr* offences and the textual authority on which they are based. The list includes consumption of forbidden substances; breach of trust; cheating in weights and measures; perjury; usury; obscenity and insult; bribery; unlawful entry into private dwellings; and espionage. In all of these the Qur'an and *sunna* provide the textual authority which renders the conduct into a *ma'ṣiya*. While meting out punishment for any of these offences, the judge must select an approved penalty, ranging from a mere warning to fines and imprisonment, and must decide whether the sentence is to be suspended or carried out promptly. The judge, in other words, enjoys discretionary powers in regard to *ta'zīr* offences, which 'Awda characterizes as *sulṭat al-ikhtiyār* (the power to select), as opposed to *sulṭat al-taḥakkum* (the power to legislate at will). In Islamic constitutional theory, neither the judge nor any other organ of government enjoys unlimited powers of this latter type.[67]

In regard to *ta'zīr* offences which violate the public interest (*al-maṣlaḥa al-'āmma*), the *ta'zīr* does not specify the nature of the offence, but provides only general guidelines on the type of conduct deemed harmful to society, the reason being that offences of this type are, on the whole, unpredictable and cannot be specified in advance. An act may be permissible, and yet the circumstances in which it is committed, or some of its attributes, are such that this would violate public interest. While in principle the Sharī'a penalizes only such acts which amount to transgression, it makes an exception by authorizing the judge to penalize the conduct, which, though not forbidden by textual authority, and therefore not a *ma'ṣiya*, is prejudicial to public interest and causes harm (*ḍarar*) to society.[68] Examples of this kind of *ta'zīr* are: restrictions on the liberty of the insane for the sake of public safety and preventing him from harming the community, or detention of an accused without proof on grounds of public interest, that is, to facilitate investigation and prevent a possible escape.[69]

In all of this, whether *taʿzīr* contemplates a transgression (*maʿṣiya*) or harm (*ḍarar*), the punishment must be proportionate to the offence, and should remain within the limits of moderation. Based on the authority of the *sunna*, jurists have further added the proviso that *taʿzīr*, in general, must operate at a level below the severity of the prescribed penalties (*ḥudūd*).[70] *Taʿzīr* punishment may also be invoked in the case of prescribed *ḥadd* offences, where the specified punishment cannot be enforced due to insufficiency of evidence, or owing to doubt in the fulfilment of their necessary conditions. In both cases, the judge has powers to impose, by way of *taʿzīr*, a lesser punishment as may be considered appropriate.

There is some disagreement among the leading *madhāhib* as to the quantitative limits of *taʿzīr* penalties. While some jurists, especially of the Mālikī school, have specified no limits and have referred the matter to considerations of *maṣlaḥa* and *ijtihād* of the judge, others have held that *taʿzīr* penalties in each category must be below the level of the relevant *ḥadd* punishment. This is the view of some Shāfiʿī and Ḥanbalī jurists. According to another view, which is upheld by many Ḥanafī, Shāfiʿī and Ḥanbalī scholars, *taʿzīr* must not exceed the lowest of all the *ḥadd* penalties across the board, which means that it may not exceed forty lashes of the whip in any case. The fourth opinion, held by some Ḥanbalī *ʿulamāʾ*, is that *taʿzīr* punishment may not exceed ten lashes of the whip, and there is some authority in the *ḥadīth* in support of this. Besides this, *taʿzīr* punishment may also consist of a verbal reprimand, imprisonment or, according to some, banishment – depending on the nature of the offence, conditions of the offender and considerations of *maṣlaḥa*.[71]

Accusation (*tuhma*) and Suspicion (*ẓann*)

Accusation (*tuhma*) may be defined as 'an unproven attribution of crime to someone which is accompanied by a demand for judicial redress'. By this definition, accusation is an unproven claim, and it is this factor which differentiates accusation from indictment and sentence, which are accompanied by proof. The demand for judicial redress in this definition also differentiates accusation from a casual attribution of criminal behaviour to someone, which is not intended to involve indictment and adjudication. Accusation is often made by the crime victim or by an interested party, but it may in principle come from anyone, including members of the public and the police. It is also necessary that the subject of accusation is a crime and a violation which renders the perpetrator liable to punishment.[72]

Accusing someone of a crime without proof necessarily invokes suspicion (*ẓann*), which is generally not encouraged. The principle here is laid down in the Qur'anic address to the believers:

> *Avoid indulgence in suspicion, for suspicion in some cases is wrong; and spy not on one another.* (Q.49:12)

The *sunna* has reiterated the Qur'anic directive and warned the believers to 'beware of suspicion, for suspicion is the worst form of lying, and do not spy'.[73] Commentators have equated suspicion here to accusation. What is prohibited, as al-Qurṭubī notes, is baseless accusation, such as accusing someone of adultery and drunkenness without evidence. To say that suspicion here means accusation is also borne out by the subsequent phrase, both in the Qur'an and *ḥadīth*, '...and spy not', for it may occur to someone initially to accuse a person of some wrongdoing so as to spy on him afterwards.[74]

From the *āya* quoted above, Sayyid Quṭb has drawn the conclusion that arrest on the basis of suspicion only is a violation of the personal rights of the individual. No one may be arrested for anything other than an offence which is apparent, and no one may be chased in hidden ways or spied upon in order to be incriminated. The suspect may be arrested and convicted only for a crime that can be proved against him or her by means of lawful evidence, which must preclude espionage. In support of this conclusion, Quṭb has quoted a *ḥadīth* on the authority of Mujāhid, in which the Prophet is reported to have instructed the believers to 'avoid spying. You may accuse people for what is apparent, but leave alone that which God has concealed.'[75] The renowned Companion, 'Abd Allāh ibn Mas'ūd, is also reported to have said that 'espionage is forbidden for us. We may only incriminate people for what is apparent.'[76] Commenting on the same *āya*, al-Alwani has observed that no one may be subjected to frisking or the searching of his/her person or home, and there must be no surveillance, the recording of conversations over the telephone or elsewhere, nor invasion of privacy in any other manner, on the basis of a dubious suspicion that s/he might have committed a crime. This is because 'unfounded suspicion is the worst possible kind of suspicion, and one who acts on such suspicion is a wrongdoer'.[77] This is also the conclusion that both Awad and al-Saleh have drawn from their combined reading of this *āya* and two other Qur'anic *āyat* on the privacy of the home (Q.24:27-8). The searching of and eavesdropping on persons, personal correspondence and property are therefore unlawful, as they partake in espionage and violate the personal right to privacy.[78]

Muhammad Asad has observed concerning the same *āya* that the Qur'anic principles, when read together with the relevant *ḥadīths* on the subject of suspicion and espionage, call for a constitutional enactment that would prohibit the government from indulging in activities that compromise the inviolability of the citizen's personal dignity and right to safety. To subject the citizens, other than those previously convicted of felony and crime, to secret police supervision 'would be entirely out of bounds in a truly Islamic state. Arrest on mere suspicion would be a breach of constitutional law'. Asad adds that imprisonment or internment without previous trial and conviction by a duly established court of law would clearly 'contravene the principle of the inviolability of the human person laid down so unequivocally in the Qur'an and *sunna*'.[79]

It is further suggested that the Qur'anic *āya* quoted above alludes to two types of suspicion, one of which is permissible (*al-ẓann al-mubāḥ*) and the other blameworthy and forbidden (*al-ẓann al-sū'*, or *al-ẓann al-madhmūm*, and, according to some, *al-ẓann al-muḥarram*). When suspicion is based on conviction that is supported by clues and circumstances which may be said to be reasonable, it is permissible, and even praiseworthy, but when it lacks any such basis, then it is blameworthy and forbidden. This binary division of suspicion is indicated in the *āya* itself, which evidently does not forbid suspicion altogether. Thus it is concluded that suspicion under circumstances that give rise to reasonable doubt is permissible, and may form the basis of appropriate action. The grounds of suspicion may be related either to the attending circumstances, or to the character and reputation of the individual, to both. private (*fardī*) that is supported by these factors differs from simple doubt (*shakk*) in that, unlike doubt, which is not inclined to either side, suspicion is inclined toward the side which is supported by the attending clues.[80]

Types of Accusation (tuhma)

Accusation may be private (*fardī*) or public (*'āmm*). Private accusation is made by the victim of the crime or his representative, and usually involves litigation between the parties involved, for example, when a victim of theft accuses a person of having stolen his personal property. In this type of accusation, the claim itself is seen as grounds for suspicion, which may form the basis of arrest. Public accusation, on the other hand, is a right of the society at large, which may be exercised by any one of its members. Public accusation by a fellow citizen who is not a party to the offence partakes in *ḥisba* – that is, commanding good and forbidding evil – which is normally resorted to by one who claims to have been a witness to the offence. This type of accusation gives rise to the fear, on a wider scale than the private accusation, of abusive action, whereby individuals may accuse one another on insufficient grounds, or out of malice. The fear therefore that the reputation of innocent individuals may be jeopardized without cause, and that such individuals are put under pressure as a result, is more prominent in this type of accusation. There is also the additional concern that public accusations, if left unchecked, might strain the time and resources of law enforcement agencies. The public is encouraged to be alert to criminality and evil, yet safeguards are often necessary in order to avoid harm and suffering to innocent individuals. Whereas the private accuser is generally required to support his accusation with some form of evidence, the public accuser is not faced with a similar requirement, for he is a carrier of *ḥisba*, and his position is analogous to a witness. A witness is not normally required to support his statement by evidence. Public accusation is, however, not treated as a testimony against the accused person. This is because the judge needs to verify the probity (*'adāla*) of the witness, which he is not in a position to do in a public accusation, and until this has actually taken place, the allegation is not given the same weight as that of a private accusation. Public accusation is therefore treated as a weak form of accusation, which carries a lesser weight than the testimony of witnesses.[81]

From the viewpoint of its validity or otherwise, accusation is once again divided into two types: valid accusation *al-tuhma al-ṣaḥīḥa*) and void accusation (*al-tuhma al-fāsida*). Valid accusation is credible accusation that is granted a hearing by the judge. Accusation is valid when it fulfils the following three conditions. First, it must be well-defined and specific, as it is addressed to a particular person and solicits adjudication, which is not possible unless the subject matter and person(s) involved therein are clearly identified. An example of unclear accusation would be when someone accuses another of theft in which the stolen goods are not identified, or when the accuser mentions a name and simply says 'I accuse so-and-so', without mentioning what that person might have done or is accused of.[82]

Second, a valid accusation is one which is susceptible to proof, and must be free of inconsistency and contradiction. Accusation is thus not credible in a murder where the victim's body is not found; nor is it credible when the accuser accuses two persons, saying in each case that 'this person alone has murdered my father', or, when a man known for poverty claims that so-and-so has stolen a huge sum of money from him. Third, a valid accusation is one where the end result of the accusation is feasible, and the accusation, when proven, can lead to indictment and sentencing; in other words, it is not an exercise in futility. An example of an unfeasible accusation would be to accuse someone of stealing his own property, or to accuse someone of something trivial, such as stealing 'a grain of wheat'.[83]

Without wishing to enter into minutiæ, Muslim jurists have also sub-divided valid accusation into three types: strong, weak and average. A strong accusation (*al-tuhma al-qawiyya*) is one which is supported by apparent circumstances, such as accusing someone of theft who is known for having committed similar offences in the past. A weak accusation (*al-tuhma al-ḍa'īfa*) is one that is not supported by circumstances, for example, accusing an upright person of good reputation of theft. An average accusation (*al-tuhma al-mutawassiṭa*) is one where neither of the two sides of the claim can be given preference over the other, such as accusing someone who is obscure of theft, and where no information is available concerning his past behaviour.[84] Lastly, a void accusation is one that is devoid of credibility and does not warrant attention. It is an accusation which fails to fulfil one or more of the requirements of a valid accusation, as discussed above.

Arrest and Detention

In an attempt to specify the powers of the law enforcement authorities with regard to arrest and detention, Muslim jurists have discussed two sets of criteria: one which refers to the character of the accused, and the other to the objective bases of suspicion. With reference to the former, the accused may fall under one of three categories. The first of these is where s/he is not known for criminality and corruption, there is no criminal record and the person evidently does not belong to what is phrased in Arabic as *ahl al-tuhma*, or the 'deviant' type. The jurists are in agreement that this type of accused may not be arrested or detained on the basis of mere suspicion; it is added that this is precisely the type of suspicion which the Qur'an has proscribed and declared to be sinful. A mere suspicion in this case is not enough to warrant arrest, unless it is accompanied by credible evidence. There is disagreement, however, as to whether the accuser himself may be liable to punishment, and the dominant of the two variant views on this validates a deterrent punishment for the accuser. This is necessary in order to prevent the miscreants from soiling the good name of upright and innocent individuals by launching hostile and malicious claims against them. Imām Mālik has held the view that the accuser should not be punished unless it can be proved that he acted out of malice in order to harm the accused. The judge should not pay heed to such claims and should not even grant the claimant the opportunity to take an oath to fortify his claim. The Mālikī and the majority rulings on this issue pursue the same objective, which is to deter attacks on the good name and reputation of upright individuals.[85]

The second category is that where the accused person is obscure and has no reputation either for piety or deviation. This type of accused may be arrested and detained according to the majority ruling for the purpose of investigation. Imām Mālik is also in agreement with the majority on this, and the ruling here is founded in a *ḥadīth* in which Abū Hurayra reported that 'the Prophet detained the accused for a day and a night', apparently for the purpose of investigation.[86] While quoting this *ḥadīth*, Ibn Qayyim wrote on the same page that 'the agreed-upon principles among the leading *imāms* support this position', for they agree that the judge is under duty to summon the defendant when there is a claim against him, in order to adjudicate between them. But then, if the accused has travelled a distance and it is not possible to adjudicate the case within the same day, the judge would have little choice but to detain the accused. This is valid, Ibn Qayyim adds, not only in criminal litigation but also in financial disputes. Ibn Qayyim adds further that detention does not necessarily mean imprisonment in a confined space. It means restricting a person's freedom of movement, and it may be in any place, including his own house. The judge may also assign a person to watch over the accused and follow his movements, or take a surety from him.

To limit the initial period of preventive detention to 24 hours, as indicated in the *ḥadīth*, seems to be the preferred position to begin with. Some jurists have recorded the view that this may be extended to two days and then to three, but there is disagreement as to the maximum duration of preventive custody. There are basically two opinions on this, one of which, held mainly by the Shāfiʿīs, has determined it to be one month; if by this time the facts are still not known, the accused should be released forthwith. The second view refers the matter to the discretion and *ijtihād* of the head of state and his representatives, with the recommendation that the detention should not be lengthy, and should be terminated without delay whenever possible.[87]

Māwardī explains that some jurists, like ʿAbd Allāh al-Zubayrī al-Shāfiʿī, have stated a maximum limit of one month's detention, for purposes of investigation. Others have suggested different time limits, 'but the best view is that the *imām* may specify the limit as he deems fit'.[88] This latter view would bring the issue under the umbrella of *siyāsa sharʿiyya*, a subject which I have discussed elsewhere.[89] Suffice it here to note that *siyāsa sharʿiyya* itself may be regulated by means of statutory legislation, and it would in principle be valid for the *imām* to impose statutory limitations on preventive detention.

The third category is that where the accused is known for wrongdoing and the accusation against him appears consistent with his reputation and record. The majority of jurists have in this case validated preventive detention for purposes of investigation. According to one view, the accused may be detained for a period longer than one month, if the charge against him gains further ground, but he may neither be beaten nor presented. The preferred view is that the matter should be determined by the authorities, who should mainly consider the strength or weakness of the accusation, and may detain the accused for a period longer than the accused whose condition is unknown.[90] The detention here is basically aimed at facilitating investigation, and it is not meant to punish or intimidate the accused. It seems that beating this type of person is also permitted, although the *ʿulamāʾ* have recorded different views on this, as I shall elaborate later. A denial, even under oath, by the accused of the charges laid against him is not enough to warrant his release, and it is essential that the truth or falsehood of the accusation be established through evidence. The ruler and judge may consequently detain him for the duration of the investigation. Those who have validated beating, and this includes Mālikī and Ḥanbalī jurists, maintain that beating should be by the whip. The length of detention is not specified according to the preferred view, although some *'ulamā'* have held, as noted above, that detention for investigation may not exceed one month.[91] In response to the question as to whether the judge or the *imām* (or both) have discretion to order detention for the purpose of investigation, jurists have disagreed, but the preferred view is that the order may be issued by either.[92]

The second of the two sets of criteria under discussion here refers to the nature of the activity itself and the visible aspects of suspicious conduct which prompt the arrest and detention of a suspect. The proponents of this view proceed on the assumption that knowledge of the personal character of individuals is often not available to law enforcement authorities, and it is therefore preferable that the decision over whether or not to detain a person should be based on objective and visible factors, which must contemplate the violation or suspicious conduct itself. Thus, a person may not be arrested on suspicion only, which is not substantiated by circumstantial evidence, and clues (*al-adilla wa'l-qarā'in*). Suspicion alone should not be mistaken for evidence, for it is neither evidence nor a clue, and if an arrest were to be based on it, there must be something more than a mere doubt (*shakk*) which turns it into a permissible suspicion (*al-ẓann al-mubāḥ*). An example of unfounded suspicion would be to arrest someone on suspicion of burglary without there being any clue to support that suspicion. This is impermissible, or malicious suspicion (*al-ẓann al-sū'*), which the Qur'an has proscribed, and which violates the individual's right to personal safety. The Prophet has equated this kind of suspicion with the worst kind of lie, *akdhab al-ḥadīth*, as it has no basis in reality and originates in malice.[93]

In their attempt to distinguish permissible suspicion (*al-ẓann al-mubāḥ*) from blameworthy suspicion (*al-ẓann al-madhmūm* or *al-ẓann al-sū'*), the majority of *'ulamā'* prefer to combine the two criteria (i.e. the subjective and the objective) into a single formula. It is accordingly held that suspicion is forbidden in regard to individuals who have no reputation of wrongdoing and who are, by all appearances, upright, and there is also no objective basis nor apparent motive or circumstance for suspicion.

Whether Preventive Detention is Permissible

Since accusation is an unproven claim, and preventive detention is a serious restraint on personal liberty, the question naturally arises as to whether it is at all justified to detain a person on the basis of a mere accusation. The other and equally persuasive side of this argument – as already indicated – is that it is often necessary to detain the accused for the purpose of investigation, so as to prevent his possible escape. Muslim jurists have held three different views on this, one of which maintains that pre-trial detention is unlawful; the second view validates preventive detention only in crimes that invoke a prescribed (*ḥadd*) or retaliatory (*qiṣāṣ*) punishment. The third view, which is held by the majority of jurists, validates preventive detention generally.

The first view, held by Ibn Ḥazm al-Ẓāhirī and some Shāfiʿī and Ḥanbali *ʿulamā'*, proceeds from the original principle of non-liability (*barā'a al-dhimma al-aṣliyya*), and maintains that the accused is not liable to anything prior to proof. Detaining the accused on the basis of accusation alone is tantamount to oppression and a violation of his right, which must be avoided. The proponents of this view have quoted in support the precedent of the Caliph ʿUmar, in a case in which one ʿAbd Allāh ibn Abī ʿĀmir had his leather bag stolen while on a journey together with a group of others. One of the men in the group was suspected of the theft and was questioned for it, but he denied the charge. Abū ʿĀmir later reported the case to the Caliph, who asked as to how many of them were travelling, and the Caliph was informed of this. Abū ʿĀmir then said: 'O Commander of the Faithful! I had intended to bring the accused tied up before you.' To this, the Caliph expressed anger, and said, 'You tie him up and bring him without any evidence? I shall not write nor ask anything about this.' Abū ʿĀmir then said that the Caliph refused to take any action.[94] The Caliph evidently disapproved of the accused being in fetters, which is equivalent to detention, while there was no evidence to support the accusation.

Imām Abū Ḥanīfa's disciple, Abū Yūsuf, has also advanced a forceful argument to the effect that no one should be detained on the sole basis of a claim made by another person:

> It is not permissible to imprison a person because of the accusation of another person. The Prophet did not arrest people on the basis of accusation only, but it is proper to bring the accuser and the defendant together. If the former produces positive evidence in support of his claim the judgement will be issued in his favour, otherwise a surety is taken from the defendant and he is released. If the defendant subsequently clarifies something [it may be considered], otherwise he should not be pressurized. This should also apply to everyone who is detained on suspicion. The Companions of the Prophet were cautious about imposing punishments [lest they harm the innocent].[95]

The second view on preventive detention is held by the majority of the Ḥanafīs, and validates preventive detention of the accused in the prescribed offences of *ḥudūd* and *qiṣāṣ*, but not in pecuniary claims. This view is based on the analysis that imprisonment is the most that can possibly be ordered in pecuniary claims, after the claim is proven, hence it would be excessive to impose that punishment prior to proof. But since the *ḥudūd* and *qiṣāṣ* offences involve punishment of greater severity than imprisonment, the latter may be imposed for the purpose of investigation.[96]

Third, the majority view which validates preventive detention in all crimes, including financial crimes, is based on the analysis that setting the accused free during the investigation and trial is likely to lead to a miscarriage of justice, should the accused escape, try to influence the witnesses, or destroy incriminating evidence. The majority have also quoted a *ḥadīth* which reports that 'the Prophet detained a man under accusation'.[97] According to yet another *ḥadīth*:

> A group of people brought a claim of theft against some weavers to a Companion, al-Nu'mān ibn Bashīr, who detained the accused persons for a few days and then released them. The plaintiffs protested to Nu'mān that 'you released them without beating them or testing their veracity', to which Nu'mān replied: 'What would you have done? You might have beaten them and procured your goods, but if you punished them wrongfully, you would be liable to retaliation yourselves.' The accusers then asked: 'Is this your judgement?' Nu'mān replied: 'This is the judgement of God and His Messenger.'[98]

The conclusion has thus been drawn that, if detention were impermissible, Nu'mān would not have detained the accused persons, nor would he have said that this was 'the judgement of God and His Messenger'.

The majority have also quoted in support another *ḥadīth*, on the authority of Abu Ḥurayra, that 'the Prophet detained [on occasions] for a day and a night for investigation on precautionary grounds'.[99] Quoted in support is also the Qur'anic *āya* which validates a brief detention of witnesses, in the case of a bequest which is made during a journey, but where the testator has later died. The text provides:

> *If you doubt their testimony, then detain them after the prayer, and let them swear by God [saying]: We will not take for it a price though there be a relative nor will we hide the testimony* ... (Q.5:106)

The text thus permits temporary detention of witnesses that are suspected of perjury, in order to verify the truth of their testimony. The detention here is evidently precautionary, not punitive, and is intended to prevent misappropriation of the property of a deceased person, and the text is therefore quoted to validate preventive detention for the purpose of investigation. 'Detain them after the prayer' in the *āya* quoted above evidently contemplates a brief detention, presumably until the next prayer time on the same day, which may well be within the perimeters of the mosques and may not even involve detention in the usual sense of the word.

As for the argument that detention violates the presumption of innocence, it is stated that the presumption remains intact and detention prior to proof is not a punitive but a precautionary measure which is justified to prevent escape, especially in claims that are supported by credible clues *(qarā'in)*.[100]

The Issue Over Beating the Accused

Al-Shāṭibī writes that the *'ulamā'* are in disagreement over beating the accused; those who validate preventive detention of the accused also validate beating him, since both inflict punishment and partake in the attributes of one another. Imām Mālik has validated detention of the accused, and his followers also upheld the permissibility of beating. Al-Shāṭibī himself tends to concur, as he adds: 'For if beating and detention were not permitted, it would be difficult to retrieve the properties of the people from thieves and usurpers.'[101] It is difficult to ascertain the majority position over this issue, as some of the references made in *fiqh* books to 'majority ruling' or 'predominant position' turn out to be somewhat doubtful. What seems certain is that many jurists have upheld beating during detention only of the accused who is a known criminal, and they are almost unanimous in saying that beating is not permissible when the accused is known to be a person of good reputation and integrity.

Disagreement prevails among the *'ulamā'* over the permissibility or otherwise of beating a person who is obscure and whose past record cannot be verified. A number of early jurists, including Aṣbagh, Ibn Ḥazm and al-Ghazālī proscribe beating during investigation altogether, even in cases where the accused has a criminal record.[102] Both the opponents and the proponents of beating have referred to evidence that consists of several reported *ḥadīths* and incidents that took place during the time of the Companions. The evidence remains to be somewhat interpretational and inconclusive, some of which has been quoted by both sides, with each drawing an entirely different conclusion. A contemporary writer on the subject, Fahd al-Suwaylim, has reviewed the detailed evidence and reached the conclusion, albeit without specifying any particular type or class of accused persons, that beating is permissible. This is provided that it is not excessive, but enough to pressurize the accused, whose accusation is supported by circumstantial evidence, including his past record. Al-Suwaylim adds that this does not include inhumane methods of torture, such as electric shocks, nail-pulling and the like.[103]

My own examination of the evidence leads me to the conclusion that passing an affirmative judgement on the permissibility of beating during interrogation can at best be sustained with reference only to dangerous criminals, but that taking a general position of the kind that al-Suwaylim has taken is ultimately self-defeating and futile. To validate beating during interrogation is untenable simply because it fails to meet the basic requirement of Sharīʿa that confession must be voluntary and free of duress. The accused may not, in other words, be forced to make a confession. He is entitled to remain silent and to refuse to give self-incriminating evidence. The accused may also choose not to respond to questions. If s/he does respond, and it is later determined that the answers were false, s/he may not be charged with or punished for giving false testimony. In the event where the accused confesses to a *ḥadd* offence, s/he may retract his/her statement and thereby nullify the confession. Likewise, the accused may not be made to make a confession under hypnotism, truth serum or under the influence of drugs.[104] The main argument against the exercise of coercion in order to extract a confession is presented by al-Ghazālī, and although it is said to be a minority view,[105] it stands on a stronger foundation, and draws support from several *ḥadīths* which al-Ghazālī has quoted. These may be summarized as follows:

First, there is the *ḥadīth* of the Farewell Pilgrimage (*ḥajj al-wadāʿ*), in which the Prophet declared in an address to the believers: 'Everything that belongs to a Muslim, his blood, his property and his honour is forbidden to his fellow Muslim.'[106] Naturally, 'everything that belongs to a Muslim' includes his personal safety from beating and persecution, which are forbidden, unless it is in the course of justice. The substance of this *ḥadīth* is confirmed by the *ḥadīth* quoted above, of al-Nuʿmān ibn Bashīr, who released a group of persons that were accused of theft for lack of evidence. Had beating and torture been permissible, Nuʿmān might have beaten the accused person in order to procure a confession. This also recalls the *ḥadīth* where the Prophet said, concerning a woman who had a reputation for debauchery and corruption, 'If I were to stone anyone without evidence, I would have stoned this woman.'[107] It is thus concluded that the Prophet did not resort to punishment, even concerning a person who had a reputation for wrongdoing.

Ibn ʿAbbās has reported an incident in which a slave woman complained to the Caliph ʿUmar that her master had accused her of adultery and had forced her to sit on fire, resulting in injury to her vagina. The Caliph then asked her if the man had seen her doing what he had accused her of, to which she is reported to have said, 'No.' She was then asked if she had confessed to anything, to which she also replied in the negative. The Caliph then asked the man the same questions: whether he had seen her committing adultery, and whether she had confessed to anything herself. To both of these, the man replied in the negative. The Caliph then said, 'By God, had I not heard the Messenger of God saying that "the master is not retaliated for his slave, nor the father for his son", I would have retaliated in the like manner.' Then the Caliph flogged the man with one hundred lashes, and told the woman, 'You are now free from his bondage.'[108] The conclusion has thus been drawn that the Caliph 'Umar was so incensed that he punished the man for the torture he had inflicted on the woman based only on suspicion and unproven accusation.

Al-Ghazālī has gone so far as to say that beating is prohibited, even in accusations involving hardened criminals. A bad reputation or past record of criminality is not enough to warrant beating the accused before trial. If the accused had committed a crime in the past and was punished for it, then punishing him again on that basis is oppressive. To say that one accusation is proven by a previous incident is equally imaginary and unjustified. The life and right to safety of every individual are sacrosanct, and departure from this position is warranted only on the basis of proof of criminality.

As for the relevance of *maṣlaḥa* to the issue over pre-trial beating, al-Ghazālī has observed that punishing the accused on the basis of the *maṣlaḥa* of the community in the name of crime prevention, is tantamount to overruling certainty on the basis of doubt. The certainty here is the right to safety of the accused person, and what is in doubt is the *maṣlaḥa* of the community. Al-Ghazālī has thus reached the conclusion that *maṣlaḥa* is not the correct context by which to determine this issue, for there are opposing interests involved, one of which is that of the accuser and the society at large, while the other is that of the accused. The former is in need of proof, whereas the latter is not; the latter should therefore take priority, not vice versa. This is the view, as already noted, of Ibn Ḥazm al-Ẓāhirī and one of the early Mālikī jurists, Aṣbagh, both of whom consider beating the accused entirely impermissible.[109] The proponents of this view have added that there is no report of any incident where the Companions might have beaten or tortured the accused, despite the relatively high crime rate that was experienced in that period. Al-Ghazālī also wrote that beating the accused forces him to make a confession, and confession under duress is of no value.[110] A reference is here made to the *ḥadīth* in which the Prophet proclaimed: 'God has forgiven my community for what they do by mistake, forgetfulness, and under compulsion.'[111]

There is general agreement on the principle that confession obtained under duress is null and void. Imām Mālik has said that confession to a crime obtained 'after a threat, a promise, imposition of restriction on one's movement, beating or imprisonment is invalid and fails to provide a basis for punishment'.[112] The Ḥanafī jurist al-Sarakhsī also wrote that 'when the judge compels a man by threatening him, beating him, or subjecting him to restriction or imprisonment to incriminate himself in respect of a *ḥadd* or *qiṣāṣ* offence, the confession is null and void'. Al-Sarakhsī then quotes Caliph 'Umar's statement, cited above, that a man is never secure when he is in pain and frightened and incriminates himself.[113]

The proponents of pre-trial beating have quoted the following evidence in support of their position:

> Anas ibn Mālik reported that a Jewish man crushed the head of a woman in between two stones and the case was brought before the Prophet where the victim barely managed to identify her attacker. The Prophet did not release the accused until he confessed to his crime for which he was retaliated in the like manner.[114]

The conclusion drawn from this *ḥadīth* is that the Jew did not make a confession at first, and it appears that he was threatened or beaten until he made one, hence the permissibility of beating the accused during investigation. In another *ḥadīth*:

> It is reported in conjunction with the story of Ḥāṭib ibn Abī Balta'a that when the Prophet decided to conquer Mecca, Ḥāṭib wrote the Meccans a letter about the Prophet's intention, and sent it with a woman he trusted. When the Prophet learned of this, he sent 'Alī ibn Abī Ṭālib, Zubayr and Miqdād to stop her and retrieve the letter. So they went riding on horses until they found the woman and asked her to hand over the letter. She said, 'I have no letter with me', but she was told, 'Either you hand over the letter or you will be stripped naked.' Then she brought the letter out of the pleats of her hair.[115]

The fact that the said Companions threatened the woman and pressurized her is taken to mean the permissibility of applying punitive tactics on the accused for the purpose of investigation.[116] In yet another *ḥadīth*:

> Anas ibn Mālik has reported that the Prophet sent out a reconnaissance party to Badr. On their way to Badr, they met some camel riders of the Quraysh tribe and there was among them a black slave of the clan of Banī al-Ḥajjāj. The Companions seized the man and questioned him about Abū Sufyān and his followers. The man said, 'I do not know about Abū Sufyān, but these are Abū Jahl, Shihāb, 'Utba and Umayya ibn Khalaf.' They beat him until he said, 'Yes I can tell you this is Abū Sufyān.' So they let him go, but then he was asked the same question again, and again he denied knowing anything about Abū Sufyān. Upon hearing this, they beat him again.

> The Prophet had by then finished his prayer, and when he noted what had happened, he said, 'By the one in whose hands my life reposes: you beat him when he told you the truth and you released him when he lied to you.'[117]

In this episode, in which the Companions beat the man on the basis of suspicion, it is said to be indicative of permissibility for the authorities to threaten the accused, and to beat him until he tells the truth. In one last example:

> In conjunction with the incident of the slander of the Prophet's wife, 'Ā'isha, it is reported that the Prophet summoned 'Ā'isha's servant, Barīra, and questioned her over the incident. 'Alī, who was present on the occasion, struck Barīra hard, and told her to reveal the truth to the Prophet. Barīra spoke and said all that she knew about 'Ā'isha, and it was nothing but good. She then told about the household work she had done during the day, but this did not bring any new information either.[118]

It is concluded from this incident that 'Alī suspected Barīra of hiding information and struck her on that basis, which indicates the permissibility of what he did, especially in view of the fact that the Prophet did not object to his action.[119] Ibn Qayyim has observed: 'Beating is permissible of someone who is believed to know the truth but denies it, and the *'ulamā'* are in agreement on this.'[120] With reference specifically to

> ...the accused who is known to be in possession of [stolen] goods, but who conceals and denies it, he is beaten in order to confess, and there is no doubt in this. He is beaten in order to fulfil an obligation, which is to return the stolen property to its owner.[121]

Ibn Farḥūn has also referred to Ibn Qayyim on the issue of beating and has, in fact, quoted the above passage in reference only to

> ...one who is accused of crimes such as theft, highway robbery, murder and adultery. These may be interrogated and pressurized in proportion to the nature of the accusation and their reputation for such [crimes]. They may sometimes be beaten or detained without beating, depending on their past record and reputation. Ibn Qayyim al-Jawziyya al-Ḥanbalī has said ... [here follows the passage I have quoted above].

Ibn Farḥūn closes his discussion by saying once again that 'it is permissible to beat or detain this category of accused persons when there is valid Sharī'a evidence [to warrant it]'.[122]

The Mālikī jurist al-Bājī has written with reference to

> ...the accused who is obscure and has no criminal record, the manifest (*ẓāhir*) ruling of the *mudawwana* requires that he may not be beaten but may be asked to take an oath (as to his innocence) and, according to one opinion, should be released without taking an oath. The position therefore is that if the accused has a corresponding reputation, he may be threatened, detained and put on oath, but if he has no such reputation, he may not be subjected to any of these, and if he is an upright person, his accuser may be punished.[123]

Ibn Farḥūn has once again verified the position, and has quoted al-Bājī's statement as quoted above *in toto*, agreeing with and confirming it.[124]

Al-Alwani has also discussed the views of some *'ulamā'* on this issue, and has, in particular, quoted Ibn 'Ābidīn's opinion, which is as follows:

> Beating one accused of theft is a matter of judicial policy. So opined al-Zayla'ī. A *qāḍī* may do what is politically expedient, as policy matters are not the exclusive domain of the *imām* [...] There is nothing to support the opinions offered by these scholars [...] Moreover none of these reasons refutes or even weakens the evidence gathered by the majority of jurists that it is illegal to obtain a confession through the use (or threat) of force. Their opinions would be valid if there were contributing circumstances that indicated clearly that the accused was guilty ...[125]

Clearly, the *'ulamā'* are in disagreement over the legality of beating. Ibn Qayyim, al-Baji and Ibn Farḥūn have reserved beating during interrogation to only one class of the accused, namely notorious criminals, especially in cases of theft and highway robbery, where the veracity of a possible confession can be ascertained by the subsequent discovery or otherwise of the stolen goods that the accused might have concealed. Moreover, having summarized the evidence in the *sunna* that is quoted in support of beating the accused, we note that none of the four *ḥadīths* that have been quoted above is conclusive, as virtually every one of them is open to some level of doubt. Ibn Ḥazm al-Ẓāhirī has discussed most of the relevant *ḥadīths*, and has explained why they are doubtful: 'With regard to the first report, Ibn Ḥazm has noted that it is vague and does not establish for a fact that the Prophet either threatened or punished the Jew before he made a confession; it remains in other words, inconclusive.'[126]

With reference to the second report, it is suggested that the Prophet knew for a fact that the woman was carrying the letter in question; so it was not a case merely of accusation, but one which involved acting on the basis of knowledge. The *ḥadīth* is therefore not relevant. As for the third *ḥadīth*, the Prophet actually expressed disapproval of punishing the black man, and his remark intimates that those who punished the accused should have been more careful in the first place. It cannot therefore establish the permissibility of pre-trial beating. With reference to the fourth *ḥadīth* concerning Barīra, there is once again some doubt in respect of the precise detail of what happened on that occasion, for the same *ḥadīth* has been reported in some collections with the words that 'some of the Companions rebuked her (*intaharahā*), and told her to tell the truth to the Messenger of God'. There is no mention of beating Barīra in this version of the *ḥadīth*, and the facts as presented remain doubtful.

To sum up, the permissibility of beating the accused during investigation requires decisive proof, which is not available in either the Qur'an or *sunna*. What remains for us to discuss here is the case of consideration of *maṣlaḥa*, which the advocates of beating have used as the centrepiece of their juristic reasoning. Al-Shāṭibī has examined the evidence and his argument is summarized as follows: with regard to beating the accused, the *'ulamā'* are in disagreement. Those who have validated detention of the accused have also validated beating, for detention is a form of torture and so is beating. The advocates of this view make the analogy of the responsibility of a trustee in the manufacture of goods, such as a tailor who receives a piece of cloth from a client to make a dress. The trustee (*amīn*) is normally not responsible for damage or loss to the goods in his custody unless he is shown to be negligent. But the *'ulamā'* have held that the trustee in the manufacture of goods is a guaranteur, who is responsible for the loss of goods that are placed in his custody.

Here, let us intervene to explain that the analogy between beating the detainee and the responsibility of trustee have an aspect in common: both involve a measure of arbitrary judgement, as the upright and the miscreant are in both cases placed on the same footing. But then, if beating and detention of the accused were not allowed, it would be difficult to protect private property against thieves and usurpers, as producing incriminating evidence is usually difficult, especially in the case of theft. The benefit of *maṣlaḥa* that is involved in holding the trustee responsible for the loss of goods in his custody is upheld by general consensus (*ijmā'*), and the same logic is now extended to the case of beating the accused.

As for the objection that beating in this case might mean torturing the innocent which amounts to prejudice (*ḍarar*), al-Shāṭibī wrote that to do otherwise might be even more harmful. This is notwithstanding the fact that no one validates beating on the basis merely of a claim, but only when the latter is accompanied by supportive clues (*qarā'in*) that penetrate the thought and judgement of the observer and create a reasonable suspicion on his part. The innocent is therefore not very likely to fall victim to prejudice, but if he does so, then that partakes in a pardonable error, somewhat similar to the error that is possible in the case of a craftsman who is held responsible for the goods he has received into his custody.

As for the question that beating is futile if it leads to a confession that is null and void, it is said that 'if it leads to retrieving the stolen property, then it is beneficial'. If the accused who is beaten or threatened with beating makes a confession which leads to the discovery of the stolen goods, then the confession in question may also be validated. Beating the accused also serves as a deterrent, which dissuades people from criminality and corruption.[127] The whole of this argument is thus premised on considerations of *maṣlaḥa*, which also involves the possibility of mischief (*mafsada*) arising in the process. In the event of a conflict between *maṣlaḥa* and *mafsada*, the issue is normally determined on rational grounds, which takes into consideration the balance of evidence and the attending circumstances of each case.

One has to submit that the *maṣlaḥa* in question might have warranted a judgement in favour of beating the accused in earlier times, when the police were, on the whole, poorly equipped with crime detection facilities. Although criminality remains no less a menace to society than it ever was, the police and law enforcement agencies are nevertheless better equipped now and can utilize more advanced methods, from fingerprinting to laboratory analyses and data collection methods that were not possible in medieval times. This might mean that we ought now to give preference to the prevention of evil (*dar' al-mafsada*) in the case before us, over securing the benefit that might be involved, a position which is in harmony with the general guidance of Sharī'a and the legal maxim that 'prevention of harm takes priority over the attraction of benefit'.

Comparing the evidence for and against the permissibility of pre-trial beating, it seems that the evidence against it is more persuasive, and is also in harmony with the basic presumption of Sharī'a, which maintains original non-liability (*barā'a al-dhimma al-aṣliyya*) to be the normal state, unless proven otherwise. The case of dangerous criminals against whom society needs to be protected may be looked at individually within the context perhaps of *siyāsa shar'iyya*. As already noted, this doctrine entitles the head of state and the judge to exercise discretion, so as to provide an adequate response to exceptional situations where the normal rules of law might fall short of providing one. The government may accordingly devise a special procedure for dangerous criminals and treat the issue on that basis. As for the permissibility in principle of pre-trial beating, the case against it is clearly a stronger one. Since pre-trial beating is aimed at extracting self-incriminating confession from the accused, and confession under duress is invalid, it must therefore be seen as an exercise in futility and *ultra vires*.

The Right to Counsel

The Sharīʿa recognizes the right of both plaintiff and accused to present evidence and to have access to counsel during pre-trial interrogation, at the trial and, if the accused is convicted, at the execution of the sentence. The principle that applies here is that of agency (*wakāla*), while both parties are equally entitled to appoint a representative. This is because it is possible that the party concerned is not sufficiently knowledgeable to present his case effectively, or that s/he is unable to attend the court. There is no disagreement among the *ʿulamāʾ* over the validity of representation in all civil claims involving disputes over the Right of Man (*al-ḥaqq al-ādamī*), but the *ʿulamāʾ* have held different views on *wakāla* concerning matters that involve violation of the Right of God (*ḥaqq Allāh*).

The Ḥanafīs have expressed reservations over *wakāla* in regard to the prescribed *ḥudūd* offences, that consist mainly of the Right of God. Thus it is said that in *ḥudūd* offences, such as adultery and wine drinking, the issue before the judge is usually over the sufficiency or otherwise of proof, as these offences usually do not involve litigation, and judicial proceedings over them consist mainly of presentation of evidence, often with no plaintiff or private litigant. Since the *ḥudūd* offences of adultery and wine drinking do not usually involve a private claim, representation is said not to be necessary. If the proof consists of confession, then *wakāla* is not valid in confession, and if it consists of testimony, once again, there is no need for *wakāla*. But if the offence in question consists mainly of violation of the Right of Man, such as slanderous accusation, the dominant Ḥanafī view permits representation on either side.[128] The Shāfiʿīs have basically concurred with the Ḥanafīs, and consider representation in *ḥudūd* offences generally invalid, except in slanderous accusation, on the analysis that the Sharīʿa advises restraint in the proof of the *ḥudūd* offences, whereas representation usually seeks to promote and facilitate proof.

It will be noted, however, that this whole argument is somewhat lop-sided, as representation may seek to disprove and deny the charge, just as it may also seek to secure the proof of the *ḥudūd*.[129] This is basically why the Mālikīs and the Ḥanbalīs maintain the view that representation is valid in all offences, including the *ḥudūd*. The head of state may be represented as public prosecutor in such offences, just as the defendant may also wish to be represented in the court. This is the majority view, and it applies equally to offences involving *qiṣāṣ* and *ta'zīr*, for they too involve violation of the Right of Man and *wakāla* over them is valid, despite some differences of opinion that have arisen over details. The right to retain counsel is thus a general right that extends to all disputes.

A question has arisen concerning the consent of one's opponent, in the event where only one of the two sides resorts to *wakāla*. Imām Abū Ḥanīfa has held that *wakāla* in such a case is not valid without the consent of the other litigant, who may be unable to have a representative (*wakīl*) and may also be unable to defend himself equally well. The opponent's consent is not necessary, according to this view, in situations such as travelling or illness, or when a woman who is not wont to mix with men appoints a *wakīl* to handle the case on her behalf. This is valid even without the consent of the other party. The majority – that is, the Shāfi'īs, Mālikīs, Ḥanbalīs and the two disciples of Abū Ḥanīfa, Abū Yūsuf and al-Shaybānī – have ruled, however, that *wakāla* is permissible generally with or without the consent of the opponent. They maintain that the disagreement of one litigant should not deprive the other of his right to representation. One of the parties may well be unable to defend himself and wish to be represented, just as it is possible that the other party is more capable of defending himself personally and may decide not to appoint a *wakīl*. If we make these decisions contingent on the consent of the other party, it might cause harm, and lead to delays if the consent is not granted in good time.[130]

The *'ulamā'* are generally in agreement that the purpose of representation, whether in civil litigation or crimes, is to vindicate the truth and facilitate justice. Representation may not, in other words, seek to distort justice and advocate falsehood by recourse to deceitful and time-consuming methods. Hence it is forbidden for a person to represent another in the event where the former knows that his principal is in the wrong.[131] Representation is valid, however, in the event where the representative only doubts the veracity of his client's claim. Textual authority for these views is found in the Qur'anic address to the Prophet to 'be not a pleader on behalf of the treacherous' (Q.4:105). Some *'ulamā'* have gone so far as to maintain that it is not permissible for anyone to litigate on behalf of another unless he knows the truth of the matter. If it appears to him to be a right cause, he should accept representation, but he should reject it otherwise. Representation is therefore unlawful in the event where it seeks to distort the truth in pursuit of falsehood.[132] Support for this position also comes from the *ḥadīth* reported by 'Ā'isha, in which the Prophet said: 'The most disliked man before God Most High is one who stubbornly litigates in pursuit of falsehood.'[133] According to another *ḥadīth*: 'One who litigates in pursuit of falsehood while he knows it shall remain afflicted with the wrath of God until he disengages himself from it.'[134] Court decisions must accordingly be founded on what is known to be the truth, and everyone involved – including the judge, witnesses and litigants – are bound by this requirement.

Conclusion

I conclude here by affirming once again that criminal judicial procedure in Islamic Sharī'a remains largely open to the prospects of refinement and growth within the general framework of *siyāsa shar'iyya.* The textual guidelines of the Qur'an and *sunna* on criminal procedure examined in this essay point generally to the same direction, that Islamic law supports any procedure that advances the cause of justice and fair treatment and does not, in the meantime, violate considerations of public interest, or *maṣlaḥa. Siyāsa shar'iyya* is itself predicated on *maṣlaḥa,* and is, as such, changeable, as it must respond to the exigencies of time and circumstance and cannot, as it were, be entirely predicted and legislated in advance. Even if the broad outlines of *siyāsa shar'iyya* on criminal procedure were to be codified, the head of state and judge would still be left with a measure of discretionary powers under *siyāsa shar'iyya,* which they may utilize in response to exceptional and emergency situations that cannot be adequately dealt with under the normal rules of the Sharī'a.

Finally, it should be mentioned that there is a daunting gap between the theory and practice of Islamic Sharī'a in this area. Even a cursory glance at the juridical guidelines of the Sharī'a and the prevailing practices of government in present-day Muslim countries is enough to show the nature of the challenge. One can hardly be more explicit in conveying this concern than al-Alwani, who observed in his recent article that

> ...it is indeed shameful for us today to see that certain Muslim majority states are not at all concerned with human dignity and rights and that they wilfully ignored the guarantees designed to protect those rights ... Their tyranny serves only to distort the truth of Islam and the ways in which it upholds justice.[135]

Some of these governments have indeed become immersed in mistrust, suspicion and espionage against their own people to an alarming extent. The sensitivities that are voiced by the normative guidelines of Islam and the juristic heritage of its leading *'ulamā'* is a far cry from what is being practised in many quarters of the Muslim world today. It is not surprising therefore to see that resistance and insurgency in Muslim societies have consistently found cause to wage a campaign against oppressive government practices, and have usually done so from an Islamic platform. Without wishing to condone insurgency and violence in any quarters, the fact remains that resistance movements are often driven to despair, extremism and violence by the barbarism of these rulers, and the absence of reciprocity and dialogue. If the world community views Muslims as generally trigger-happy and violent, it is due, in no small measure, to the mistrust, conspiracy and suspicion that oppressive Muslim governments have practised against their own citizens.

Notes

[1] c.f. Herbert Packer, *The Limits of the Criminal Sanction* (Stanford, 1969), p 140 ff

[2] c.f. 'Abd al-Ḥamīd al-Mutawallī, *Mabādi' Niẓām al-Ḥukm*, 4th ed (Alexandria, 1974), p 148; Osman Abd el-Malek al-Saleh, 'The right of the individual to personal security in Islam', in Cherif M. Bassiouni (ed), *The Islamic Criminal Justice System* (London, 1982), p 56

[3] Ismā'īl Badawī, *Da'ā'im al-ḥukm fi'l-Sharī'a al-Islāmiyya wa'l-Nuẓum al-Dustūriyya al-Mu'āṣira* (Cairo, 1980), p 91; Fu'ād 'Abd al-Mun'im Aḥmad, *Uṣūl Niẓām al-Ḥukm fi'l-Islām* (Alexandria, 1991), p 263; 'Abd al-Ḥakīm Ḥasan al-'Ilī, *al-Ḥurriyyāt al-'Āmma* (Kuwait, 1983), p 363

[4] Muḥammad Salīm Ghazzāwī, *al-Ḥurriyyāt al-'Āmma fi'l-Islām*(Alexandria, n.d.), p 25

[5] c.f. al-Saleh: 'The right of the individual', p 19

[6] Muslim, *Mukhtaṣar Ṣaḥīḥ Muslim*, 2nd ed, ed Muḥammad al-Albānī (Beirut, 1984), p 473, *ḥadīth* no 1775

[7] Muslim: *Ṣaḥīḥ Muslim*, p 473, *ḥadīth* no 1775

[8] Al-Bukhārī *Ṣaḥīḥ al-Bukhārī*, VIII, trans Muḥammad Muḥsin Khān (Lahore, 1986), K. al-Ḥudūd, p 510, *ḥadīth* no 776; Abū Yūsuf, *Kitāb al-Kharaj* 2nd ed (Cairo, 1352 AH), p 163

[9] Abū 'Īsā Muḥammad al-Tirmidhī, *Sunan al-Tirmidhī*, III (Beirut, 1980), p 255, K. al-Birr, *ḥadīth* no 84

[10] Al-Tirmidhī: *Sunan al-Tirmidhī*, IV, K. al-Diya, p 16, *ḥadīth* no 1395

[11] Al-Bukhārī: *Ṣaḥīḥ al-Bukhārī*, I, p 110, *ḥadīth* no 48

[12] Abū 'Ubayd al-Qāsim ibn Sallam, *Kitāb al-Amwāl* (Riyad, 1353 AH), p 42

[13] *Ḥadīth* uttered at the farewell pilgrimage (*ḥajj al-wadā'*)

[14] Al-Bukhārī: *Ṣaḥīḥ al-Bukhārī*, VIII, p 512, *ḥadīth* no 778

[15] 'Abd al-Wahhāb Khallāf, *al-Siyāsa al-Shar'iyya aw Niẓām al-Dawla al-Islāmiyya* (Cairo, 1972), p 31

[16] 'Abd al-Malik ibn Hishām, *Sīrat al-Nabīy*, ed M. 'Abd al-Ḥamīd Muḥammad, I (Beirut, n.d.), p 625; Muḥammad Abū Zahra, *Tanẓīm al-Islām li'l-Mujtama'* (Cairo, n.d.), p 230

[17] Abū 'Abd Allāh Muḥammad ibn Sa'd, *al-Ṭabaqāt al-Kubrā*, III (Beirut, n.d.), p 293; Aḥmad: *Uṣūl*, p 266; Muḥammad Fatḥī 'Uthmān, *Ḥuqūq al-Insān Bayn al-Sharī'a al-Islāmiyya wa'l-Fikr al-Qānūnī al-Gharbī* (Cairo, 1962), p 79

[18] c.f. Abū Isḥāq Ibrāhīm al-Shāṭibī, *al-Muwāfaqāt fi Uṣūl al-Aḥkām*, ed Muḥammad al-Khiḍr Ḥusayn al-Tūnisī, II (Cairo, 1922), pp 3-5 and *passim*; Mohammad Hashim Kamali, *Principles of Islamic Jurisprudence* (Cambridge, 1991), p 271 ff

[19] c.f. al-'Ilī: *al-Ḥurriyyāt*, p 369; al-Saleh: 'The right of the individual', p 56

[20] Abū Yūsuf: *Kitāb al-Kharaj*, p 190

[21] Muḥammad ibn 'Abd Allāh al-Khaṭīb al-Tabrīzī, *Mishkāt al-Maṣābīḥ*, ed Muḥammad al-Dīn al-Albānī, III (Beirut, 1979), *ḥadīth* no 3570; Abū Yūsuf: *Kitāb al-Kharaj* p 164

[22] Abū Yūsuf: *Kitāb al-Kharaj*, p 175; see also Burhān al-Dīn Ibrāhīm ibn 'Alī ibn Farḥūn, *Tabṣirat al-Ḥukkām fī Uṣūl al-'Aqdiyya wa Manāhij al-Aḥkām*, ed 'aha A. R. Sa'd, II (Cairo, 1986), p 158

[23] Abū Yūsuf: *Kitāb al-Kharaj* pp 190-1

[24] 'Alī ibn Muḥammad al-Māwardī, *Kitāb al-Aḥkām al-Sulṭāniyya* (Cairo, 1986), p 193

[25] Abū Yūsuf: *Kitāb al-Kharaj*, pp 51-63; al-'Ilī: *Ḥurriyyāt*, p 369; see also al-Saleh: 'The right of the individual', p 85

[26] Abū Yūsuf: *Kitāb al-Kharaj* p 162; al-'Ilī: *Ḥurriyyāt*, p 370

[27] c.f. Ṣubḥī Rajab Mahmassānī, *Arkān Ḥuqūq al-Insān fi'l-Islām* (Beirut, 1979), pp 107-8

[28] Muḥammad Fārūq al-Nabhān, *Niẓām al-Ḥukm fi'l-Islām* (Kuwait, 1974), p 167

[29] Hamid Enayat, *Modern Islamic Political Thought* (London, 1982), p 128

[30] c.f. Abū Zahra: *Tanẓīm*, pp 34-5; al-Mutawallī: *Mabādi'*, p 387; Ghazzāwī: *al-Ḥurriyyāt*, p 26

[31] Muslim: *Ṣaḥīḥ Muslim*, K. al-Amāna, *ḥadīth* no 39. This *ḥadīth* is reported unanimously (*muttafaq 'alayh*)

[32] Abū Dāwūd al-Sijistānī, *Sunan Abī Dāwūd*, trans Aḥmad Ḥasan (Lahore, 1984), *ḥadīth* no 2285

[33] Al-Māwardī: *Kitāb al-Aḥkām*, p 33

[34] Mahmassānī: *Arkān*, p 94

[35] Abū Yūsuf: *Kitāb al-Kharaj* p 152

[36] Abū Dāwūd: *Sunan*, III, *ḥadīth* no 3582; Mahmassānī: *Arkān*, p 107

[37] 'Abd al-Wahhāb ibn Aḥmad al-Sha'rānī, *Kitāb al-Mīzān*, II (Cairo, 1329 AH), p 165; see also Awad, 'The rights of the accused under Islamic criminal procedure', in Bassiouni: *The Islamic Criminal Justice System*, p 94

[38] c.f. al-Saleh: 'The right of the individual', p 66

[39] Mahmassānī: *Arkān*, p 106

[40] Abū Bakr Aḥmad ibn al-Ḥusayn al-Bayhaqī, *al-Sunan al-Kubrā* (Beirut, n.d.), K. al-Da'wa wa'l-Bayyināt

[41] Muslim: *Ṣaḥīḥ Muslim*, p 280; *ḥadīth* no 1053; Ibn Qayyim al-Jawziyya, *al-Ṭuruq al-Ḥukmiyya fi'l-Siyāsa al-Shar'iyya* (Cairo, 1953), p 94

[42] Ibn Qayyim: *al-Ṭuruq al-Ḥukmiyya*, p 28

[43] Taqī al-Dīn ibn Taymiyya, *al-Siyāsa al-Shar'iyya fī Iṣlāḥ al-Ra'y wa'l-Ra'īya*, 2nd ed (Cairo, 1951), p 153

[44] Shihāb al-Dīn al-Qarafī, *Kitāb al-Furūq*, IV (Cairo, 1346 AH), p 54; Ibn Farḥūn: *Tabṣirat al-Ḥukkām*, I, p 131; Ibn Qayyim al-Jawziyya, *I'lām al-Muwaqqi'īn 'an Rabb al-'Ālamīn*, II (Beirut, 1973), p 87

[45] Al-Sha'rānī: *Kitāb al-Mīzān*, II, p 137; Mohamed Selim El-Awa, *Punishment in Islamic Law* (Indianapolis, 1982), p 128

[46] Ibn Qayyim: *al-Ṭuruq*, p 5; 'Abd al-Salām ibn Sa'īd Saḥnūn, *al-Mudawwana al-Kubrā*, VI (Beirut, 1994), p 293; Bandar ibn Fahd al-Suwaylim, *al-Muttaham, Mu'āmalātuhu wa Ḥuqūquhu fi'l-Fiqh al-Islāmī* (Riyad, 1988), p 184

[47] Muḥammad al-Khaṭīb al-Sharbīnī, *Mughnī al-Muḥtāj ilā Ma'rifat Ma'ānī al-Minhāj*, IV (Cairo, n.d.), p 150; al-Suwaylim: *al-Muttaham*, pp 187-8

[48] Al-Sha'rānī: *Kitāb al-Mīzān*, II, p 166

[49] Abū Dāwūd: *Sunan*, III, p 1016, *ḥadīth* no 3576

[50] Al-Sha'rānī: *Kitāb al-Mīzān*, II, p 169

[51] Maḥmūd Shaltūt, *al-Islām, 'Aqīda wa Sharī'a* (Kuwait, *c.* 1966), p 327; see also al-Sha'rānī: *Kitāb al-Mīzān*, II, p 125

[52] Muḥammad ibn 'Alī Shawkānī, *Nayl al-Awṭār*, VII (Cairo, 1347), p 70

[53] c.f. Muḥammad al-Bahīy, *al-Dīn wa'l-Dawla min Tawjīhāt al-Qur'ān al-Karīm* (Beirut, 1971), p 394
[54] Shaltūt: *al-Islām*, p 327
[55] Abū Muḥammad 'Alī ibn Aḥmad ibn Ḥazm, *al-Muḥallā*, II (Cairo, 1347), p 55
[56] Shaltūt: *al-Islām*, p 327
[57] 'Abd al-Qādir 'Awda, *al-Tashrī' al-Jinā'ī al-Islāmī* I (Beirut, 1983), p 115
[58] Abū Ḥamīd Muḥammad al-Ghazālī, *al-Mustasfā min 'Ilm al-Uṣūl*, I (Cairo, n.d.), p 63; Sayf al-Dīn al-'Āmidī, *al-Iḥkām fī Uṣūl al-Aḥkām*, 2nd ed, I (Beirut, 1982), p 130
[59] 'Abd al-Wahhāb Khallāf, *'Ilm Uṣūl al-Fiqh*, 12th ed (Kuwait, 1978), p 173
[60] c.f. 'Awda: *al-Tashrī' al-Jinā'ī*, I, p 117
[61] 'Awda: *al-Tashrī' al-Jinā'ī*, I, p 115
[62] 'Awda: *al-Tashrī' al-Jinā'ī*, I, p 133
[63] Khallāf: *'Ilm Uṣūl al-Fiqh*, p 98
[64] Muḥammad Abū Zahra, *al-Jarīma wa'l-'Uqūba fi'l-Fiqh al-Islāmī* (Cairo, n.d.), p 185
[65] Muslim: *Ṣaḥīḥ Muslim*, K. al-Īmān, *ḥadīth* no 192; Abū Zahra: *al-Jarīma*, p 343
[66] Abū Zahra: *al-Jarīma*, p 323; al-Saleh: 'The right of the individual', p 63
[67] Abū Zahra: *al-Jarīma*, pp 138-49; al-Saleh: 'The right ofthe individual', p 60
[68] Abū Zahra: *al-Jarīma*, p 209
[69] Māwardī explains that some jurists, like 'Abd Allāh al-Zubayrī al-Shāfi'ī, have stated a maximum limit of one month of detention for purposes of investigation. Others have suggested different time limits, but the best view is that the *imām* may specify the limit as he deems fit. *Kitāb al-Aḥkām*, p 192; 'Awda: *al-Tashrī' al-Jinā'ī*, p 150
[70] Abū Zahra: *al-Jarīma*, p 208; 'Awda: *al-Tashrī' al-Jinā'ī*, p 308
[71] See, for details, Ibn Qayyim: *al-Ṭuruq*, p 124; see also al-Māwardī: *Kitāb al-Aḥkām*, p 205
[72] c.f. Ibn Qayyim: *al-Ṭuruq*, pp 93-4, al-Suwaylim: *al-Muttaham*, p 23
[73] Bukhārī: *Ṣaḥīḥ al-Bukhārī*, VIII, p 58, *ḥadīth* no 90; Muslim: *Ṣaḥīḥ Muslim*, K. al-Birr wa'l-Ṣila, Bāb al-Nahy 'an al-Tajassus
[74] c.f. Abū 'Abd Allāh Muḥammad bin Aḥmad al-Qurṭubī, *al-Jāmi' li-Aḥkām al-Qur'ān*, XVI (Cairo, 1967), p 331
[75] Sayyid Quṭb, *Fī Ẓilāl al-Qur'ān*, VI (Beirut, n.d.), p 3346
[76] Quṭb, *Fī Ẓilāl al-Qur'ān*, VI, p 3343; al-Sha'rānī: *Kitāb al-Mīzān*, p 166
[77] Taha Jabir al-Alwani, 'The rights of the accused in Islam', *American Journal of Islamic Social Sciences*, II (1994), p 363
[78] Awad: 'The rights of the accused', p 104; al-Saleh: 'The right of the individual', p 68
[79] Muhammad Asad, *Principles of State and Government in Islam* (Berkeley, 1966), pp 85-6
[80] c.f. al-Qurṭubī: *Aḥkām al-Qur'ān*, XVI, pp 331-2; Shams al-Dīn Muḥammad ibn 'Arafa al-Dusūqī, *Ḥāshiyat al-Dusūqī 'alā'-Sharḥ al-Kabīr*, IV (Cairo, n.d.), p 144; Ḥusnī al-Jundī, *Ḍamānāt Ḥurmat al-Ḥayāt al-Khāṣṣa fi'l-Islām* (Alexandria, n.d.), pp 185-6
[81] 'Alā' al-Dīn al-Kasānī, *Badā'i' al-Ṣanā'i' fī Tartīb al-Sharā'i'*, VI, 2nd ed (Beirut, 1982), p 277; Muḥammad ibn Aḥmad ibn Juzayy, *Qawānīn al-Aḥkām al-Shar'iyya* (Beirut, 1979); al-Sharbīnī: *Mughnī al-Muḥtāj*, IV, p 437
[82] Al-Dusūqī: *Ḥāshiya*, IV, p 144; al-Sharbīnī: *Mughnī al-Muḥtāj*, IV, p 46
[83] Ibn 'Ābidīn: *Ḥāshiyat Radd al-Muḥtār 'alā Durr al-Mukhtār* V (Damascus, 1421 AH), p 544; al-Qarāfī: *Kitāb al-Furūq*, IV, p 72; Ibn Farḥūn: *Tabṣirat al-Ḥukkām*, I, p 148; Ibn Juzayy: *Qawānīn*, p 304
[84] Ibn Farḥūn: *Tabṣirat al-Ḥukkām*, II, p 145; al-Māwardī: *Kitāb al-Aḥkām*, p 219
[85] Ibn Farḥūn: *Tabṣirat al-Ḥukkām*, II, p 156; Taqī al-Dīn ibn Taymiyya, *Majmū' Fatāwā Shaykh al-Islām Ibn Taymiyya*, XXXIV, ed 'Abd al-Raḥmān ibn Qāsim (Beirut, 1398 AH), p 236; Ibn Qayyim: *al-Ṭuruq*, p 101; al-Jundī: *Ḍamānāt*, p 182

---

86 Al-Ḥākim al-Nīshābūrī, *al-Mustadrak 'alā al-Ṣaḥīḥayn*, IV, ed Yūsuf 'Abd al-Raḥmān al-Mar'ashlī (Beirut, n.d.), p 102; Ibn Qayyim: *al-Ṭuruq*, p 102

87 Al-Māwardī: *Kitāb al-Aḥkām*, p 152; Ibn Qayyim: *al-Ṭuruq*, p 103; Ibn 'Ābidīn: *Ḥāshiya*, IV, p 188; Abū'l-Walīd Sulaymān ibn Khalaf ibn al-Bājī, *al-Muntaqā Sharḥ al-Muwatta'*, VII (Cairo, 1332 AH), p 166

88 Al-Māwardī: *Kitāb al-Aḥkām*, p 150

89 Mohammad Hashim Kamali, '*Siyāsah shar'iyyah* or the policies of Islamic government', *American Journal of Islamic Social Sciences* 6 (1989), pp 59-81

90 Ibn Farḥūn: *Tabṣirat al-Ḥukkām*, II, p 158; al-Bājī, *al-Muntaqā*, VII, p 166; Zayn al-'Ābidīn al-Zayla'ī, *al-Baḥr al-Rā'iq Sharḥ Kanz al-Daqā'iq*, V (Beirut, n.d.), p 46

91 Ibn Qayyim: *al-Ṭuruq*, pp 104-105; al-'Ilī: *Ḥurriyyāt*, p 369

92 Al-Māwardī, *Kitāb al-Aḥkām*, p 220; Ibn Qayyim: *al-Ṭuruq*, p 104; Ibn 'Ābidīn: *Ḥāshiya*, IV, p 15

93 Al-Qurṭubī: *Aḥkām al-Qur'ān*, VII, p 6152; al-Jundī: *Ḍamānāt*, pp 185-6

94 Abu Bakr 'Abd al-Razzāq al-Ṣan'ānī, *al-Muṣannaf*, I, ed Ḥabīb al-Raḥmān al-A'ẓamī (Beirut, 1972), p 217; Ibn Ḥazm: *al-Muḥallā*, II, p 16

95 Abū Yūsuf: *Kitāb al-Kharaj*, II, pp 190-1

96 Al-Zayla'ī: *al-Baḥr al-Rā'iq*, V, p 6; al-Suwaylim: *al-Muttaham*, p 92

97 Abū Dāwūd: *Sunan*, III, p 314; Ibn Qayyim: *al-Ṭuruq*, p 102

98 Abū Dāwūd: *Sunan*, IV, p 135, *ḥadīth* no 4382

99 Al-Ḥākim: *al-Mustadrak*, IV, p 102; Ibn Qayyim: *al-Ṭuruq*, p 102

100 Al-Māwardī, *Kitāb al-Aḥkām*, p 220; Ibn Farḥūn: *Tabṣirat al-Ḥukkām*, II, p 329

101 Abū Isḥāq Ibrāhīm al-Shaṭibī, *al-I'tiṣām*, II (Beirut, 1982), II, p 120

102 Ibn Taymiyya: *Majmū' Fatāwā*, XXXIV, p 238; see also al-Māwardī: *Kitāb al-Aḥkām*, p 220; Ibn Qayyim: *al-Ṭuruq*, p 105; Ibn Farḥūn: *Tabṣirat al-Ḥukkām*, II, pp 154; 158

103 Al-Suwaylim: *al-Muttaham*, pp 116-7

104 Al-Alwani: 'The rights of the accused', p 507

105 Al-Suwaylim: *al-Muttaham*, pp 101-2

106 Al-Bukhārī: *Ṣaḥīḥ al-Bukhārī*, VIII, p 51, *ḥadīth* no 776; al-Ghazālī, *Shifā' al-Ghalīl*, ed Ḥamd al-Kubaysī (Baghdad, 1981), p 229

107 Al-Bukhārī: *Ṣaḥīḥ al-Bukhārī*, VIII, p 559, *ḥadīth* no 839; Ibn Taymiyya: *al-Siyāsa*, p 153

108 Al-Ḥākim, *al-Mustadrak*, II, p 216; al-Bayhaqī: *al-Sunan al-Kubrā*, VIII, p 36

109 Al-Ghazālī: *Shifā' al-Ghalīl*, p 229; al-Ghazālī: *al-Mustaṣfā*, I, p 297; Ibn Ḥazm: *al-Muḥallā*, VIII, p 141; al-Bājī: *al-Muntaqā*, VII, p 166; Ibn Farḥūn: *Tabṣirat al-Ḥukkām*, II, p 158

110 Al-Ghazālī: *Shifā' al-Ghalīl*, p 229

111 Al-Ḥākim: *al-Mustadrak*, II, 198. Al-Bukhārī has recorded the same *ḥadīth* with a slight variation in wording. See *Ṣaḥīḥ al-Bukhārī*, VIII, p 527, *ḥadīth* no 805

112 Saḥnūn: *al-Mudawwana al-Kubrā*, VI, p 293

113 Shams al-Dīn Muḥammad al-Sarakhsī, *al-Mabsūṭ*, XXIV (Beirut, n.d.), p 70

114 Muslim: *Mukhtaṣar Ṣaḥīḥ*, p 272, *ḥadīth* no 1028

115 Al-Bukhārī: *Ṣaḥīḥ al-Bukhārī*, IV, p 19; Muslim: *Ṣaḥīḥ Muslim*, IV, p 1941; Abū Dāwūd: *Sunan*, III, p 47

116 Ibn Qayyim: *al-Ṭuruq*, p 9; Ibn Farḥūn: *Tabṣirat al-Ḥukkām*, II, p 139

117 Muslim: *Ṣaḥīḥ Muslim*, III, p 1404; Abū Dāwūd: *Sunan*, III, p 58

118 Al-Bukhārī: *Ṣaḥīḥ al-Bukhārī*, VI, p 12; Muslim: *Ṣaḥīḥ Muslim*, IV, p 2138

119 Ibn Farḥūn: *Tabṣirat al-Ḥukkām*, II, p 137; 'Alā' al-Dīn al-Ṭarābulsī, *Mu'īn al-Ḥukkām* (Cairo, 1323 AH), p 171

120 Ibn Qayyim: *al-Ṭuruq*, p 106; al-Shāṭibī: *al-I'tisam*, II, p 120

[121] Ibn Qayyim: *al-Ṭuruq*, p 108
[122] Ibn Farḥūn: *Tabṣirat al-Ḥukkām*, II, pp 157-8
[123] Al-Bājī: *al-Muntaqā*, VII, p 166
[124] Ibn Farḥūn: *Tabṣirat al-Ḥukkām*, II, p 162
[125] Al-Alwani: 'The right of the accused', p 512, quoting Ibn 'Ābidīn:*Ḥāshiya*, III, p 259
[126] Ibn Ḥazm: *al-Muḥallā*, VIII, p 132; al-Suwaylim: *al-Muttaham*, p 116
[127] Al-Shāṭibī: *al-I'tiṣām*, II, p 120
[128] Al-Kasānī: *Badā'i' al-Ṣanā'i'*, VI, p 21
[129] Abū Isḥāq Ibrāhīm ibn 'Alī al-Shīrāzī, *al-Muhadhdhab fī Fiqh al-Imām Shāfi'ī*, I (Cairo, n.d.), p 349; al-Sharbīnī: *Mughnī al-Muḥtāj*, II, p 221; Awad: 'Rights of the individual', p 97
[130] Al-Kasānī, *Badā'i' al-Ṣanā'i'*, VI, p 22; Ibn Qudāma al-Maqdisī, *al-Mughnī* (Riyadh, n.d.), V, pp 89-90; al-Shīrāzī, *al-Muhadhdhab*, I, p 355
[131] 'Alā' al-Dīn ibn al-Ḥasan 'Alī ibn Sulaymān al-Mardawī, *al-Inṣāf fī Ma'rifat al-Rājiḥ min al-Khilāf 'alā Madhhab al-Imām al-Mubajjal Aḥmad Ibn Ḥanbal*, V (Cairo, 1956), p 394; Manṣūr ibn Yūnus Idrīs al-Buḥūtī, *Kashshāf al-Qinā' 'an Matn al-Iqnā'*, III (Beirut, 1982), p 483
[132] Ibn Farḥūn: *Tabṣirat al-Ḥukkām*, I, p 159
[133] Al-Tirmidhī: *Sunan al-Tirmidhī*, *ḥadīth* no 2976
[134] Abū Dāwūd: *Sunan*, III, p 305; al-Bayhaqī: *al-Sunan al-Kubrā*, VI, p 82
[135] Al-Alwani: 'The rights of the accused', p 518

5

Compensation for Homicide in Islamic Sharīʿa

Muhammad Abdel Haleem

The first legal objective of the Sharīʿa is to protect the life of the individual; indeed, life takes priority over religion itself. The Qur'an sets the highest penalty for taking life deliberately, and is categorical in its treatment of homicide and its consequences, employing language that addresses both reason and emotion. It forbids killing thus:

> *Do not kill the soul which God has made inviolable, except as justice requires.* (Q.17:33)

Anyone violating the sanctity of the life of another lays him or herself open to *qiṣāṣ*, a penalty similar to what he or she has done. But the matter does not end there; the Qur'an stands firmly with the victim and his/her heirs, calling the victim 'unjustly slain' (*qutila maẓlūm*), and awarding the heirs special power (*sulṭān*) to demand *qiṣāṣ* from the murderer. God speaks in the first person plural of majesty, saying:

> *Whoever is slain unjustly, We have given his heirs a power* ... (Q.17:33)

This power is given as a right: Muslim jurists call this power 'the right of the individual' (*ḥaqq al-ʿabd*). It is one of three categories of rights, which jurists define as follows: those regarded as exclusively involving the Right of God, that is the right of society as a whole (this includes theft and brigandage); those in which both the Right of God and the Right of the individual are recognized, but where the Right of God predominates (this includes unproven slander of a chaste person); then there are those in which the Right of the individual is predominant (this includes homicide and wounding). The difference between these three categories is that, in the first two cases, neither the contending parties nor the court may drop the case or allow a settlement once proceedings have started, while in the latter case the injured party may do either.

The Qur'an defines major offences and sets punishments for them but, as always, it endeavours to restrict the application of these punishments whenever possible. Strict conditions are set for proving guilt, as the Prophet Muḥammad commanded: 'Avert the application of *ḥudūd* penalties when there is any doubt, as much as you can, for it is better for a judge to err on the side of pardon than on the side of punishment.'

The Style of the Qur'an Regarding Penalties for Homicide

In the Sharī'a, the provisions for the crimes of murder and manslaughter are based exclusively on the Qur'an. However, whereas jurists and modern legislators formulate the provisions of penal systems in legal language (as we see in acts of parliaments and legal text-books), when introducing penalties for homicide, the Qur'an has its own unique style, combining legal formulations with emotive appeals and offering a comprehensive and all-embracing means of dealing with crime.

I shall present here the Qur'anic texts that deal with murder and manslaughter. It is these texts, and not legal clauses, that Muslims read and hear in their daily prayers and lives, and it is these texts that form their attitudes and affect their practice. Moreover, these texts are quoted by prosecutors and lawyers in their pleadings in Muslim courts. Two texts will be discussed here: Passage A (Q.2:178-9 from *Sūrat al-Baqara*) and Passage B (Q.4:92-3 from *Sūrat al-Nisā'*).

Passage A:

You who believe, just retribution is prescribed for you in cases of murder: the free man for the free man, the slave for the slave, the woman for the woman.[1] *But if something is waived for the culprit by his* [*aggrieved*] *brother, this shall be adhered to in fairness, and he shall pay what is due in a goodly manner. This alleviation is from your Lord, an act of mercy, but if anyone wilfully exceeds the limits after that, a grievous suffering is in store for him. In just retribution there is life for you, people of understanding, so that you may guard yourself against what is wrong.*

This passage deals with murder. It begins by appealing to all believers, including the parties to the murder and the authorities, to tell them that *qiṣāṣ*, which involves similar, and thus fair, treatment is prescribed for them. To do this, it uses the verb *kutiba* ('it has been written or prescribed [by God]'), which it also uses, for instance, to describe the obligation to fast in the month of Ramadan. By addressing the entire community in this way, it puts the whole of society under the obligation of accepting this teaching and adhering to it. Commentators say that, in the case of murder, there is a religious obligation on the murderer to hand himself over to the authorities, unlike with the adulterer, for instance, who, if not witnessed, is recommended to conceal his crime. Nor is the penalty for adultery introduced as a religious obligation in this way.[2] The text then counteracts the pre-Islamic tribal practice of excessive demands for retaliation, as when a superior tribe would demand that two free men be killed from the tribe of the offender for each free man, or a free man for a slave, or a man for a woman.[3]

Having established the principle of equity, the Qur'an then goes on to recommend pardon in return for compensation. Here, it departs from legal vocabulary to use emotive words, even calling the culprit a 'brother' of the victim's representative (*walīy al-dam*). It instructs them that the settlement should be made 'in a goodly manner' and compensation 'handed over generously', pointing out to the two parties and to the whole community that 'this is an alleviation and a mercy from your Lord'. In this section, the words *'ufiya* (pardoned) and *akhīh* (his brother), *bi'l-ma'rūf* (in a fair way) and *b-iḥsān* (in a good way) are calming words that call for magnanimity and generosity on all sides. It should be pointed out that, when discussing retaliation, the Qur'an always suggests pardon and compensation. For instance, *Sūrat al-Mā'ida* (Q.5:45) calls these measures 'a charitable act that expiates the [aggrieved] person's own sins'.[4]

Having effected reconciliation, the passage ends with a stern warning to anyone who commits aggression after that. Again, this is a reminder of the pre-Islamic practice of committing violence against the murderer after compensation and pardon. The passage ends with an appeal to common sense and social benefit, stating: 'In *qiṣāṣ* there is life for you, men of understanding', explaining that the institution results in the saving of the lives of individuals and of society. '*La'allakum tattaqūn*' has the double meaning of (i) 'that you may be conscious of God', and (ii) 'that you may avoid committing wrong'. In this passage, the Qur'an follows its normal practice of always justifying its teachings with reasons, while appealing to the feelings and common sense, a style that contrasts vividly with normal legal texts and acts.

Thus, the heirs of the murdered person have three rights: first, to demand *qiṣāṣ* by due legal process, but not to do it themselves,[5] since the implementation is solely vested with the state; second, to accept compensation; or, third, to pardon completely without any financial settlement, as a charitable act. It should be pointed out here that, for the implementation of *qiṣāṣ*, all the heirs of the victim must agree on this course of action. If anyone disagrees or opts for compensation or pardon, *qiṣāṣ* cannot be carried out. Thus, the number of cases in which *qiṣāṣ* is effected is further diminished in this way. Similarly, any heir can waive his or her share of the compensation if he/she so desires. This is constructive because it empowers the victim's family, calms people and promotes reconciliation, and compensates the heirs for the loss of the earning power of the victim. Furthermore, it saves life, and does not involve long prison sentences for the culprits, which use state money and deprive the culprits' families of their personal, financial and social support.

Compensating the Heirs by *Diya*

Diya is not 'blood money', as it is normally translated. The *Oxford English Dictionary* gives the primary meaning of the term 'blood money' as 'a reward for bringing about the death of another'. The word *diya* has no such association in Arabic, and is therefore better translated as 'compensation'. Furthermore, it is not a fine, since fines go to the state. Here is but one example of how translating Islamic terminology has been responsible for the traditional, bad image of Islam in the West. It should also be remembered that compensation is an option, and that both parties, heirs and murderer, must agree to it. The option of compensation is constructive and fair, and can be seen to obviate the criticism levelled against capital punishment, namely that it might be proved later to have been inflicted on an innocent party.

Passage B deals with killing by mistake:

> *Never should a believer kill another believer,*[6] *except by mistake, and anyone who kills a believer by mistake must free one Muslim slave and pay compensation to the victims' relatives, unless they forgo it charitably. If the [believing] victim belonged to a people at war with you, then the obligation is only to free a believing slave. If he belonged to a people with whom you have a treaty, then the compensation should be paid over to his relatives, and a believing slave should be set free. Anyone who lacks the means to do this must fast for two consecutive months by way of repentance to God: God is all-knowing, all-wise. For anyone who kills a believer deliberately, the punishment is Hell, where he will remain: God will be angry with him, and will reject him, and He has tremendous torment in store for him.*

The passage begins with the fact that killing ought not to be done, unless by mistake, and then there would have to be an act of expiation and compensation; expiation (*kaffāra*) here takes the form of freeing a slave.[7] All acts of expiation in the Qur'an benefit society and the individual performing them. It is interesting that the expiation is placed first, before compensation, and then the compensation (*diya*) is described as being handed over (*musallam*) to the victim's family, a word which suggests being 'sound' and 'undiminished'. This is followed by the exception 'unless they forgo it charitably', being a recommendation for the victim's family to forgo it if they can do so. If the victim had been living in enemy territory, then what is required is expiation only. If the culprit is one of the People of the Book in Muslim lands (*dhimmī*), then compensation must be paid to the victim's family; it is interesting to note that here it is placed before expiation. If the person cannot pay the expiation of freeing a slave, then s/he must still make amends by fasting for two successive months, by way of repentance. The verse then reminds the believers that God is all-knowing and all-wise in introducing these teachings, and that therefore they should accept them and apply them in good faith. The passage then states the penalty in the hereafter for deliberate murderers, whose recompense will be hell fire, and in which they shall stay. This emphasizes that God will be angry with such persons, and will keep them at a distance and prepare woeful torment for them.

The legal penalty in this world for a murderer is stated in Passage A. There is discussion amongst jurists as to whether murderers should also pay the expiation in addition to going through *qiṣāṣ*. Abū Ḥanīfa states that they should not pay expiation, on the basis that the above verse does not mention expiation for murder, whereas al-Shāfiʿī argues that they must do so, basing the obligation on the *ḥadīth* in which the family of a murderer came to ask the Prophet what they should do, and he told them to free a slave, in the hope that God would free the murderer from the suffering in the fire. Another basis for al-Shāfiʿī's opinion is analogy, saying that if the person who kills by mistake should pay expiation, then the one who murders with intent should pay more.[8]

In the Sharīʿa, then, the penal system deals both with the culprit on the one hand, and the victim and his family on the other. The consideration of the victim and his family is epitomized in the juristic rule '*lā yuṭallu dam fi'l-islām*' (no blood will go to waste under Islamic law [without retribution or payment of compensation]).[9]

Who Pays the *Diya*?

The burden of paying the *diya* falls first on the murderer, and if he is unable to do so, it will fall on his *ʿāqila* (blood relatives). If they cannot pay, it will be the responsibility of the Muslim state, since it owed the slain person the right of protection and it owed his family the right of care. If the state cannot obtain payment from the murderer, then the *diya* is incumbent on the treasury. If payment to the victims' families will burden the treasury, the state can levy a general tax for this purpose, since the whole nation becomes like an *ʿāqila*,[10] on the basis of the following Qur'anic teachings: 'The believers, men and women, are supporters of each other' (Q.9:71), and 'aid one another in what is good and righteous' (Q.5:2). In any case, the blood of the victims must not be allowed to go uncompensated.

The Amount of *Diya*

According to Abū Ḥanīfa, in murder cases the amount of *diya* that must be paid is what the two parties agree to,[11] but traditionally the *diya* itself has been fixed from the time of the Prophet. For people whose wealth consisted of livestock, it was then estimated at one hundred camels or one thousand sheep. For those whose wealth was not in livestock, *diya* was paid in money: one thousand *dīnārs*. Deliberate homicide caused the penalty to be accentuated in three ways: it was to be paid promptly, not in instalments; it was to be paid from the culprit's own fortune; and it was to be qualitatively higher than for accidental killing (e.g. forty of the camels had to be pregnant). In the case of accidental killing, the penalty was extenuated by being payable in instalments, the camels did not have to be pregnant, and it could be paid by the extended family of the culprit. This is part of a wider system of social security within the family, in which the right to inheritance, and hence the obligation to maintenance and compensation for murder, went beyond the nuclear family.

In traditional Arab society nowadays, such as in the Gulf for instance, the system still functions and the tribe as a whole pays the *diya*. In Saudi Arabia, wealthy princes pay the *diya* on behalf of culprits that do not have the means. In opening the way for the culprit to make amends for the damage he has inflicted on the family of his victim, the Sharī'a makes the best of the situation. Locking him up in prison for a long time is not seen to benefit the victim's family, while the state itself is penalized.[12] By handing over the *diya*, the culprit makes amends with the family and in addition makes amends with society as a whole, as well as correcting himself by making *kaffāra*. This is defined in the Qur'an in the same verse that introduces the institution of *diya*, and thus has the same degree of obligation. *Kaffāra*, as mentioned before, is to free a slave, but if this is not possible, then it is to fast for the full duration of two successive months, being the maximum period in the Qur'an for expiation. All acts of expiation in the Qur'an carry benefit to society and self-correction for the culprit, and can take the form of freeing a slave, fasting for a certain period, or feeding the poor.[13]

Murder, then, gives the family of the victim 'an authority' to demand retaliation, or to pardon the culprit in exchange for compensation, or 'to be charitable' and freely waive its right to compensation. This 'authority', which the Sharī'a gives to the family of the victim, led one scholar of Islamic law to conclude that 'murder in Sharī'a can be classified as a tort which gives damages rather than a crime committed against the law and entailing a penalty imposed by the court.'[14] The Sharī'a thus divests the state of the power to punish the criminal. However, the Islamic viewpoint is different: it is seen as a penalty and compensation at the same time.[15] The Sharī'a gives due regard to the feelings of the victim's family, unlike the position in other legal systems that pay no regard to their feelings, and which might leave some to take revenge against the culprit. It is also seen to be reforming for the culprit, should he be pardoned by the victim's family.

The Sharī'a also pays due regard to what actually benefits the victim's family, should they opt for compensation. Sending the culprit to prison for years does not benefit the victim's family in any way; it burdens the state with the cost of keeping him in prison, and possibly of maintaining his family. Nor does the Sharī'a divest the state of authority to punish the criminal. In giving the family of the victim power to demand the execution of the murderer, to accept compensation or to pardon him, there is healing for them, and the satisfaction that the Sharī'a and society stand with them. In the Islamic penal system, the heir of the victim has the satisfaction of knowing that the Qur'an recognizes the fact that the victim is *maẓlūm,* having suffered the wrong of having his life unjustly ended, and that the relative is *manṣūr,* being given assistance and power (Q.17:33). In legal systems that do not give the relatives of the victim such power, they are left to feel disregarded and abandoned. However, even after the victim's family has accepted compensation or freely pardoned the culprit, courts still have power under the Sharī'a to impose a fitting punishment, by way of *ta'zīr* on the culprit for having offended against the law.[16] Courts in Saudi Arabia now impose a prison sentence of up to five years as *ta'zīr.*

Penalties

In the Sharī'a, penalties come in three categories: *qiṣāṣ, ḥudūd* and *ta'zīr. Qiṣāṣ* penalties are for murder and deliberate wounding. We have seen that with murder and manslaughter goes *kaffāra,* or expiation. *Ḥudūd* are fixed penalties, and are for other major crimes. The root of this word relates (i) to the limits set by God, which must not be transgressed, which is how the word is used in the Qur'an (ii) to what is being defined or specified, hence, the technical meaning of the penalties of *ḥudūd* as 'specified' penalties. The crimes in this category, which all jurists agree upon, are adultery, theft, slander, and brigandry. These represent very serious crimes, which undermine Islamic social order, and both the crime and its penalty are specified by the Qur'an. The penalties are unchangeable: they cannot be increased or decreased, nor can they be pardoned or waived.

The Sharī'a has been strict in defining the crimes in cases of *qiṣāṣ* and *ḥudūd* and in setting penalties for them, due to the seriousness of such crimes and their effect on the individual and society. Such crimes represent only a small percentage of the total body of crimes committed in society, but statistics have shown that, overall, this small category of crimes is committed much more frequently than other crimes, which explains the weight laid on them by the Sharī'a in contrast to other, lesser crimes, which are punished by *ta'zīr*.[17]

Ta'zīr is technically defined as a discipline for an offence which has neither a fixed penalty nor penance prescribed in the Qur'an or *sunna*. Lexically, it is derived from a verb meaning (i) to aid and support (ii) to restrain or prevent. A connection can be seen between the second and the first meanings since, according to Islamic ethics, to restrain someone from committing an offence is to help him, as the Prophet said in one of his *ḥadīths*: 'Help your brother whether he is committing wrong or being a victim of wrong.' When his Companions asked him, 'We can understand helping a victim, but how can we help the wrongdoer?' he said, 'By stopping him from committing a wrong: that is helping him.'[18]

The objectives envisaged by *ta'zīr* are to prevent the recurrence of the crime by the culprit and others, and to correct the culprit. This is done through selecting a punishment that is suitable for the individual and his circumstances. N. J. Coulson states that in substantive law 'the sovereign is completely free, outside the *ḥadd* offences to determine what behaviour constitutes an offence and what punishment is to be applied in each case.'[19] This is not correct. It is not the sovereign who determines offences and punishments, but scholars of law, legislators and judges. In his comprehensive and excellent study of the Islamic penal system as compared with secular law, 'Abd al-Qādir 'Awda, an Egyptian judge, states:

> The statement that a judge has arbitrary power in *ta'zīr* offences has no real foundation, and we would not be exaggerating to state that such a statement is based on insufficient familiarity or insufficient understanding of Sharī'a. Anyone who has sufficient knowledge of the Sharī'a texts and the ability to understand the terminology and style of writing of the jurists knows perfectly well that the judge has no authority to determine the offences or the penalties. The texts of the Sharī'a have explained the offences and the penalties. The judge's authority is confined to applying the text to the case under consideration. If it applies to the case, he will apply the penalty. The freedom given to the judge is in choosing the penalty he considers fit from those stated for the crime. The Sharī'a leaves it to the judge, in choosing the penalty, to consider the character of the accused, his past record and the effect of the penalty on him, and consider also the offence and its effect on society. It gives the judge the freedom to apply the maximum down to the minimum penalty. He can

> implement the penalty or suspend it. This is the extent of the authority given the judge by the Sharī'a. It is not arbitrary and he is given such authority to enable him to deal with both the offender and the crime. It is an authority of choice and assessment and not an arbitrary authority, - [one] that is more likely to achieve justice. This is the method introduced by the Sharī'a nearly fourteen centuries ago for *ta'zīr* offences and it is the method which modern legal systems have recently adopted.[20]

All offences, then, have been decided by the Sharī'a:

> Every act of disobedience to God (*ma'ṣiya*) is considered, in Islamic law, an offence that entails a penalty (*jarīma*). Since the *ma'ṣiya* is a commission or an omission that is forbidden in Sharī'a, it is considered an offence. It is inaccurate to think that the *ma'ṣiya* for which no penalty has been specified falls outside the realm of criminality. Such an understanding disregards the extent of the connection between legal provision on the one hand and religion and ethics on the other.[21]

When judges decide which particular penalty to apply in *ta'zīr* offences, they are governed by the injunctions to 'judge with justice' (Q.4:58), and to find a punishment that fits the crime (Q.42:40). Furthermore, the flexibility of application which *ta'zīr* affords makes the Islamic legal system as suitable for application now as it was in the past.[22]

Muslim scholars[23] have observed that, in the Sharī'a, *ta'zīr* penalties can come in many forms, such as *wa'ẓ* which is reminding the person that what they were doing is wrong, and recalling to them God and His teachings. This is suitable primarily in domestic situations. Other penalties include restitution; reprimanding the offender; cautioning the offender and suspending the sentence, under threat of imposing it should they re-offend (*ḥudūd* penalties, however, may not be suspended); *hajr* (deserting or boycotting the offender); *tashhīr* (publicising the wrong-doing); and financial penalties (although traditionally there has been disagreement among jurists as to whether imposing fines and confiscation are permissible as penalties: Abū Ḥanīfa disallowed them, whereas the three other schools permitted them and Ibn Qayyim al-Jawziyya (d. 751/1350) defended them strongly). Lastly, there are the penalties of imprisonment, if deemed fitting by the court; exile, which was discussed by jurists in the past as a means of taking away an offender from an environment in which he offends; and corporal punishment.[24]

In the Qur'an, corporal punishment is prescribed only for proven fornication and unproven slander against chaste individuals. In *ta'zīr* it is an option, available in some Muslim countries, and is normally defended on the grounds of its deterrent effect, and the fact that it does not burden the state by having to support the prisoner and perhaps also his family outside. Forms of corporal punishment include the death penalty and combined penalties. The Ḥanafīs consider that criminals from whose crimes society cannot be protected by any other punishment may be executed, whereas the Mālikīs hold that serious crimes, such as high treason, and regular re-offenders from whom society cannot be protected by other means, may be executed in *ta'zīr*. As for combined penalties, Ḥanafīs and Mālikīs consider it admissible to combine more than one penalty, if this is more likely to deter the culprit and others.[25]

It is clear that the discussions of Muslim jurists affirm the principle that the penalty must fit the crime and the circumstances of the culprit, and what is seen as most conducive to the protection of society – all within the general principles of justice. If the judge exceeds these limits, his verdict would be an act of aggression and a violation of the consensus of Muslim jurists.[26] The practice now is that several judges sit together in Sharī'a criminal courts, and appeals are held to correct excessive or unsuitable sentences. In Muslim countries which have codified their Sharī'a laws, *ta'zīr* penalties are determined by the legislature, and judges must act within this body of legislation. In such countries, jurists and legislative bodies have the traditional, rich resources of Islamic legal opinions on which to draw.

Conclusion

In cases of murder and manslaughter involving *qiṣāṣ* or *diya*, even if the heirs of the victim accept compensation or pardon the culprit, it is still open to the court under Islamic law to apply a fitting penalty from the wide area of *ta'zīr*, in order to protect society from the wrong committed against it, and as a punishment for violating its laws. It is, however, the victim of murder or manslaughter and his family who are more directly and immediately wronged. Any legal system that concentrates entirely on punishing the culprit for offending against the law leaves the family of the victim feeling disregarded and abandoned to their 'bad luck'.[27] Thus the Sharī'a punishes the culprit and stands firmly with the victim as *maẓlūm*, or having suffered the wrong of having his life unjustly ended. It also stands with the victim's family by giving them *sulṭān* (power), and making them *manṣūr* (assisted by God and the legal provisions of the Sharī'a). By compensating the victim's family in this way, Islamic law is constructive and consistent with justice. In *ta'zīr*, the system is seen to be flexible, allowing for developments according to changing times and circumstances, while being within the limits of justice, which is the ultimate objective of the Sharīʿa. As God states in the Qur'an:

> *We have sent Our messengers with clear signs and with them we sent down the scripture and the balance, so that people may uphold justice.* (Q.57:25)

Notes

[1] Before Islam, the Arabs, as will be seen below, did not observe equality in retribution and financial compensation. The intention of this verse is to insist on equality.
[2] Fakhr al-Dīn al-Rāzī, *al-Tafsīr al-Kabīr*, V, 3rd ed (Beirut, n.d.), p 48
[3] Al-Rāzī reports that someone murdered a man from a noble tribe, and that the family of the culprit came to the father of the victim, asking, 'What do you want from us now?' He answered, 'One of three things: to bring my son back to life, or fill my house with stars from the sky, or hand me all your people to kill, and even then I would not consider myself to have had appropriate compensation for my son.' In *Tafsīr*, V, p 46. On killing a free man for a slave and a man for a woman in Islamic Sharīʿa, see Ibn Rushd, *Bidāyat al-Mujtahid wa Nihāyat al-Muqtaṣid* (Cairo, 1981), pp 398-9
[4] In fact, whenever the Qur'an mentions any wrongdoing which entails punishment in this world or the next, it opens the door for repentance and pardon. We find this, for instance, in cases of homicide (Q.2:178; 4:92), theft (Q.5:39), brigandry (Q.5:34), sexual offences (Q.4:15-18), and perjury (Q.24:68-71), to mention but a few.
[5] Muḥammad Salīm al-ʿAwwā, *Fī Uṣūl al-Niẓām al-Jinā'ī al-Islāmī*, 2nd ed (Cairo, 1983), p 254
[6] The Qur'an mentions homicide between believers because this is the context of these verses. Should a Muslim kill a *dhimmī*, a non-Muslim living in a Muslim society, according to the Ḥanafī school, the Muslim must still pay the same amount of *diya*. See ʿAbd al-Qādir ʿAwda, *al-Tashrīʿ al-Jinā'ī al-Islāmī Muqāran bi'l-Qānūn al-Waḍʿī*, I (Alexandria, 1949), p 399
[7] If a slave cannot be found, then the value should be paid out in charity. If the person does not have the means he should fast for two successive months. See ʿAwda: *al-Tashrīʿ al-Jinā'ī*, pp 684-5
[8] Al-Rāzī: *al-Tafsīr*, p 230
[9] ʿAwda: *al-Tashrīʿ al-Jinā'ī*, p 676
[10] ʿAwda: *al-Tashrīʿ al-Jinā'ī*, pp 674; 677
[11] Ibn Rushd: *Bidāyat al-Mujtahid*, p 409
[12] The cost of maintaining a prisoner in a British prison at present is estimated at £25,000 per annum. In addition, the state may have to maintain his family outside who would, moreover, be deprived of him.
[13] ʿAwda: *al-Tashrīʿ al-Jinā'ī*, pp 683-5
[14] N. Anderson, 'Homicide in Islamic law', *Bulletin of the School of Oriental and African Studies*, VIII, 1949-50, pp 811-28
[15] ʿAwda: *al-Tashrīʿ al-Jinā'ī*, pp 668-9
[16] ʿAwda: *al-Tashrīʿ al-Jinā'ī*, p 696
[17] ʿAwda: *al-Tashrīʿ al-Jinā'ī*, p 710
[18] Al-Bukhārī, *Ṣaḥīḥ al-Bukhārī*, Bāb al-Maẓālim, 4

[19] N. J. Coulson, *History of Islamic Law* (Edinburgh, 1971), pp 132-3. Readers should note that this book has been translated into Arabic by Professor M. A. Sirāj of the American University of Cairo. In his excellent translation, *Fī Tārīkh al-Tashrī' al-Islāmī* (Cairo, 1992), Sirāj has written extensive footnotes, comments and corrections of views expressed in the original text. To get the most out of Coulson's important text, the reader should benefit from these excellent footnotes.

[20] 'Awda: *al-Tashrī' al-Jinā'ī*, pp 148-9

[21] Al-'Awwā: *Uṣūl*, pp 260-1

[22] Al-'Awwā: *Uṣūl*, p 260

[23] 'Awda: *al-Tashrī' al-Jinā'ī*, pp 685-708; al-'Awwā: *Uṣūl*, pp 268-297; Sirāj: *Tārīkh al-Tashrī'*, p 174 fn

[24] The Arabic word *jald* is used for this, which is related to 'skin'. It does not necessarily mean flogging, whipping or caning. It is reported in the *ḥadīth* that, at the time of the Prophet, it was sometimes done with the hands, clothing, or sandals.

[25] 'Awda: *al-Tashrī' al-Jinā'ī*, p 130

[26] Shihāb al-Dīn al-Qarāfī, *Kitāb al-Furūq* III, pp 16-20; IV, p 182

[27] In 1961, the Criminal Compensation Board was set up in Britain to offer limited compensation for the victims of crime on application. Such compensations are paid by the state, so the principle has now been accepted. The Islamic system is fairer, as it is the culprit who is responsible, and the process is carried out within the criminal proceedings, and not by a separate application, which can be accepted or rejected

Part Three

Evidence and International Crimes

6

Confession and Other Methods of Evidence in Islamic Procedural Jurisprudence

Mohamed Selim El-Awa

The intricate relationship between the implementation of punishment on the perpetrator of a given crime and the veritable means of proof which the law requires in order to determine the guilt of an alleged culprit, is one that is permanently binding. Indeed, in the event of a court of law not being utterly convinced of the accused person's guilt in committing a crime, then it is not possible for it to demand the prescribed penalty for the crime. The study of the rules of evidence in any system of law reveals the extent to which the legislator endeavours to restrict, or indeed extend, the instances in which it is either permissible or necessary to implement a particular punishment against someone who has committed a crime. Therefore, any examination of the penal code of Islam is incomplete without a careful study of the established rules of evidence relating to that code. Moreover, it is these established rules which ultimately determine the innocence or guilt of the accused.

It is important to note that the rules of evidence in Islamic criminal law are not aimed solely at establishing the guilt of the criminal; equally, they endeavour to determine the possible innocence of the accused. These rules have been rightly described by Coulson as 'aimed at the establishment of the truth of claims with a high degree of certainty'. The principal forms of evidence used in Islamic law for substantiation are as follows: a confession or an admission of guilt on the part of the criminal, and the statements of witnesses, who should be two upright Muslim persons, who are intimately aware of the happenings or events to which they are bearing witness. It is also the case that any statements should be offered in the presence of a judge in a court of law; it matters not whether the case is of a civil or criminal nature. Furthermore, circumstantial details and contingencies relating to the events surrounding the case also have enormous bearing. Some jurists also suggest that the knowledge of the judge also plays an important role in the processes of substantiation in criminal law.

With the above contexts in mind, we shall attempt to review briefly the rules pertaining to confession, statements of witnesses, and the role played by the judge in relation to establishing evidence in Islamic law. Owing to the fact that the statements of witnesses in cases of adultery and fornication differ, especially regarding the number of witnesses, we shall devote a small section to the specifics therein. Our study will consider the extent to which a judge is expected to adhere to the established rule of evidence, particularly in relation to the statement of witnesses and, moreover, to the extent of his discretion in exacting the tenor of proof embodied within such statements, deriving proof of guilt or innocence based upon the particulars seemingly furnished by the weight of evidence.

Confession as Evidence

The most authoritative form of evidence establishing the perpetration of a given crime is undoubtedly a confession by the person who committed the crime. It matters not whether this confession proceeds from or precedes the formal levelling of an accusation against the person in question, especially when such a person voluntarily presents himself before a judge and confesses openly to having perpetrated the crime. It is agreed that the confession itself represents sufficient proof of a person's perpetration of a crime, without the need for a formal accusation. Indeed, the consequence of such a confession predicates the implementation of the prescribed punishment for the crime. Yet the confession itself establishes only the guilt of the person confessing; it cannot be extended to prove the guilt of others. Hence, if a person admits to having committed adultery or theft, then the admission becomes binding *per se* against the person confessing to the crime. Although such a confession may implicitly implicate a certain partner in a given crime, it cannot be used against the second implicated person; that person can only be punished if he similarly confesses to the same crime, or if the due processes of law positively establish that person's guilt according to the aforementioned rules of evidence.

It is also the case that the confession does not need to be repeated: a single admission suffices as proof. This applies to cases of retribution (*qiṣāṣ*), deterrents and the general framework of the *ḥudūd* (the Islamic code for crimes and punishment), with the exception of adultery, as there are considerable differences amongst the schools of jurisprudence as to the sufficiency of a single confession and its scope in relation to establishing guilt.

The reason for such a diversity of opinion on this matter emanates from the level of evidence, along with the stringent conditions applied in the cases of adultery or fornication. The Ḥanbalīs, the Ḥanafīs and the Zaydīs stipulate that, in the case of adultery or fornication, the confession should be repeated four times in order to establish guilt. They employ an analogy of the statement of witnesses required for cases of adultery and extend it to the very confession itself. They also refer to the practice of the Prophet in dealing with a figure called Mā'iz, who confessed four times to having committed adultery. The Zaydīs attach greater significance to the proof of confession, which in essence allows the confessor the opportunity to retract his confession, and thus avoid the punishment for that crime. They accentuate the redemptive aspect of this as being enshrined in the tradition of Islam; this is deemed more virtuous than an exacting of punishment.

The Mālikīs, Shāfi'īs and Ẓāhirīs, meanwhile, state that one single confession suffices in establishing guilt in relation to adultery. This opinion is based on the manifest distinction between the 'statement of witness' and the act of 'confession'. It is assumed that establishing the perpetration of a crime and attributing it to the accused by virtue of the 'statements of witnesses' depends upon an absolute presupposition *à propos* the veracity of those bearing witness. For this reason, Islamic law applies stringent conditions concerning their number. In the case of confession, however, there is no reason to doubt the probity of the statement of someone confessing to a crime, and it follows that there is no need for the stringent demand that the confession be repeated more than once. The proponents of this opinion base it upon the account of Mā'iz and other similar traditions, in which the Prophet did not insist upon a repetition of the confession.

The Ḥanafīs have two opinions on the subject of the repetition of the confession in cases other than adultery or fornication. Abū Yūsuf, the disciple of Abū Ḥanīfa, takes the view that two repeated confessions or admissions of guilt are required in respect of theft, the consumption of alcohol, and slander, whilst Abū Ḥanīfa takes the opinion that one single confession suffices for all of these determinate categories of crimes. Abū Yūsuf bases his opinion on the device of approbation, which demands a measure of reservation in the implementation of prescribed penalties decreed by the law. Conversely, Abū Ḥanīfa expresses the view that there is nothing in the repetition of a confession which effectively substantiates further the commission of a crime other than that already provided by the initial confession. According to him, the confession is a declarative statement; the act of repetition does not accentuate its worth. Evidently, the opinion of Abū Ḥanīfa holds sway amongst the Ḥanafīs, as opposed to the opinion of Abū Yūsuf.

It is stipulated that the confession should be well detailed, such that it confirms to the judge that the confessor is fully aware of the committed crime to which he or she has confessed. A plain confession to a crime devoid of actual detail may well result in the administering of punishment to someone who does not deserve the prescribed penalty. Thus, if someone were to confess to committing theft, slander or adultery, then it is incumbent upon the judge that he request the particulars relating to the supposed crime from the person confessing. This ensures that he does not pass judgement upon the confessor until it is confirmed that the confines of the law relating to crimes have been clearly encroached upon. A further condition relating to the nature of a confession stipulates that it be articulated in a candid form, which distinctly indicates the confessed crime. A confession which is allusive or of a dissimulated nature cannot be accepted as a means of criminal proof in Islamic law. Moreover, as a result of this, the Ḥanafīs and some Shāfiʿīs have argued against the acceptance of the confessions of those who are dumb, even if such confessions are written. This is because such a person's written confession, together with their gesticulation, is not considered a candid representation of a person's will, as stipulated above. Another opinion adopted by some of the other schools accepts the validity of the confession of the dumb, whether this is by way of gesticulation or in written form, as long as such demonstrations of confession indicate a clear intention which leaves no room for ambiguity or doubt.

The Possibility of Retracting a Confession

Given that the confession functions as a proof in establishing the nature of the confessed deed and its link to the person confessing, it therefore follows that in respect of criminal (but not civil) matters, it is possible for a person to retract his or her confession. This applies both before and after the process of sentencing and during the actual administering of punishment. However, the effect of retracting a confession differs in criminal matters, and is governed by the nature of the offence which initially warranted the confession. If the confessed act is one which falls into the category demanding penalties sanctioned by the *ḥudūd*, then a retraction unconditionally prevents the process of passing sentence; this would also be the case if sentencing had already taken place. If, however, a retraction were to be enunciated whilst the sentence was being administered, expressly in cases involving the punishments of lashing or stoning for adultery and fornication, then this would instantly invoke a halt to the administering of the punishment.

It is interesting to note that, in the case of deterrents and retraction therein, jurists from the four schools of jurisprudence accept that it is possible to continue with the procedural aspects of the due processes of law, including the issuing of a guilty verdict and, indeed, the execution of the prescribed punishment, if the retraction occurs after its issue. The reason for the distinction between the retraction of confessions relating to transgressions within the confines of the *ḥudūd* and those relating to deterrents stems from a legal ground rule which underlines the necessity of 'averting prescribed punishments (*ḥudūd*) when ambiguities persist'. However, the execution of prescribed punishments in the case of deterrents can take place even when ambiguities persist. It is reasoned that retracting a confession immediately creates an ambiguity which hinders ascertaining the veracity of the criminal's confession, hence it is impossible to implement punishment, given the existence of this ambiguity. Nevertheless, this ground rule does not extend to the case of deterrents, thus the retraction of a confession which occurs within the confines of deterrents has no effect on the prescription and execution of punishment.

It is fair to state that this position is subject to some criticism, as the ground rule of 'averting prescribed punishments (*ḥudūd*) when ambiguities persist' emerges from the two legal precepts upon which all the schools of jurisprudence are agreed: the first precept predicates the presumption of innocence, while the second precept stipulates that 'it is not possible to retract that which has been incontrovertibly established save by virtue of an imminent fact which is similarly incontrovertible'. In essence, the first precept operates from the hypothesis that no punishable crime has been committed by any person; anyone alleging otherwise must produce irrefutable evidence to the judicial authorities substantiating such allegations. The second precept intimates that when a person accused of perpetrating a crime stands before a judge, it is inconceivable that the judge would declare the guilt of the accused unless he is convinced that the allegation against that person has been undeniably proven. Every man is presumed to be innocent, and this is an incontrovertible axiom; furthermore, only incontestable proofs are capable of negating this presumed axiom. For this reason, we take the view that the retraction of a confession in cases relating to deterrents should have the same effect as a retraction within the confines of the punishments prescribed by the *ḥudūd*.

It is obvious from what has followed that confession has an attenuated role in respect of establishing proofs of a criminal nature, particularly when one compares this with the role of confession in civil cases. It appears that, in respect of proving civil offences, the law clearly upholds protecting the interests of the individual (hence, retractions of the confession are not accepted), preventing persons from encroaching upon the rights of one another. One normally finds that humans in general refrain from devouring the assets of their fellow men, accepting the sanctity of the rights of one another. In criminal cases of law, the permissibility of one voluntarily retracting a confession, whether the case be in the procedural or executive stages of administration, underlines the restricted nature of the significance of a confession as a means of proof in such cases. If one reflects upon the severity of punishment in criminal offences as imposed by the *ḥudūd*, one notes that it is difficult to conceive that a criminal would offer a confession, admitting to having committed a crime and thereby exposing himself to punishment. Besides, it is also the case that the fundamentals of Islam advocate the importance of repentance and provide 'protected' cover for the contrite offender, as a means of coveting the mercy and forgiveness of God. This is more important than openly exposing the offences such a person had committed; likewise, it is more meaningful than seeking purification from sins by the infliction of punishment.

The Invalidity of a Forced Confession

It is paramount to point out that a confession articulated by a person which implicates that person as having committed a crime, and the consequences of that in terms of punishment, must be the result of an utterly voluntary and independent act. A confession cannot be forcefully obtained; moreover, a confession which is obtained as a result of the use of force should not be used in a legal context against the person forced to confess. This is the position of most of the Islamic schools of jurisprudence, although some of the schools differ regarding the conditions which render confessions invalid. The Ḥanbalīs state that there are three conditions which nullify a coerced confession: first, that the act of compulsion originated from a person who has dominance and authority over the compelled person; second, that it is also likely that the person compelled to confess was threatened with violence if he refused to comply; and third, that the threat used to obtain the confession was of a life-threatening nature, such as murder or severe physical violence, or carried the threat of lengthy imprisonment.

The Ḥanafīs distinguish between the severe use of force and that of a more moderate kind, extending this distinction to the duration of the threatened term of imprisonment, i.e. a short or lengthy period. Ibn Ḥazm, a Ẓāhirī, criticizes this differentiation; he draws no distinction in the length of the threatened imprisonment, nor in the severity of the torture used to extract the confession: in his view, such methods render the confession extracted from the coerced legally invalid. If a person who has confessed to a particular crime is brought before a judge, it is imperative that the judge ascertain whether that person's confession was voluntary and genuine, and that he was not compelled into such an act. If, however, he suspects or it is established that compulsion was employed, then it is his duty to annul the confession, ruling against its admissibility as evidence. Moreover, the person responsible for compelling someone to confess to a crime for which he is not responsible has himself transgressed; the same is true of a judge who fails to establish whether a confession is wholly voluntary.

The Limited Role of Confession in Islamic Criminal Law

We have seen that the function of confession as a form of evidence in Islamic jurisprudence is to a great degree governed by a judge's evaluation of its significance; accordingly, a confessor is not a hostage to his own confession. It is possible for him to retract his confession, should he find reason for that, while it is the prerogative of the judge to decide whether to accept or reject a retraction. The application of the precept of a presumption of innocence in Islamic jurisprudence, based on authentic prophetic practice, leads to the endorsement of the right to retract a confession, particularly when the prescribed punishment for the associated crime is a capital one, as stipulated in cases of adultery and retribution for murder. It is our view that there should be no distinction therein between crimes which fall within the jurisdiction of the *ḥudūd* and those pertaining to deterrents, as opposed to the predominant view amongst jurists. Therefore, the role of confession as a form of criminal evidence in the system of Islamic law is particularly limited.

The Testimonial Value of Witness Statements and the Probity of Witnesses

The established form of substantiating the vast majority of criminal cases in Islamic jurisprudence is the testimony of two honest witnesses. Offences which fall within the confines of *ḥudūd* endorse this form of substantiation in the crimes of slander and theft; the use of the testimony of two upright witnesses is also sanctioned in serious offences relating to deterrents, and such testimony is valid in cases of retribution for murder and in offences of serious injury or assault. The Mālikī school of jurisprudence, along with a number of Ḥanbalī scholars, offer a subtle distinction in relation to the number of witnesses required for retribution in the case of deliberate murder and the number required for crimes of physical assault or bodily harm. In the case of the former, the testimony of two honest witnesses is required to substantiate the charge of murder, whilst in the latter instance, the testimony of a witness in addition to the sworn oath of the victim of a crime suffices, or the testimony of one man and two women.

The jurists have devoted considerable attention to the nature of testimony, reviewing associated aspects of its form, mode of function, application, the responsibilities it entails, and the issue of the grounds for accepting or rejecting testimony. In our view, one of the most important studies on the subject of testimony relates to the question of the integrity of witnesses, as the Islamic system of law accepts only the testimony of the honest and upright, whilst the testimony of a person without these essential qualifications, or a person whose propriety is questionable, is rejected outright. The grounds for stipulating probity in potential witnesses is provided by the following Qur'anic prescriptions:

> *And seek the testimony of those amongst you who are upright.* (Q.65:2)

> *O you who believe, the provision of testimony in the event of a death and for the purpose of a will is the responsibility of two honest men amongst you or around you.* (Q.5:106)

According to the Ḥanafis, the Mālikīs and the Shāfi'īs, a Muslim is considered honest and upright if it is known that he performs what is expected of him and refrains from that which is prohibited. The Ḥanbalīs, and some Shāfi'īs, add to this a quality defined as the 'espousal of benevolence', namely, avoiding all forms of demeanour which diminish the reverence and esteem in which a person is held. It is reasoned that a person who relinquishes benevolence cannot be trusted to desist from bearing false witness, for he who feels no embarrassment in disregarding benevolence cares not for the consequences of his actions. The proof for this is found in the prophetic tradition narrated by Abū Mas'ūd al-Badrī on the authority of the Prophet, who said: 'That which mankind had retained from the chronicle of early prophecy asserts, "If you feel no shame, then do as you please."'

Ibn Ḥazm reported al-Shāfi'ī's stipulation of 'benevolence', but rejected it, stating:

> The reference to religious obedience or disobedience, as the case may be, should have sufficed for him. The reference to benevolence at this juncture is superfluous and impaired, because if it were enjoined as being integral to religious obedience, then that would suffice for it. If, however, it is not enshrined within obedience, then it is not permissible to impose it as a condition in religious affairs, particularly when it is not sanctioned by Qur'anic or Prophetic sanction.

Ibn Ḥazm and Ẓāhirī jurists define an honest and upright Muslim as someone who has neither committed a grave sin nor who has plainly committed a lesser one. According to their view, a grave sin is that which the Prophet expressly defined as grave, or an act with which severe caution is associated, while a lesser sin is that concerning which no caution has been associated. The caution itself is defined as a threat of punishment or reprimand in the hereafter. Ibn Ḥazm finds support for his opinion and those of the Ẓāhirīs in the Qur'anic verse:

> *If you avoid sins which are grave and prohibited, we will forgive for you your bad deeds and grant you an entrance of splendour.* (Q.4:31)

He states that it is correct to infer that, by shunning grave sins, one earns the right to have his lesser sins forgiven. Moreover, when a sin has been excused and disregarded by God, it is improper for someone to censure the culprit, or to use the sin to besmirch that person. This also applies to a person who repents from disbelief or an equally grave offence, for the state of disbelief of that person is relinquished by virtue of his repentance. Thus, it is improper to impute a person for something which has been relinquished, nor is it befitting to use it as an epithet to describe him.

It is worthy to note that the Qur'an makes honesty a condition for testimony, adding in the verse which follows the aforementioned verse that believers 'are satisfied with them', without stipulating probity. Considering both verses, it is fair to define probity as satisfaction with the testimony of a person, in line with the prevailing customs and conventions at a given location and time when such testimony is proffered. There are, however, crucial exceptions in this respect, as there are types of conduct unacceptable to Muslim society. Nor can the testimony of someone who indulges in such conduct be accepted, regardless of the circumstances of location and time.

There are a number of preconditions imposed by jurists to decide the probity of witnesses, although these are essentially contingent upon time, place and prevailing convention. This is seemingly recognised by the Qur'an, as it speaks of 'those whom you are satisfied of amongst witnesses' (Q.2:282). It is known that some schools of jurisprudence actually stipulate that the validity of testimony can rest on whether the witness is amongst those known to have eaten in the vicinity of a public highway, or who goes about his affairs with his head uncovered. Likewise, there are other examples in which the conventions and customs of a given society differ. It is therefore appropriate that one applies the rule that 'satisfaction is one of the bases of testimony'. Furthermore, it is fair to state that, in the absence of specific textual proof which negates the value of someone's testimony, the honest and upright amongst Muslims is the one whose testimony is accepted by the vast majority of his peers in society. Besides, probity is a relative quality which is regulated by custom and convention.

The jurists differ regarding the detection of probity in witnesses: if a Muslim is considered honest and upright in the absence of any proof, should it be suggested otherwise, or does one have to actively prove a person's probity? There are two main points of view on this topic: Abū Ḥanīfa and the Ẓāhirīs take the position that all Muslims are intrinsically upright unless the contrary is proven. Therefore, the testimony of a Muslim should be accepted without necessarily probing the issue of his integrity. If it is proven that the conditions of probity have not been preserved, then his testimony is discarded. Jurists from other schools, including the Ḥanafīs Abū Yūsuf and Muḥammad al-Shaybānī, maintain that, prior to delivering a decision based on the testimony of witnesses, a judge should review the probity of witnesses, particularly if he does not know of their integrity. If the probity of the witnesses is established, he can then rule on the basis of their testimony, or he can request either that the plaintiff supply other witnesses or other proof. On this basis, one can say that if two upright witnesses provide testimony before a judge, then that judge is directed to rule on a given case, basing his decision on the content of such testimony. The only exception here is the penalty of adultery, to which we shall now turn our attention.

Testimony in Cases of Adultery

The Qur'an has stipulated the requirements regarding the obligatory number of witnesses in the case of adultery, confining this to the testimony of four Muslim witnesses:

> *Those of your women who commit debauched acts, seek proof for that through the testimony of four.* (Q.4:15)

Meanwhile, the Qur'an says:

> *Those who cast serious aspersions against married women and are unable to provide four witnesses, then their recompense is eighty lashes and their testimony can never be accepted; indeed, they are the depraved.* (Q.24:4)

In another verse in this chapter, the Qur'an states:

> *If only they came forth regarding this with four witnesses; for if they cannot bring forth four witnesses, then they are perjurers as far as God is concerned.* (Q.24:13)

The requirement of providing four male witnesses to substantiate the offence of adultery and the prescribed penalty for that offence is agreed upon by the majority of jurists, although the Ẓāhirīs take the view that the testimony of women is accepted in cases relating to *ḥudūd*. In addition, therefore, the testimony of two women suffices for that of one man. Indeed, one can apply this criterion to the four witnesses required for adultery. Hence, it is possible to have a number of combinations in obtaining the quorum for male or female witnesses: three men and two women; two men and four women; one man and six women; or eight women. Nevertheless, only two honest male Muslims, one man and two women, or four women are the stipulated requirement in respect of testimony for the vast corpus of legislative practices: those enshrined within the *ḥudūd*, *diya* and *qiṣāṣ*; and civil law such as marriage, divorce and financial transactions. In support of his position of accepting the testimony of women in matters pertaining to the *ḥudūd* (including adultery), Ibn Ḥazm adduces the Qur'anic verse which, when speaking generally of testimony, states: 'And seek two male witnesses: but if you do not have two males then (seek) one male and two females' (Q.2:282). However, it is only the Ẓāhirīs who accept the testimony of women in *ḥudūd* and *qiṣāṣ* cases; moreover, the majority of scholars take the position that only the testimony of men is appropriate as corroborative proof.

In order to establish the offence of adultery, it is necessary that the witnesses should, in the presence of a judge, define in their testimony the time and place of the alleged offence and the persons committing that offence. This should be accomplished in one sitting before the judge, and the witnesses should relate in explicit detail exactly what they witnessed as regards the punishable offence. It is not sufficient that they bear witness to the fact that they saw a man alone with a woman, or that they were found naked in bed. Moreover, their testimony should be submitted on the basis that the actual act of explicit sexual intercourse was witnessed. If, on the other hand, the number of witnesses is insufficient, i.e. there were only three witnesses, these witnesses should then be punished for slander, each of them receiving eighty lashes. Whether the witnesses were truthful or not bears no relevance, for it is assumed that, in failing to provide the four witnesses required to legally substantiate the offence, the witnesses are lying.

The requirement for four witnesses in such cases is stipulated by texts from the Qur'an. In the event that there are four witnesses to the offence of adultery, but one of those witnesses decides to withdraw his testimony during the court proceedings, the three remaining witnesses can expect to be punished for the offence of slander: this is irrespective of the reasons for the fourth witness withdrawing his testimony. A summary of the aforementioned requirements in relation to substantiating adultery as cited by the jurists indicates the difficulty of scrutiny therein: a quorum in respect of witnesses; specific details which render the testimony valid; that the testimony be provided by the witnesses in one sitting; and the necessity of a positive identification of the culprits together with the need to confirm the explicit nature of the offence. These all point to the fact that proving the offence of adultery by means of testimony is somewhat burdensome. It is an unquestionable fact that the committing of this offence in a form which would furnish the required number of witnesses and the type of statement needed to substantiate the offence would constitute an affront to moral and social values. This applies not only from an Islamic legal perspective, but also from the standpoint of other legal systems. The perpetration of such an offence in a manner which makes it possible for the required number of witnesses to bear testimony is itself described as a crime even in the English legal system, which permits sex to take place outside the institution of marriage.

It is for these reasons that, in the entirety of Islamic history, there has not been one single case of the offence of adultery being substantiated by the testimony of witnesses. This offence is mostly substantiated by way of confession, when the culprit wishes to purify himself and atone for his sin and thereby meet his Lord without the burdens of his vices. However, such a confession is confined to its confessor; it cannot be used to indict anyone other than the confessor. Islamic law deems concealing such offences by way of God's grace as more virtuous. It is said that if a judge is approached by someone who wishes to confess to such an offence, it is more fitting that the judge persuade him to do otherwise, as the Prophet did. This occurred in the case of Māʿiz, whom he rebuffed four times, saying that perhaps he had been pardoned or had merely 'implied' such an act, and in the case of the Ghāmidī woman, whom he rebuked, saying: 'Woe to you, seek God's forgiveness and repent.' Moreover, the Prophet said to the person who encouraged Māʿiz to confess to him: 'If only you had "sheltered" him with your robe, that would have been better.'

The purpose of the imposition of punishment for adultery, or indeed any other *ḥudūd* type offence, is not to pursue and chastise one who has given in to the whims of his or her soul on an occasion. The aim of these punishments is to warn those whose souls are irredeemable: since the instruments of conscience have no effect upon them, only punishment prevails as a remedy for them.

Criminal Substantiation and the Role of Circumstantial Evidence

We have mentioned that one of the basic forms of substantiation in criminal proceedings is the testimony of witnesses. We surveyed the differences amongst scholars regarding the testimony of women with those provided by men, and concluded that the predominant view in Islamic jurisprudence is that the testimony of a woman is invalid in cases of *ḥudūd* and *qiṣāṣ*. It is my opinion that the stipulation of special conditions regarding testimony in criminal proceedings, along with the various forms of substantiation, is essentially a restriction established for the benefit of the accused. It is aimed at the judge in that he should not accept lesser evidence in substantiating the guilt of a person accused of committing a crime. Moreover, a judge should not pronounce a guilty verdict without being unquestionably convinced of the guilt of the accused.

The question we shall endeavour to answer here is: has the system of Islamic law confined the forms of substantiation to testimony and confession, as appears at first sight to students of Islamic jurisprudence as preserved in texts? Alternatively, are there forms of substantiation by other means, particularly the factual contexts of contingency or circumstance, permitted in criminal cases? Ibn Qayyim deals trenchantly with this issue in his *Methods of Judgement in Applied Legal Theory*, in which he states:

> If a judge is not able to discern perceptively the significance of signs; appreciate the indicators of contingency; contemplate the relevance of evidence; grasp the axiomatic subtleties of circumstantial and textual issues, including an appreciation of the specific and general aspects of law; then he has squandered the rights of people, for he proffers invalid judgements to which people are oblivious and concerning which they have no doubts. This is because he has depended upon a patently apparent definition, failing to ponder the more profound significance of such matters and the relevance of context and circumstance.

Ibn Qayyim regards the resort to taking contingency in legal abstraction into account as legitimate, citing instances of this from the Qur'an, Prophetic practice, and the actions of the *ṣaḥāba* and succeeding generations of scholars. We shall limit ourselves to quoting a number of instances relating to criminal cases adduced by Ibn Qayyim. One of these instances relates to the Qur'an's recollection of the story of Yūsuf, and the circumstantial evidence in relation to the torn shirt, as a means of proving his guilt or confirming his innocence in allegedly desiring the minister's wife against her will. The Qur'an states:

> *And a spectator amongst them [suggested], if his garment is found to be torn from the anterior then she has spoken the truth and he is amongst those who lie; [however], if his garment is ripped from the rear, then she has lied and he is amongst the truthful; and when they noticed his garment was ripped from the rear they said: 'Indeed, it is the plot of women and their plot is a tremendous one.'* (Q.10:26-8)

Another example is the oath of condemnation: if a woman abstains from proffering the oath of condemnation as a result of the same oath having been used against her by her husband, then the penalty for adultery (stoning) is pronounced against her due to the fact that she abstained. Such an abstention from the oath of condemnation is seen as circumstantial proof of the husband's allegation of adultery. It is the case that such procedures become evidentiary, in the same manner as the testimony of witnesses.

Referring to the *sunna*, Ibn Qayyim illustrated the authority of contingency and circumstantial evidence. He cited the case of a woman who went to perform the Morning Prayer at the mosque before being sexually assaulted by a man, who then absconded. She pleaded for help, and a passer-by came to her aid. Meanwhile, a group of people was alerted to the incident and made its way to the scene of the crime. The group of people took the woman, along with the man who had come to her aid, to the Prophet. She related the details of her ordeal, claiming that the person who had come to her aid was the perpetrator of the rape, whereupon the man exclaimed that he had actually come to help her. The group of people reported that this man had, strangely, tried to flee when they had come upon the crime scene. The man responded by saying that he had come to the woman's rescue when he heard her cries for help, but that he had been detained by the approaching group of people and brought to the Prophet. However, the woman continued to assert to the Prophet that this man had raped her, and so the Prophet ordered that the punishment for rape be imposed against the man. It was then that a man amongst those gathered in the presence of the Prophet cried out: 'Do not impose this penalty against him: impose it against me. It was I who committed this crime against her.' Commenting on this, Ibn Qayyim adds:

> This is an example, God only knows, of imposing penalties on the basis of manifest circumstantial evidence which taints the accused. This person was found running away from the scene of the crime before being apprehended by these people. He admitted to having been at the scene of the crime (being in the presence of the assaulted woman), although he claimed to have come to her aid. The woman claimed that he was the culprit. These are all manifest stains against the character (circumstantial proofs).

Ibn Qayyim also recounts the ruling of 'Umar ibn al-Khaṭṭāb and other *ṣaḥāba* concerning the imposition of the penalty for adultery in the case of a pregnant woman who has no husband or master; this extends to the imposition of the penalty for the consumption of alcohol if the smell of alcohol is detected on the breath of a man or if a person vomits the substance. He adds:

> Proof is the name given to something which elucidates and reveals truths. Those who stipulate that truth can only be discerned by virtue of the testimony of witnesses have not accorded this quality its due merit. Moreover, the term 'proof' in the Qur'an does not exclusively denote the testimony of witnesses, whatever their number; it

> symbolizes a form of distinct evidence, a type of proof, or demonstrator of fact; it matters not whether these are in collective or singular format, just as the two witnesses are a form of proof. Undoubtedly, other forms of evidence might prove to be more convincing. The Islamic system of law has not invalidated the efficacy of circumstantial, token and contingent proofs. Indeed, anyone analysing this system of law in terms of its sources and resources will find it taking into consideration such proofs and resolving rulings on their basis.

It is clear that Islamic law, according to the majority of its schools of jurisprudence, award the judge the power to rule based on there being sound evidentiary proof. This can be in the form of testimony or other types of evidence. However, Islamic law does not permit a judge to accept the validity of the testimony of witnesses if it transpires that that to which they testify has not occurred: thus, if four men accuse a women of adultery and it is found that she is still a virgin, then it cannot be said that the requirements of testimony (the statements of four witnesses) have been satisfied, and that such testimony should form the basis of a ruling. This is unanimously agreed upon by the jurists. A judge should evaluate the presented proofs which form the basis of a legal case, taking into account its circumstantial aspects and contingencies. His ruling should only follow when he has satisfied himself that his decision is substantiated by the evidence placed before him.

One cannot repudiate this fact by stating that the schools of jurisprudence are agreed that the form of substantiation is provided by the testimony of a man or two women. This form of substantiation is mentioned in the Qur'an in respect of civil transactions and not corporeal offences (those which confirm or repudiate criminal accusations). The Qur'an states that the testimony of two male witnesses, or a male and two women, is relevant to substantiating a loan or cases of divorce. The contrast between criminal and civil proceedings underlines the need to differentiate between the type of proofs employed in each of the two proceedings. Civil actions are carefully prepared: a point is made of recording them and cataloguing the testimony of witnesses in the event of any unfolding developments, such as doubts or future denials. In the case of offences of a capital nature, particularly those to which serious penalties are attached, the perpetrator is generally careful not to leave behind incriminating evidence, and conceals his crime from the glare of the public. It is inconceivable that any person in his right mind would commit a crime in the presence of four honest witnesses who would then implicate him as the culprit. Therefore, it is imperative that the forms of substantiation be broadened in every possible way in serious criminal cases, particularly if this would, to a large degree of certainty, aid the accused or absolve him of any guilt. Conversely, this should be restricted in civil cases, especially when these impinge upon the individual rights of a person in relation to his property, assets, marriage or divorce, and result in his being punished or something of this nature.

It is clear therefore that Islamic law restricts considerably the latitude of the capacity to substantiate serious crimes, taking great care to advocate the principle of 'averting prescribed punishments (*ḥudūd*) when ambiguities persist'. However, one finds that the forms of substantiation are not restricted when it comes to proving the accused person's innocence. Indeed, Islamic law has neither proposed a specific way of substantiating the flawed nature of the testimony of witnesses, nor proposed a format for negating their claims; there has to be incontrovertible proof of a person's guilt. As Ibn Taymiyya says:

> The Qur'an did not mention the witnesses (be they two men or a man and two women) in relation to the method of ruling decided by a judge, but rather it recalled these two types of proofs as a means for man to preserve his rights: that which preserves the rights of someone differs from that which forms the decision of a judge. The methods of ruling are greater in latitude than the testimony of witnesses (male or female).

In relation to the testimony of witnesses, a number of researchers have attempted to identify a restrictive seal of substantiation with Islamic law. There are two important observations to be made in this respect: from the previous paragraphs it follows that, just as Islamic law achieves substantiation via a number of proofs, it also allows other ways and forms of proof for substantiation, if these clearly implicate an accused person as having committed a crime with a considerable degree of certainty or seeming sureness. The whole purpose of Islamic law's stringency towards substantiation aims at protecting the accused, as opposed to restricting the authority of the judge. This can be proved by the fact that, according to the authenticated opinions amongst the schools of jurisprudence, it is permitted for a judge to use forms of evidence other than the instruments of testimony and confession when ruling. He can also discard a proof which is provided from these instruments of evidence if its veracity is dubious, or something has transpired which authoritatively contradicts and repudiates that which has been hitherto substantiated. The second observation is that, in stipulating the plurality of witnesses, Islamic law has taken into consideration the frailties of human nature: the propensity to forget and to make mistakes in the understanding or recounting of events. Furthermore, the law also accounts for the possibility that witnesses might fabricate lies for their own benefit or, indeed, because of a whimsical flaw which effectively leads one to err from probity and the path of rectitude.

It is worthy to note that, in respect of the plurality of witnesses, as sanctioned by Islamic law, there has been a shift towards adopting this feature by a number of contemporary legal systems. These systems stipulate that in certain instances there should be at least two witnesses, whilst in all cases the testimony of a single witness should be supported by circumstantial evidence. It is imperative that the judge inform the jury (those who determine a person's guilt or innocence) of the need to ascertain and affirm the accuracy and probity of the presented testimony, especially when the only proof in a given case is provided by the testimony of a single witness. This was the position adopted by the cardinal law of the Iraqi petty divisional courts in its canon issued in 1971. Clause 213 of the law states that testimony provided by a solitary witness is insufficient as the basis of a ruling, unless it is supported by convincing circumstantial or secondary proof, or is buttressed by the accused's confession, or unless the law has set out a particular form of substantiation which is binding *per se.*

The fact that a system of law depends upon a certain form of evidentiary proof should not be construed as an imperfection which taints the apparatus of law, nor is it an attribute worthy of praise. The crux of the matter is that all forms of evidentiary proofs which lead ultimately to the manifestation of right warrant support, while those which hinder the exploration of truth and the just resolution of disputes deserve criticism. It has been indisputably shown that Islamic law firmly upholds all methods of substantiation which assist the positive disclosure of truth or, indeed, that which comes as close to the truth as is possible. This alone is a virtue of the system of criminal substantiation in Islamic law, moreover, it represents an objective which any system of law aspires to achieve through its forms of substantiation.

A Judge's Knowledge and Foresight in Substantiating Criminal Matters

The Ẓāhirī school of jurisprudence is alone in giving consideration to the knowledge and foresight of a judge as a means of substantiation in criminal cases; it is their opinion that a judge ought to rule by virtue of his knowledge and wisdom in all cases presented before him, be they civil or criminal. Ibn Ḥazm comments on this, saying:

> It is incumbent upon a judge to use his knowledge and foresight to decide cases relating to life and limb, retribution, assets, intimate human relationships, and prescribed penalties of the *ḥudūd.* This applies whether he was aware of the profundities of such matters before his taking office or following his appointment. The most forceful of proofs used to decide rulings proceeds from his

> knowledge, for it is founded upon certitude. This is followed by confession and then evidentiary proof.

The basis upon which the opinion of Ibn Ḥazm is predicated is the connection between an equitable approach to legal rulings, as set out in the Qur'an:

> *And be upholders of equity bearing witness for God's [sake]* (Q.65:2)

It is also predicated upon the confirmed appeal of the Qur'an and *sunna* to enjoin good and desist from evil. That which the judge knows to be right must form the basis of his legal ruling, otherwise, he would lose sense of the quest for upholding equity and, more seriously, he would be advocating evil, as opposed to discouraging it.

The other schools of jurisprudence precluded a judge's use of his 'knowledge' in determining criminal cases, although some of them accepted its use in the case of deterrents and rights pertaining to property and wealth. They deduced that it is only proper that a judge's decision in a given case be based exclusively upon the forms of established evidence presented to him for that case. A judge should not add his own testimony to that of others in order to attain a required level of attestation: if he were to do so, he would be both judge and witness at the same time, and this is not permissible. Moreover, those who disagree with the Ẓāhirīs concerning their interpretation of the significance of the Qur'anic verse 'And be upholders of equity bearing witness for God's (sake)', have argued that a judge is vindicated in not using his knowledge and foresight in deciding a case, for he cannot rule in favour of a wronged person unless there is plain evidence to support the ruling. As the Prophet said: 'You are bringing your quarrels before me: it might be that some amongst you are more eloquent in arguing his case than his rival, and I might assume the former to be truthful and therefore pass judgement in his favour.'

As to adducing the relevance of 'enjoining good and desisting from evil', I would suggest that a judge is commanded to alter that known to people as evil in such a way that does not impinge upon his own integrity. Actions which bring his integrity into disrepute are utterly prohibited. In firm support of the view that the knowledge and foresight of a judge (in relation to the attributes of perception and perspicacity) should not form the basis of his own ruling, Ibn Qayyim presents the following view:

> If it were the case that there was a time when an equitable judgement was one formed on the basis of a judge's knowledge and awareness, the judges of today should be prevented from doing the

> same. Moreover, even if one were speaking of the eminent Shurayḥ, the Kufan judge, K'ab ibn Siwār, or al-Ḥasan al-Baṣrī, the same criterion would apply. The Master of Judges (peace and blessings of God be upon him) knew things about the hypocrites which would make lawful their blood and assets, yet he did not use his knowledge of that to rule against them, even though he was free from any reprehension in the eyes of God, His angels, and the believers, lest it be said 'Muḥammad is murdering his companions.' He who reflects upon Islamic law and the way it incorporates general interests and blocks certain means [to evil] would appreciate the correct opinion in this respect.

It follows that the knowledge of a judge alone cannot be considered sufficient proof for establishing the perpetration of a crime and the identity of the culprit and providing a ruling to that effect. Such a ruling must be based firmly on the forms of evidences and substantiation sanctioned by Islamic jurisprudence. It is fair to say that the Ẓāhirī position on this matter distinctly contradicts the text of the Qur'an in at least one place. The Qur'an stipulates that in order to prove adultery the testimony of four male Muslims is required, yet the Ẓāhirīs allow the testimony of a single witness to substantiate this offence, if it so happens that this witness is the judge. Furthermore, it matters not if he was aware of the offence before or during his tenure as judge. Consequently, the passing of judgement upon persons without a distinct form of proof sanctioned by sacred texts and the legal principles derived from these texts is in itself a form of evil that should be opposed. The fact that the Ẓāhirī position on this point is flawed stems from its providing immense latitude for the arbitrary and capricious excesses of judges; it also furnishes grounds for an attack against the integrity of the judicial system and cultivates a lack of confidence in it. These are reasons enough to renounce and reject their position.

Translated by Mustafa Shah

7

Genocide from the Perspectives of International and Islamic Law

M. Shokry El-Dakkak

The crime of genocide is the most fundamental of all assaults on human rights.[1] Nothing is graver in a criminal sense than a deliberate policy of systematically exterminating a people based on its particular ethnic identity.[2] This essay discusses the crime of genocide from the comparative and, frequently complementary, perspectives of international and Islamic law.

Genocide under International Law

The need to prohibit and punish genocide committed during peacetime gave rise to the Convention on the Prevention and Punishment of the Crime of Genocide, adopted 9 December 1948.[3] At the first session of the United Nations' General Assembly in 1946, a unanimous resolution defined genocide as a denial of the right to existence of entire human groups, just as homicide is the denial of the right to existence of individual human beings. Furthermore, it declared genocide a crime under international law. The framing and adoption of the Convention demonstrated that genocide was of prime concern to the international community at that time, and was indicative of the revulsion felt against the 'odious scourge' of this crime.[4]

Article II of the Genocide Convention, which entered formally into force on 12 January 1951, defines the crime of genocide in terms of an intent to destroy human groups. More specifically, the Article speaks of the intent to destroy, in whole or in part, national, ethnic, racial or religious groups.

The Material Element of Genocide (Actus Reus)

According to Article I of the Genocide Convention, the following acts constitute the crime of genocide: killing members of the group; causing serious bodily or mental harm to members of the group; deliberately inflicting on the group conditions of life calculated to bring about its physical destruction in whole or in part; imposing measures intended to prevent births within the group; and forcibly transferring children of the group to another group.

'Killing members of the group' refers to acts committed against a civilian population, whether in times of peace or war, such as the Nazi killings of Jews during the Second World War,[5] the massacres of Armenians by Ottoman troops in 1915,[6] and the killings of Vietnamese by United States troops in 1970.[7] Likewise, in the disputed region of Jammu and Kashmir, acts of deliberate killing and rape have been committed by Indian military troops and policemen during raids launched there against Muslim civilians; in addition, uncounted numbers of Muslim detainees have been executed without trial.[8] Among the Muslim minority in Bulgaria, some members of the community have also been subject to deliberate killing by Bulgarian security forces.[9]

'Causing serious bodily or mental harm' encompasses a variety of injuries inflicted upon group members in order to undermine the group's physical or mental health, and includes the crime of torture. The act of 'deliberately inflicting on the group conditions of life calculated to bring about its physical destruction' refers to the imposition of measures causing death or, at least, serious bodily harm, to a number of group members. The term 'deliberately' embraces so-called 'slow death measures', or subjecting the group to conditions such as a lack of proper housing, food, clothing or medical care, which are likely to result in death or debilitation. For example, a central government may deprive an ethnically distinct, antagonistic opponent of its population of food, so as to starve it into submission, as has been alleged in several African inter-ethnic conflicts, such as those in Nigeria and Somalia, and among the Eritreans in Ethiopia. Should this deprivation result in the decimation of the target group, it amounts to genocide.[10]

'Imposing measures intended to prevent births within the group' relates to practices aimed at the prevention or limitation of births, such as compulsory sterilization or abortion, the separation of the sexes and the prohibition of marriages.[11] Lastly, 'forcibly transferring children of the group to another group', refers to the compulsory transfer of children away from their home within the group to a different environment.[12] An example is that of some 28,000 Greek children, who were abducted by Communists at the close of the Second World War, and transferred to several countries in Eastern Europe. The forced separation of children from their families by the expulsion of adults and the holding back of the young constitutes the crime of genocide as provided in Article I (e). In such a case, the significance of the crime derives from the keeping of the child from his relatives and culture, and the placing of him in an environment different to that of his ethnic group, in order to utilize him in the future.[13]

The Mental Element of Genocide (Mens Rea)

In order to constitute the crime of genocide, all of the foregoing acts should be committed intentionally. The Convention expressly indicates *mens rea*, stipulating '... with intent to destroy, in whole or in part, a national ethnic, racial or religious group'. By this, it implies a special intent which constitutes the mental element of the crime of genocide. The Act enumerates in subsections (a) to (e) that acts constitute genocide only when committed with the intent to destroy the group as such. Without such intent, the killing of members of the group may be homicide, but does not constitute genocide.[14] Although genocide is usually considered an attack against a large number of people, the murder of even a single individual may constitute genocide if committed with the requisite intent. Conversely, the mass murder of persons who are members of one group, without the intent to destroy the group as such, would not constitute genocide. In other words, the *actus reus* may be restricted to one human victim, but the *mens rea* must be directed against the life of the group.[15]

Similarly, the word 'deliberately' was added in subsection (c) of the Genocide Convention in order to denote the premeditated planning of the imposition of deadly conditions of life.[16] Therefore, even if such measures do not actually bring about the physical destruction of the group, they still constitute genocide. The same applies to practices such as forced sterilizations and abortions, the purpose of which is to prevent a group from replenishing itself, so that it may eventually be destroyed. Again, whatever measures might be employed, they must be carried out with the intent to destroy a group, either in whole or in part.[17]

We usually perceive genocide as a 'completed' crime, and rarely view it as an 'attempt'. Yet, aware of the gravity of such a crime, the international community is keen to halt the international repercussions thereof. Therefore, it holds both State and individuals criminally liable for the commission of any act which may constitute the crime of genocide, even if the criminal results thereof have not yet been attained.

The International Element of Genocide

The crime of genocide not only breaches the right to life as it falls under domestic criminal law, but is also prohibited by and penalized according to international conventions, whether in times of peace or war,[18] and for so long as the state is involved in the crime.[19] This is demonstrated by UN Resolution 180 (II), of 21 November 1947, which declares: 'Genocide is an international crime.'[20]

Furthermore, it should be clarified here that not only those states party to the Genocide Convention are compelled to abide by its rules, but also non-party states, since the rules thereof protect the collective interest of the international community, i.e., the rules of *jus cogens*, which are mandatory to all nations, including those not party to international conventions.[21] Therefore, the International Court of Justice emphasizes the points of *jus cogens* as related to the special nature of genocide, saying:

> The origins of the Convention show that it is the intention of the United Nations to condemn and punish genocide as 'a crime under international law' involving a denial of the right of existence of entire human groups, a denial which shocks the conscience of mankind, etc. (Resolution 96 (I) of the General Assembly, December 11th, 1946). The first consequence arising from this conception is that the principles underlying the Convention are principles which are recognized by civilized nations as binding on States, even without any conventional obligation. A second consequence is the universal character both of the condemnation of genocide and of the co-operation required 'in order to liberate mankind from such an odious scourge' [...] The Genocide Convention was therefore intended by the General Assembly and by the Contracting Parties to be definitely universal in scope.[22]

Homicide and Genocide

Homicide is intentional killing without lawful justification. Lawful justification refers to those legal justifications, excuses and defences known to the world's major criminal justice systems, e.g. self-defence, coercion, necessity and reasonable mistake of law of fact.[23] Thus, the drafters of the Genocide Convention distinguished between the crimes of homicide and genocide. As they saw it, homicide becomes genocide when the underlying intent relates to a group. Clearly, individuals are the victims in the commission of both crimes, but in genocide they become the victims on account of their group identity, and not because of anything particular to them as individuals. It was necessary for the drafters to recognize that even the partial destruction of a group could constitute genocide, for otherwise the concept would not have been applicable until a very high proportion or all the members of a group had been killed. In fact, it was for this reason that a Norwegian delegate at the Sixth Committee of the General Assembly proposed that the words 'in whole or in part' be included in Article II of the Convention.[24]

Mass killing as a form of genocide may not necessarily be intended as homicide. Hence, killing and particularly extermination include other forms of international and unintentional killing, for so long as the eventual target is to destroy an ethnic group.[25] Lastly, genocide is distinguishable from homicide in connection with the material element (*actus reus*), where the earlier crime may, besides killing, include other culpable acts, as mentioned in Article I (clauses [b] through [e]) of the Convention.

Conversely, extrajudicial executions could be characterized as crimes of homicide for which governments and their agents are responsible under national and international law. Their accountability is not diminished by the commission of similarly abhorrent acts, or by considerations of national security. Thus, governments are duty-bound not to commit or condone extra-judicial executions, and to take all legislative, executive and judicial measures necessary to ensure that those directly or indirectly responsible for such acts are brought to justice.[26]

Genocide against Muslims in Bosnia and Herzegovina

In both distant and recent times, the Muslims of Bosnia and Herzegovina have been the victims of genocidal acts perpetrated by Serbs. While western writers have been inclined to focus on the genocide committed against Jews by the Nazis during the Second World War, genocide simultaneously committed against Bosnian Muslims has been largely ignored. In a report produced in 1992, it was documented that some 100,000 Muslims were killed in a programme of genocide perpetrated by Fascists and others collaborating with Nazi Germany, and that hundreds of mosques, libraries and other monuments were destroyed.[27]

In 1990, the collapse of the Yugoslav Federation began as a result of multi-party elections held first in Slovenia and Croatia, where Communist reformers lost to parties favouring national sovereignty within a decentralized and re-organized Yugoslavia. In the same year, similar non-Communist nationalist parties emerged victorious in elections in Macedonia and Bosnia and Herzegovina. The Serbian leadership rejected proposals for a looser federation of sovereign Yugoslav states, prompting the Croatian parliament to declare independence in June 1991. This in turn led the Yugoslav federal army to seize and destroy Croatian territory, and to terrorize and expel Croatian citizens there. When it became known that Bosnia and Herzegovina also intended to declare its independence,[28] Serbian forces launched a campaign of territorial conquest and 'ethnic cleansing' against the local Muslim (and, to a lesser degree, Croat) population, which may now be seen to have taken the form of a genocide operation. This consisted in the main genocidal crimes, such as armed aggression by the Yugoslav People's Army, its agents and surrogates of Bosnian Serbs and Croats; acts of terror; land usurpation; mass killing; mass deportation; mass torture in concentration camps; summary executions of individuals and groups; mass rape; and the wanton devastation of villages, towns, cities, districts and religious institutions. Centres, including Sarajevo, were turned into concentration camps, where slow, mass killing through starvation took place, along with an enforced denial of basic needs, especially during the harsh conditions of winter.[29]

Thereby, Yugoslavia (Serbia and Montenegro) breached its legal obligations towards the predominantly Muslim population of Bosnia and Herzogovina, under Articles I ([a], [b], [c], [d]), II ([a], [b], [c], [d], [e]), IV and V of the Genocide Convention, in addition to the four Geneva Conventions of 1949 and their additional Protocol of 1977. In its treatment of the Muslim citizens of Bosnia and Herzogovina, Yugoslavia also violated its obligations under Article I (3), 55 and 56 of the UN Charter. Furthermore, by recruiting, treating, arming, equipping, financing, supplying and otherwise encouraging, supporting, aiding and directing military and paramilitary actions in and against the Muslims of Bosnia and Herzogovina, by means of its agents and surrogates, Yugoslavia (Serbia and Montenegro) violated its express charter and treaty obligations and, in particular, its charter and treaty obligations under Article II (4) of the UN Charter,[30] as well as its obligations under general and customary international law.[31]

It is worth noting that the operation by Yugoslavia against the Muslims of Bosnia and Herzegovina was not the result of a civil war or an ethnic conflict between Bosnian Serbs and Muslims, but was a genocide operation committed during a time of war waged by the aggressor State of Yugoslavia against the Muslims of Bosnia and Herzegovina, with the aim of cleansing Yugoslavia, and potentially the whole of Europe, of Muslim communities.[32]

On 13 September 1993, the International Court of Justice asserted that what took place in Bosnia and Herzegovina constituted a crime of genocide committed by the State of Yugoslavia against the Muslim population. In its judgement, the International Court of Justice stated:

> (1) The Government of the Federal Republic of Yugoslavia (Serbia and Montenegro) should immediately, in pursuance of its undertaking in the Convention of the Prevention and Punishment of the Crime of Genocide of 9 December 1948, take all measures within its power to prevent commission of the crime of genocide;
>
> (2) By 13 votes to 1, the Government of the Federal Republic of Yugoslavia (Serbia and Montenegro) should in particular ensure that any military, paramilitary or irregular armed units which may be directed or supported by it, as well as any organizations and persons which may be subject to its control, direction or influence,

> do not commit any acts of genocide, of conspiracy to commit genocide, of direct and public incitement to commit genocide, or of complicity in genocide, whether directed against the Muslim population of Bosnia and Herzegovina or against any other national, ethnical, racial or religious group.[33]

Thus, it is clear that the crimes committed by Yugoslavia against the Muslims of Bosnia and Herzegovina are equivalent to those committed by the Nazis against the Jews of Europe. However, despite the fact that the crimes of Yugoslavia were committed under the many conventions protecting human rights and condemning genocide, regrettably, the response of international bodies to Yugoslavia's acts has been cool. Furthermore, this attitude has generated scepticism – notably among the international Muslim community – regarding the United Nations' credibility, particularly when it comes to dealing with international crimes against humanity.

Genocide under Islamic Law

Since genocide is a denial of the right to existence of an entire human group, frequently on the basis of its particular ethnic identity, the first point that should be considered here is the situation of ethnic groups within the Islamic State. Islamic Sharīʿa contains explicit injunctions, hailing from the time of revelation, which declare that the principle of equality is mandatory in Islam. This is expressed in the Holy Qur'an, as follows:

> *O mankind, We created you from a single* [*pair*] *of a male and a female, and made you into nations and tribes, that ye may know each other* [*not that ye may despise each other*]. *Verily, the most honoured of you in the sight of Allah is the most righteous.* (Q.49:13)

The Prophet Muḥammad also emphasized this principle, when he said:

> 'O, men, verily your God is one, and your father is one. No Arab is superior to a non-Arab except in righteousness, nor black to red or red to black except in righteousness.' Then he [the Prophet] said: 'Did I convey?' and they said: 'Yes.' He said: 'Hence, he who is attendant ought to convey to who is absent.'[34]

Thus, God and his Messenger have condemned in their statements all aspects of discrimination on the grounds of race or colour. Moreover, one of the Prophet's closest companions, Bilāl, was black, and his wife was related to one of the highest Arab tribes.[35] It is also reported that a slave quarrelled with ʿAbd al-Raḥmān ibn ʿAwf, another great Companion of the Prophet, and he (the slave) complained to the Prophet that 'Abd al-Raḥmān ibn 'Awf had called him a 'son of a black woman'. The Prophet was enraged by this, and raised his hand and exclaimed: 'No son of a white woman is superior to a son of a black woman, except in respect of truth.' At this, 'Abd al-Raḥmān ibn 'Awf was so ashamed of his conduct towards the slave that he determined to apologize to him, so he put his cloak on the ground and asked the slave to trample on it, in order that he may be consoled.

With regard to other faiths, Christians and Jews are viewed in Islam as the recipients of previous divine revelations. They are known as *ahl al-kitāb*, or 'People of the Book', an indication of Islamic respect for their scriptures. In general, non-Muslims living in Islamic states (*dhimmīs*)[36] are protected, as their lives and properties are deemed to be as 'sacred' as those of Muslims.[37] The Qur'an and *ḥadīth* stress Muslim obligations to protect *dhimmīs* from possible attack and molestation, for as long as they maintain peaceful relations with Islam. Abū Yūsuf and al-Balādhurī report several charters issued by the Prophet Muḥammad to the *dhimmīs* of Jarash, Khaybar, Najrān and other places, in which they were promised the protection of their lives, property and beliefs.[38]

As for polytheists or unbelievers, when the Islamic State expanded eastwards, premodern doctrines had to be adjusted, and Muslims had to learn to co-exist with Hindus and other polytheists.[39] So, it is fair to say that, when judged by today's standards, the Muslim world has historically showed far greater tolerance and humanity in its treatment of religious minorities than has the Christian West.[40] In particular, the treatment of the Jewish minority in Muslim societies stands out as fair and enlightened, especially when compared to the dismal record of Christian Europe's persecution of Jews over the centuries.[41]

Genocide in the Qur'an and Sunna

In connection with the Genocide Convention, we have found that the crime of genocide is committed intentionally in order to destroy an ethnic group, either by killing the members of the group or causing serious harm thereto or persecuting them through other acts. It goes without saying that Islamic Sharī'a prohibits persecution and makes criminal any genocidal acts committed against ethnic groups who are covered by the protection of the Islamic State. Accordingly, murder of the members of an ethnic group is strictly prohibited in Islam,[42] be it committed against individuals or groups. According to the Holy Qur'an:

> *Whosoever slays a person for other than manslaughter or corruption in the earth, it would be as if he had slain all mankind.* (Q.5:32)

The scholars of Islam give different commentaries on this verse, the most appropriate in this regard being that 'God regards the sin of one murder like the murder of the whole people, however, the judgement is due eventually from Him'.[43] In our opinion, this commentary conforms with the characterization of the crime of genocide with respect of intent (*mens rea*). Hence, the wrongdoer shall be accountable for genocide if he had the intent to commit such a crime, even if he killed just one person. This view can be supported by the well-known *ḥadīth* of the Prophet: 'The reward of deeds depends upon the intention, and every person will be rewarded according to what he intended.'[44]

Accordingly, genocidal acts are condemned in Islam, and are regarded as odious crimes deserving severe punishment in both this world and the hereafter. By way of example, the Qur'an alludes to the genocidal act of mass killing when it discusses Pharaoh of Egypt's massacre of the children of Israel, saying:

> *We delivered you from the people of Pharaoh, who set you hard tasks and chastisement, slaughtered your sons and spared your women.* (Q.2:49)

Furthermore, the Qur'an warns:

> *When he turns his back, his aim everywhere is to spread mischief through the earth and destroy crops and progeny. But God loveth not mischief* (Q.2:205)

The Syrian jurist Al-Awzā'ī (d.157/774) is known to have quoted this verse in order to prohibit mass killing and other destructive measures, even if committed in the territories of the enemies (*dār al-ḥarb*). He also quoted the Caliph Abū Bakr, who warned his soldiers against committing such acts, since in Islam they constituted forbidden 'mischief'.[45]

The jurists of Islam are agreed that non-combatants who do not take part in fighting, such as women, children, monks and hermits, the aged, the blind and the insane, must be excluded from molestation.[46] Furthermore, Muslim militants are prohibited from using poisoned arrows in any form, even against their enemies,[47] and from carrying their enemies' heads on the points of lances (a practice known to Arabs before Islam).[48] This fair conduct of Muslims, whether in times of peace or war, conforms with the teachings of the Prophet, whom the Qur'an praises as follows:

> *Now has come to you a Messenger from among yourselves; it grieves him that you should suffer, ardently anxious is he over you, to the believers he is most kind and merciful.* (Q.9:128)

In this connection, the Prophet also prohibited his followers from burning anyone with fire; as he is reported by 'Abd Allāh ibn Mas'ūd to have said: 'It is not proper to punish with fire, except for the Lord of fire.'[49] He also condemned the killing of women and children: when he saw that a woman was found slain in one of his battles, he sent for Khālid ibn al-Walīd, commanding him not to kill any woman or hired servant.[50] Furthermore, he forbade mutilation, saying: 'The most merciful of people in respect of killing are believers in God.'[51]

The Companions of the Prophet followed his traditions in this regard. 'Alī is reported to have ordered his soldiers to this effect:

> When you defeat them, do not kill their wounded, do not behead the prisoners, do not pursue those who return and retreat, do not enslave their women [lit. do not undress the private parts], do not mutilate their dead, do not uncover what is to remain covered, and do not approach their property, except for what you find in their camp [in the way] of weapons, beasts, or male or female slaves.[52]

Consequently, the *imāms* al-Shāfi'ī, Aḥmad ibn Ḥanbal and Zayd ibn 'Alī take the view that, in the case of rebellion, the government is accountable for using destructive measures or weapons against rebels, such as burning cattle or attacks with mangonels, because these can cause mass killing, and because they can lead to casualties among non-combatants.[53]

On the other hand, God recommends Muslims to take care of war prisoners and even to share food with them. The Qur'an advises:

> *And feed for the love of God the indigent, the orphan and the captive.* (Q.76:8)

Moreover, the Qur'an directs Muslims to free war prisoners, even without ransom, as soon as a war is over:

> *Therefore [is the time for] generosity or ransom until the war lays down its burdens.* (Q.47:4)

The Prophet is known to have emphasized this attitude, since he too approved of the release of war prisoners, considering it a good deed amounting to the feeding of the hungry and the visiting of the sick. As he said: 'Free the captives, feed the hungry and pay a visit to the sick.'[54]

By contrast, in the Torah, the kings of Israel were urged to exterminate and enslave their enemies. The twentieth chapter of the Fifth Book of Moses (Deuteronomy) reads as follows:

> When you draw near to a city to fight against it, offer terms of peace to it. And if its answer to you is peace and it opens to you, then all the people who are found in it shall do forced labour for you and shall serve you. But if it makes no peace with you, but makes war against you, then you shall besiege it; and when the Lord your God gives it into your hand you shall put all its males to the sword, but the women and the little ones, the cattle, and everything else in the city, all its spoil, you shall take as booty for yourselves; and you shall enjoy the spoil of your enemies, which the Lord your God has given you. Thus you shall do to all the cities which are very far from you, which are not cities of the nations here. But in the cities of these peoples that the Lord your God gives you for an inheritance, you shall save alive nothing that breathes, but you shall utterly destroy them ...[55]

Western jurists have also acknowledged the histories of merciful and just Muslim leaders. Gustave Le Bon, the French historian, cites in his book *La Civilisation des Arabes* that Ṣalāḥ al-Dīn [Saladin] was so merciful with the Christians of Jerusalem that he even provided his enemy, King Richard (the Lion-Hearted), with medications for his war wounds. On the other hand, it was Richard who had initiated this war by slaying 3000 Muslim war prisoners in a heinous massacre after they had surrendered.[56] Also, Baron Michel de Taube is quoted to have said that the present international rules which govern the conduct of state in cases of war were laid down by Islamic law thirteen centuries ago, at a time when the peoples of Europe were suffering at the hands of tyrants who practised genocidal acts against them, such as Basil, Emperor of Byzantium, who committed atrocities against the Balkans and blinded 15,000 of their war prisoners.[57]

From the foregoing paragraphs, we may deduce that Islam condemns the crime of genocide as a crime against humanity, and that Muslims were commanded from the outset to renounce genocidal acts, even against their enemies, and were commanded to follow the merciful teachings of Islam, regardless of their enemies' conduct.[58]

Notes

[1] Raphael Lemkin, a Polish jurist, coined the word 'genocide' in his *Axis Rule in Occupied Europe* (Washington, 1944). He derived the term from a combination of the Greek word *genos*, which means 'race' or 'tribe', and the Latin word *cide*, which means 'killing'. See Lawrence J. Leblanc, *The United States and the Genocide Convention* (Durban and London, 1991), p 17

[2] Jean Graven, *Les Crimes contre l'humanité* (The Hague, 1950), pp 48; 55

[3] United Nations, Treaty Series, Vol 78, p 277

[4] United Nations, Treaty Series, Vol 78, p 277. See also Leo Kuper, 'Genocide and mass killing, illusion and reality', in *The Right to Life in International Law*, ed B. G. Ramcharan (Dordrecht, 1985), p 144

[5] Patrick Thornberry, *International Law and the Rights of Minorities* (Oxford, 1991), p 51

[6] See Permanent Peoples' Tribunal, 'A crime of silence: the Armenian genocide', in *The United Nations and a Just World Order*, ed Richard A. Falk, Samuel S. Kim and Saul H. Mendlovitz (Boulder, 1991). It should be noted that the Turks' conduct against the Armenians was completely in conflict with Islamic teachings, as will be seen from the details discussed hereafter.

[7] By 1970, charges that the United States was committing genocide in Vietnam were fairly widespread, and the Russell Tribunal had already rendered its judgement 'that the United States and its allies had committed genocide in Vietnam'. See Leblanc: *The United States*, p 93

[8] See the *Amnesty International Annual Report* (London, 1992), pp 288-91; 304

[9] In February 1985, Amnesty International wrote to the Bulgarian authorities calling for a full and impartial investigation into charges that ethnic Muslim Turks had been unlawfully and deliberately killed by its security forces, and for the methods and results of the investigation to be made public. The organization received no reply. See the *Amnesty International Newsletter*, September 1985

[10] See Richard Falk, 'Responding to severe violations', in *Enhancing Global Human Rights*, ed Jorge J. Dominguez et al (New York, 1979)

[11] In 1971, a group of black leaders published the pamphlet 'We charge genocide', which it submitted to the United Nations, requesting that the organization condemn the United States for its plans regarding birth control among the Black Americans, which it described as 'a genocidal practice'. See Leblanc: *The United States*, p 112

[12] See M. Cherif Bassiouni, 'Genocide', in *A Draft International Criminal Code and Draft Statute for an International Criminal Tribunal* (Dordrecht, 1987) p 72. Also Pieter N. Drost, *The Crime of State* (Leiden, 1959), p 87, and the Official Records of the General Assembly of the United Nations, C.6 82 mtg at 189-90, 1948

[13] *The Times* newspaper published on 24 June 1989 that Bulgaria had deported Turkish minority families and held back their young between the ages of 17 and 25. It was reported that the Turkish authorities wished to take these men for their army. See *The World Press on the Plight of the Turkish Minority in Bulgaria* (Ankara, 1989), pp 15-17

[14] UN Doc. A/C. 6/SR. 73

[15] Bassiouni: 'Genocide', p 73

[16] UN Doc. A/C. 6/SR. 83, p 3

[17] Leblanc: *The United States*, p 111

[18] Stanislaw Plawski, *Étude des principes fondamentaux du droit international pénal* (Paris, 1972), pp 198-9

[19] Ḥasanayn 'Ubayd, *al-Jarīma al-Duwaliyya* (Cairo, 1979), p 134

[20] Susan J. Djonovich (ed), *United Nations Resolutions* I (New York, 1988), p 320

[21] Ian Brownlie, *Basic Documents in International Law* (Oxford, 1972), p 513; Vera Gowlland-Debbas, *Collective Responses to Illegal Acts in International Law* (Dordrecht, *c* 1990), pp 531-3; Thornberry: *International Law*, p 86

[22] 'The reservations to the Genocide Convention case', quoted in Thornberry: *International Law*, pp 94-5

[23] M. Cherif Bassiouni, *Crimes Against Humanity* (London, 1992), p 290

[24] Official Records of the General Assembly of the United Nations, C.6 73 mtg at 97, 1984]

[25] Bassiouni: *Crimes Against Humanity*, p 291

[26] From 'The final statement of the International Conference on Extra-judicial Execution', Amsterdam, 30 April to 2 May 1982. Annex VIII, in Ramcharan: *The Right to Life*, p 341

[27] Fikret Karcic, 'Muslim legal religious institutions in Yugoslavia', in *IIU Law Journal*, II (1) 1992, p 32

[28] The independence of the Republic of Bosnia and Herzegonia was declared on 6 March 1992, and it was admitted to membership of the UN on 22 May 1992

[29] M. A. Mahmoud, *Bosnia and Herzegovina: A Case of Approved Genocide* (The Hague, 1993), pp 7-8

[30] Article II (4) of the UN Charter reads: 'All members shall refrain in their international relations from threat or use of force against the territorial integrity of political independence of any state, or in any other member inconsistent with the purposes of the United Nations.'

[31] Mahmoud: *Bosnia and Herzegovina*, p 8

[32] In an article entitled 'Muslims fearful of genocide', *The Times*, 28 August 1992 wrote: 'Bosnian Muslims are convinced they face extermination, Tadeusz Mazowiecki, the former Polish prime minister who is the United Nations human rights rapporteur in Yugoslavia, said yesterday. "Their situation is the most dramatic of all. Croats and Serbs, even if threatened, are conscious they have a state behind them. Ethnic cleansing by Serbs in Bosnia-Herzegovina is implemented in a very brutal way. There is a similar policy in Croatia (against Serbs) but much more subtle." Mr. Mazowiecki has just returned from a four-and-a-half day visit to former Yugoslavia with Mautner Markof, head of the UN Human Rights Centre, and Louis Joinet and Bacre Ndiaye, heads of the UN working groups on arbitrary detention and summary executions. The team is preparing a report. Mr. Mazowiecki, 65, said of their visit: "It was short but we have seen a lot, enough evidence, testimony and documents to justify what I'm saying. Human rights do not exist in Bosnia-Herzegovina." They had been appalled by the amount of weapons visible, particularly the quantity of light arms in Banja Luka. This excessive weaponry served to intimidate, so that people signed papers giving up their property before being permitted to flee.'

Also, under the title 'Kill all the Muslims', *Newsweek*, 7 June 1993, wrote: 'All-out attack: In Mostar you could show him thousands. Early in May the HVO. capped months of threats against civilians by launching an all-out attack, forcing the Muslims into a pocket on the east bank of the city. Then Croat soldiers wearing stockings over their faces began kicking down doors in predawn raids on Muslim families that had remained on the west bank. Many of the Croats also wore armbands connecting them with the Ustahe, pro-Nazi Croatian forces from World War II. At least 2000 Muslim civilians, many still in their nightclothes, were marched into HVO. detention camps. Although international pressure forced the Croats to release detainees, foreign relief officials told *Newsweek* they are still trying to locate hundreds of men who were separated from the main body of prisoners and led to an unknown destination.'

33 Thornberry: *International Law*, Appendix 4

34 'Abd al-Qādir 'Awda, *al-Tashrī' al-Jinā'ī al-Islāmī Muqāran bi'l-Qānūn al-Waḍ'ī*, 2 Vols (Cairo, 1984), I, p 26

35 'Awda: *al-Tashrī' al-Jinā'ī*, p 26

36 *Dhimmīs* are those communities tolerated within Islam, and include not only the so-called *ahl al-kitāb* (People of the Book or Scripturaries), but also idolaters (*'abadat al-aṣnām*) and fire-worshippers, provided they have accepted residence in any Muslim territory except for the Arabian Peninsula. The Scripturaries include Christians, Jews, Magians (Zoroastrians), Samaritans and Sabians. Strictly speaking, the Magians were not a Scriptuary community for, according to traditions, they neither believed in God, nor did they possess a Scripture; but since they believed in a certain deity, the Prophet Muḥammad and the early caliphs considered them in the same category as the Scripturaries and treated them as a protected community. Polytheists (*mushrikūn*) were, as a rule, denied the status of *dhimmīs*, especially in Arabia. See, Majid Khadduri, *Law of War and Peace in Islam: A Study in Muslim International Law* (London, 1940), p 176

37 Syed Abul' Ala Maudoodi, *Human Rights in Islam* (London, 1980), pp 21-2

38 Khadduri: *War and Peace*, p 179. For details on the situation of *dhimmīs* within the Islamic State, see Abū Yūsuf, *Kitāb al-Kharaj*, 2nd ed (Cairo, 1352 AH), pp 86-150; Aḥmad Yaḥyā al-Balādhurī, *Futūḥ al-Buldān* (Beirut, 1975), pp 169-72; and Sayyid Sābiq, *Fiqh al-Sunna* (Beirut, 1969), p 604

39 Ann Elizabeth Mayer, *Islam and Human Rights* (Boulder, 1991), pp 147-9

40 See also Benjamin Braude and Bernard Lewis, *Christians and Jews in the Ottoman Empire* (New York, 1982)

41 Bernard Lewis, *The Jews of Islam* (Princeton, 1984), p 83

42 'Awda rightly adopts the view of Imām Abū Ḥanīfa, who regards *qiṣāṣ* for the murder of a *dhimmī* by a Muslim as obligatory. See 'Awda: *al-Tashrī' al-Jinā'ī*, I, p 339

43 Aḥmad Fatḥī Bahnasī, *al-Qiṣāṣ fi'l-Fiqh al-Islāmī* (Cairo, 1982), pp 15-18

44 Al-Bukhārī, *Kitāb al-Jāmi' al- Ṣaḥīḥ*, I (Leiden, 1862-1908), K. al- Īmān, pp 1 and 47, nos 1 and 51

45 Quoted in 'Alī Manṣūr, *al-Sharī'a al-Islāmiyya wa'l-Qānūn al-Duwalī* (Cairo, 1982), pp 313-14

46 Muḥammad ibn al-Ḥasan al-Shaybānī, *Kitāb al-Siyar al-Kabīr* (Hyderabad, 1335 AH), I, p 33

[47] Muḥammad al-'Āmīr, *Kitāb al-Iklīl Sharḥ Muktasar Khalīl* (Cairo, 1224 AH), p 160
[48] Al-Shaybānī: *Kitāb al-Siyar*, I, p 78
[49] Abū Dāwūd, *Sunan Abī Dāwūd* (Beirut, 1980), IV, K. al-Jihād, pp 15-16, and al-Bukhārī: *Ṣaḥīḥ*, pp 160-1
[50] Abū Dāwūd: *Sunan*, II, K. al-Jihād, p 739
[51] Abū Dāwūd: *Sunan*, II, K. al-Jihād, p 738
[52] Muhammad Hamidullah, *Muslim Conduct of State* (Leiden, 1953), p 360
[53] 'Awda: *al-Tashrī' al-Jinā'ī*, II, p 693
[54] Al-Bukhārī: *Ṣaḥīḥ*, IV, K. al-Jihād, p 180
[55] *The Holy Bible* (New York, 1972), p 174
[56] Manṣūr: *al-Sharī'a al-Islāmiyya*, p 299
[57] Michel de Taube, 'Le Monde d'Islam et son influence sur l'Europe orientale', in *Recueil des Cours*, ed Académie de Droit International (The Hague, 1962), XI, pp 393-5
[58] Manṣūr: *al-Sharī'a al-Islāmiyya*, p 302

Part Four

Judges and Courts

8

The Ethical Code and Organised Procedure of Early Islamic Law Courts, with Reference to al-Khaṣṣāf's *Adab al-Qāḍī*

Muhammad Ibrahim H.I. Surty

> *O you who believe! Be you staunch in justice, witness for Allah, even though it be against yourselves or [your] parents or [your] kindred, whether [the case be of] a rich man or a poor man, for Allah is nearer to both [than you are]. So follow not passion lest you lapse [from truth] and if you lapse or fall away, surely Allah is ever informed of what you do.* (Q.4:135)[1]

The existence of judicial systems and courts of law in some form or another can be traced back to times of antiquity. Pre-Islamic Arabian society had its own methods for dispensing justice: litigating parties had the choice of taking their disputes either to a mutually-agreed *ḥakam* (arbitrator), an *amīr* (tribal head) or a *kāhin* (soothsayer possessing religious authority). Generally, cases were adjudicated based on *'urf* (custom), although this was not common among the clans and tribes of Arabia.

At this time, however, there existed neither a unified code of law nor an executive authority which could administer justice among the different tribes of the Arabian Peninsula. Therefore, one of the greatest contributions of the Prophet Muḥammad was to grant Muslims revealed law and executive authority for the administration of justice. The broad principles which emerged from the revealed law and its implementation by the Prophet provided the foundations upon which generations of jurists concerned for the promotion and development of the administration of justice were to build.

The Islamic ethical code and its procedure cannot be properly comprehended without a sound understanding of the related broad principles of the Sharī'a. In view of the nature and limited space of this essay, meticulous treatment of each aspect will be avoided. Rather, the essay will be presented with special reference to the work *Adab al-Qāḍī* (*The Judge's Etiquette*),[2] by Abū Bakr Aḥmad ibn 'Amr ibn al-Shaybānī al-Khaṣṣāf (d. 261/874), since extensive discussion of each aspect of the Sharī'a would require an independent book.

An emphasis on justice in the revealed text of the Qur'an gave birth to the institution of *al-qaḍī'*, the administration of justice, and it was not long before Islamic courts of law emerged. Their origin in a simple form can be traced easily from the time of the rise of Islam. An ever-increasing demand for courts of law by those Muslims who began to spread from the Straits of Gibraltar to the gates of India compelled jurists to compile manuals for judges, so as to enable them to administer justice on the foundations of revealed law. Such legal manuals were written generally on the themes of *adab al-qāḍī* (the etiquette, or rules of conduct, of the judge) and *al-qaḍā'*.

During the first stage of my research on the theme of *adab al-qāḍī*, which was completed in 1972, I traced 65 independent treatises on both *adab al- qāḍī* and *al-qaḍā'*, presenting them in chronological order,[3] and in the years that followed, a number of these works were published. Muḥyī Hilāl al-Sirḥān has also listed 63 independent works, and has divided them into schools of law, presenting the contribution of each school in chronological order.[4] In his recent work, Ṣiddīqī ibn Muḥammad Yāsīn lists in alphabetical order 121 books on the same themes.[5]

It would seem that *qāḍī al-quḍāh* (Chief Justice) Abū Yūsuf (d. 182/798) was the first jurist to contribute an independent treatise on *adab al-qāḍī*.[6] Three other commentaries by eminent jurists were also written during different periods.[7] Abū Yūsuf's colleague, Muḥammad ibn al-Ḥasan al-Shaybānī (d. 189/805), is known to have written a book on this topic,[8] as did Muḥammad ibn Idrīs al-Shāfi'ī (d. 204/819),[9] founder of the Shāfi'ī school. His contemporary, al-Ḥasan ibn Ziyād al-Lu'lu'ī (d. 204/819-20), a Ḥanafī jurist, also contributed a work on *adab al-qāḍī*,[10] as did Abū 'Abd Allāh Aṣbagh ibn al-Farraj (d. 225/839), of the Mālikī school,[11] followed by the Ḥanafī jurist Muḥammad ibn Samā'a (d. 233/847).[12] Unfortunately, all of these early works have been lost.

Al-Khaṣṣāf's *Adab al-Qāḍī* takes the form of eleven commentaries written during different periods,[13] and has survived on account of its many commentaries. Al-Khaṣṣāf's greatest contribution to the theme of *adab al-qāḍī* is the detailed account he gives of the administration of justice in the early Islamic period, along with the legal solutions he provides for various legal cases related to oaths; debts; correspondence between *qāḍīs*; wills; power of attorney; pre-emption; distribution of inheritance; marriage; dowry; maintenance allowance; witnesses, and so on. In the text, he argues for the acceptance or rejection of certain views, presents a case and then pronounces a judgement, providing an explanation for each judgement. He also provides ample evidence from the authoritative sources, being the Qur'an, the *sunna* and the legal opinions of the scholars of the first and second centuries of the *hijra*, be they for or against his judgements. As such, al-Khaṣṣāf's *Adab al-Qāḍī* is a valuable intellectual legal training tool for Islamic judges.

Among the early treatises on *adab al-qāḍī* mentioned above, contributions by three of the Sunni schools are evident, and the existence of a large number of books among these schools on the themes of *al-qāḍā'* and *adab al-qāḍī* indicate the importance attached to the institutions of *al-qaḍā'* and its practice in Muslim society across the generations. The pressing need for the establishment and promotion of justice in Muslim society can also be traced from the contribution of chapters on *al-qaḍā'* in celebrated books of Islamic jurisprudence and in modern works. The earliest collections of *ḥadīth* also included chapters on *al-qaḍā'*, while special biographical dictionaries for judges were prepared, and judges' anecdotes recorded. Furthermore, Muslim historians have recorded numerous chronicles relating to judicial practice.

Al-Khaṣṣāf's Ethical Code

The ethical code which al-Khaṣṣāf presents should be seen in the context of judicial ethical requirements for judges. The list of this code can be enlarged considerably in terms of Islamic ethics, which are taken for granted as being possessed by a Muslim judge, who is also regarded by the members of a Muslim society as a role model for Islamic ethics.

Affirmative Rules

According to al-Khaṣṣāf, the selection of a *qāḍī* should be inspired only by the desire to please God. Furthermore, a *qāḍī* should be distinguished by his piety, his regular observance of religious duties, and his belief in God. He must act in such a way as to obtain heavenly rewards and to avoid punishment in the hereafter.[14] To this end:

(1) He should possess a commanding personality and knowledge, and should display patience in court.[15]

(2) He should ensure that every person has easy access to the court.[16]

(3) He should consider a previous decision of the court as null and void when the falsehood of a case is apparent to him.[17]

(4) He may personally conduct a search of the accused in criminal cases.[18]

(5) He may order the accused to be held in custody even before trial.[19]

(6) He should be strict in matters of religion, but not harsh in speech.[20]

(7) He should be fair in his judgement.

(8) He should give equal response to the plaintiff and the defendant and should treat both equally. He should be attentive to their cases, and should give his judgement after hearing both parties.[21]
(9) He should order the *amīn*, or custodian with whom the wealth and property of an orphan are deposited, to render accounts for the verification of his trust.[22]
(10) He should know the manners and customs of the people to whom he has been appointed *qāḍī*.[23]
(11) He should keep a close watch on the day-to-day affairs of his court officials.[24]
(12) He should be acquainted with the jurists, as well as with the pious, trustworthy and *'udūl* (just people) of the town.[25]
(13) He may attend funerals and visit sick persons, but while doing so he should not discuss the judicial affairs of litigants.[26]
(14) He may attend general banquets. Defining a 'general' banquet, al-Sarakhsī writes: 'If the banquet can take place without the presence of the *qāḍī*, then this banquet would be taken as "general". But if at a banquet the attendance of the *qāḍī* is inevitable, then such a banquet would be called "special", that is, arranged especially for the *qāḍī*.'[27]
(15) He is permitted to accept the testimony of a dumb person, provided that person's symbolic expressions are generally understood and established by general custom. If not, then the *qāḍī* should ask for one of his trustworthy relatives, who is familiar with his expressions, to translate.[28]

Negative Rules

Among the negative rules for a *qāḍī* are the following:
(1) He must not give judgement in anger, nor when under emotional strain.[29] This is because, when a *qāḍī* is mentally or emotionally upset, his reasoning power and judgement may be impaired.
(2) He must not decide a case when sleep overcomes him, nor when he is unduly tired or overjoyed.
(3) He must not give judgement when he is hungry or has overeaten.[30]
(4) He must not accept any bribe.[31]
(5) He must not laugh at litigants, nor should he make fun of them.[32]
(6) He must not weaken himself with non-obligatory fasting when he is deciding cases.[33]
(7) He must not put words into the mouth of a victim, nor should he suggest answers, nor should he point at any of the litigants.[34]
(8) He must not permit a litigant to enter his home, although men who are not concerned with a case may visit a *qāḍī*, in order to greet him and for other purposes.[35]

(9) He must not entertain one of the litigants at his residence. He may, however, entertain both litigants together.[36]
(10) He must not persist in ignorance of something, but must ask those who have knowledge.[37]
(11) He must not crave wealth, nor should he be a slave to his lust.[38]
(12) He must not fear anyone.[39]
(13) He must not fear dismissal, nor must he eulogize, nor should he hate his critics.[40]
(14) He must not accept gifts, although he may accept gifts from his relatives, except for those awaiting trial. He may also continue to accept gifts from those who gave him gifts before his appointment as *qāḍī*, but, if they increase the value of the gift after his appointment, then it is not permissible for him to accept.[41]
(15) He must not deviate from the truth for fear of someone's anger, and must not walk in the street alone.[42] In this way, his dignity will be maintained and he will not be exposed to the undue approaches of interested parties.
(16) He must give no consideration to the emotions of litigants.[43]
During the early Islamic period, most *qāḍīs* were strict in observing these ethical principles.

The Organization and Function of the Court

This section considers matters such as the office of *qāḍī*, remuneration, insignia and dress, the seat of justice, court hours and holidays, court registers and officials.

The Office of Qāḍī

It was the duty of the caliph to appoint pious, free, learned, just, sane, adult Muslims to the office of *qāḍī*,[44] and Muslims were not permitted to solicit the office through unlawful means. According to al-Khaṣṣāf, the caliph was the deputy of the Muslim community, thus, on his appointment, the *qāḍī* became a guardian of the welfare of Muslims, and would not lose his position even with the death or deposition of a caliph.[45]

In Islam, the *qāḍī* is more than a judge; he is also a religious leader. For this reason, *qāḍīs* were called upon to consecrate the investiture of each new caliph.[46] During the first century of the *hijra*, in addition to strictly judicial functions, almost all *qāḍīs* were given additional duties, which were either related to their post – such as controller of the police – or completely unrelated – such as supervisor of the public treasury.[47]

Emile Tynan writes that, during the course of the development of the institution

> ...the *qāḍī* became increasingly conscious of the scope of his mission, which consisted in the arbitration of suits between individuals and the safeguarding of the interest of those who required the protection of the state. Thus the *qāḍī* became the guardian of the interests of orphans and absentees, whose property had been left without provision for its administration. He was a notary, the guardian of ownerless property, and the administrator of *waqfs* [pious endowments]. The *qāḍī* also exercised functions which are actually foreign to the nature of his office, but which required an identical type of knowledge. It was normal for *qāḍīs* to teach law, to write legal treatises, and to issue *fatwās*.[48]

Al-Khaṣṣāf has mentioned the following extra-judicial functions of the *qāḍī*: administration of *awqāf*; guardianship of orphans' property and estates; guardianship of the property of absentees; guardianship of unclaimed properties; and prisoners' affairs.[49] History recalls that judges have served as custodians of all these departments.

Qāḍīs could be dismissed for a number of reasons, and the caliph had the power to dismiss a *qāḍī* when the latter's integrity was called into question. The newly-appointed *qāḍī* was to appoint two persons in whom he had full confidence, in order to take charge of the *dīwān*, or court registers, from the dismissed *qāḍī*. A dismissed *qāḍī*, meanwhile, could either hand over to his successor in person, or authorize two trustworthy persons to do so. These were to put in writing all the details of the court registers of different departments, such as orphans' property, *nafaqāt* (maintenance allowance for women), *awqāf* and prisoners' affairs. They were also to check the records of every case. It was necessary for them to ask the dismissed *qāḍī* or his authorized agent about the particulars, so that no issue would remain ambiguous. They were also to take possession of *ṣukūk* (signed documents), *wadāʾiʿ* (deposits), the property of orphans, and the *qāḍī*'s register, in which all details were recorded. They were then to put all of the registers in a bag, which they were then to seal, so that they might be secure from any interference or misappropriation.

Regarding prisoners' affairs, newly appointed *qāḍīs* were to take extra care: the names of the convicted, the reason for their imprisonment and the relevant dates were to be written down, as well as being confirmed by asking the prisoners themselves, the dismissed *qāḍī*, and any claimant. On appointment, new *qāḍīs* would send their deputies in advance to their office, in order to meet the theologians, pious and just amongst the citizens, to collect information about them and other inhabitants of the station, and to ask about their personal affairs and their attitudes towards the judiciary.[50]

Remuneration

On appointing him governor and *qāḍī* of Mecca, the Prophet Muḥammad fixed the salary of 'Attāb ibn Asad (d. 23/643) at forty *uwqiyya* per month.[51] With the exception of 'Uthmān ibn 'Affān, who was wealthy in his own right, the Rightly-Guided Caliphs accepted a salary from the treasury to meet their own basic needs, and also to pay the salaries of their officials, *qāḍīs* included. The amount of the *qāḍīs*' salary was not fixed by the caliphs, rather, the *qāḍīs*' particular needs were the main criteria for their increments. Thus, Caliph 'Umar ibn al-Khaṭṭāb instructed his governors to appoint judges and pay them from the treasury, in accordance with their particular needs.[52] As far as can be deduced from available sources, the salary of *qāḍīs* during the time of the Rightly-Guided Caliphs ranged from 100 to 500 *dirhams* per month.[53]

Qāḍīs were, on the whole, well paid: during the Umayyad period, the salary of *qāḍīs* was fixed by the caliphs at 1000 *dīnārs* a year.[54] The *qāḍī* Ibn al-Hujayra, appointed in Egypt in 70/689, received an annual salary of 200 *dīnārs*. In addition, he held the posts of treasurer and state preacher, each of which earned him 200 *dīnārs* a year. Over and above that, he received a gratuity of 200 *dīnārs* plus a pension of a like amount, giving him a total annual income of 1000 *dīnārs*.[55] The 'Abbasids reduced the salary of *qāḍīs*, paying them thirty *dīnārs* a month,[56] but during the period of Caliph al-Ma'mūn, their salary was increased to 370 *dīnārs* per annum.[57] The doctrine behind fixing such handsome salaries for *qāḍīs* was to keep them financially sound, and thereby help to preserve their moral integrity.

Insignia and Dress

No special dress for *qāḍīs* was prescribed before the time of Abū Yūsuf. Previously, *qāḍīs* wore daily attire, the white and black turban being common. It is recorded that the *qāḍī* Shurayḥ wore a *khazz* (shawl), and a white turban with its end dangling down to his shoulders.[58]

Colour appears to have had particular significance under the 'Abbasids, whose 'official' colour was black. The *qāḍī* Khaṭīb Faqīh adhered to this colour, and it is said that a *qāḍī*'s refusal to wear black was considered a sign of adherence to the Umayyad cause, which would constitute a threat to his position.[59] The high *qalansuwa* (cowl or cap) was worn with a black turban and *ṭaylasān* (hooded garment). These were insignia which the *qāḍīs* and jurists claimed as their privilege, lending them exterior dignity, and being a means by which they inspired respect. *Qāḍīs* also wore the *sawadā'*, a special black robe that was rather like a shawl, over their shoulders.[60] The *qāḍīs* Ismā'īl, Yaḥyā ibn Aktham and Aḥmad ibn Abī Dāwūd are reported to have worn the *sawadā'* and *khuff* (top-boots).[61]

The Seat of Justice

According to Abū Ḥanīfa, the best place for holding the court was the *jāmiʿ*, or great or central mosque.[62] It was, however, permissible to sit in one's own house, after making adequate announcement, and provided that one allowed the admission of those who usually sat with the *qāḍī* in the mosque. Al-Khaṣṣāf describes the seating arrangements of the court as follows:

> On his arrival in the mosque the *qāḍī* would salute the audience, offer two or four *rakʿas* of prayer, and ask God to grant him success and guide him towards the right path, so as to enable him to uphold the truth and to save him from transgression. After that, he would sit facing the Kaʿba. Court ushers would stand in front of him, at such a distance that they might hear the *qāḍī*'s conversation with the litigants. The *qāḍī* placed his *qimaṭr* (box of court registers) on his right-hand side. The *kātib* (clerk of the court) sat near him, at such a distance that the *qāḍī* could watch his performance, while the *nā'ib al-qāḍī*(deputy judge) stood in front of him and called the litigants in turn. The *ḥājib* (guard) would stand near to him. The *qāḍī* allowed the jurists and other trustworthy persons to be seated near him, so that it would be easier for him to consult them on complicated legal issues. The two litigants would sit side by side in front of them.[63]

Court Hours

The early *qāḍī* were highly conscious of people's rights, and were fastidious in attending court. In particular, the administration of justice in the early morning and in darkness was not approved by al-Khaṣṣāf.[64] As mentioned earlier, mosques were sometimes used as seats of justice, and the timing of the obligatory prayers was of much help when fixing the working hours of the court. There would be a break for the *ẓuhr* (midday) prayer, which was possibly also lunch-time for the people associated with the court. Then there was another break for the *ʿaṣr* (late afternoon) prayer, and either the *ʿaṣr* or *maghrib* (sunset) prayers suspended the business of the court for the day.

Court Holidays

There is no evidence available to show which days were observed as holidays during the first century of the *hijra*. As for the second century, al-Khaṣṣāf's *Adab al-Qāḍī* is probably the only source which throws light on the holidays observed. During the time of Abū Ḥanīfa, Saturday was prescribed as a court holiday, while in al-Khaṣṣāf's time, either Monday or Tuesday was prescribed, and it was for the *qāḍī* to ascertain which of these days was to be observed.[65] Religious holidays were also recognized, such as Fridays, the days of *ʿĪd al-Fiṭr* and *ʿĪd al-Aḍḥā*, and the day of ʿArafāt (ninth of *Dhū'l-Ḥijja*). Besides these, so-called 'rainy days' (*muṭayr*) were also considered holidays. Regarding the remuneration of court officials on holidays, Ibn Māza provides legal advice.[66]

Court Registers

Al-Khaṣṣāf employs many terms with reference to court registers. Two of these require explanation here, namely *dīwān* and *qimaṭr*. A *dīwān*, as defined by Ibn Māza, was a bag which contained *sijillāt* (registers), *ṣukūk* (signed documents), *maḥāḍir* (records of the proceedings), and departmental registers.[67] The *qimaṭr*, meanwhile, was a box which contained the court records. It was introduced for the first time by the *qāḍī* Muḥammad ibn Masrūq (d. 167/783), who used to keep the box sealed.[68] Before the introduction of the *qimaṭr*, *qāḍīs* used to place the court registers in a bag, which was sealed in their presence.[69] Sulaym ibn 'Aṭr (d. 60/679), *qāḍī* of Egypt, is reportedly the first *qāḍī* to prepare a register in which the records of court proceedings were kept.[70]

Ibn Māza described the *qimaṭr* as the *qāḍī*'s 'weapon'. Al-Khaṣṣāf emphasized that the *qāḍī* should keep the *qimaṭr* with him, and that it should be on his person when he visits the court. While in court, the *qāḍī* himself should take care of the *qimaṭr*, and place it on his right-hand side.[71] The action of the *qāḍī* 'Īsā ibn Munkadir (d. 212/827) demonstrates the caution and care required of the *qimaṭr*: he kept it in the house of 'Amr ibn Khālid, but when it was discovered that the record of one case had been interfered with, the *qāḍī* arranged for special accommodation to be rented in the house of a certain 'Amr ibn al-'Āṣ, where the *qimaṭr* was kept behind a door, which the *qāḍī* himself kept locked and sealed.[72]

Court Officials

In early Islam, court officials included the following personnel: *qāḍī al-quḍāh* (the Chief Justice); *al- qāḍī* (the Judge); *nā'ib al-qāḍī* or *al-khalīfa* (the Deputy Judge); *al-kātib* (the Clerk of the Court); *al-a'wān* (the Court Ushers); *al-ḥājib* (the Bodyguard); *al-bawwāb* or *al-jilwāz* (the Doorkeeper); *al-muzakkī* (the Secret Investigator); *al-'udūl* (the Accredited Witnesses); *al-mutarjim* (the Interpreter); *al-qāsim* (the Distributor); *amīn al-ḥukm* (the Legal Trustee); and *al-wakīl* (the Agent or Solicitor).

It is said that the institution of *qāḍī al-quḍāh* was introduced by the Persians, *qāḍī al-quḍāh* being the literal translation of the Persian term *mobad mobadan*.[73] The *qāḍī al-quḍāh* was responsible for all aspects of the judiciary of the state, including the appointment, dismissal and administration of *qāḍīs*. Hārūn al-Rashīd appointed Abū Yūsuf *qāḍī al-quḍāh*, and not a single *qāḍī* in Iraq, Khurasan, Syria and Egypt was appointed without his consent.[74] Abū Yūsuf is also reported to have paid visits to *qāḍīs*, and to have tried to investigate their affairs and conduct.[75] Similarly, the Caliph al-Ma'mūn appointed Yaḥyā ibn Aktham *qāḍī al-quḍāh*, and granted him many special rights for the administration of his office. Ministers were not entitled to act upon certain resolutions without having the prior sanction of Yaḥyā ibn Aktham.[76]

The *qāḍī*, as we have seen, was responsible for the administration of his court, including the appointment and dismissal of court officials. He would appoint a trustworthy person as his deputy (*nā'ib*), who would assist him in calling the litigants to the court, in accordance with the order of the cases. This *nā'ib* would stand in front of the *qāḍī*, but was not permitted to question any of the litigants in the court regarding their disputes. Sometimes, the *nā'ib* was also placed in charge of extra-judicial functions, and was paid by the *qāḍī* for the administration of the allocated departments.

The *kātib*'s (clerk's) duties consisted of making a full written record of the statements of the parties in the law suit, the claim of the claimant, the defence of the accused, the deposition of the witnesses, the judgement of the *qāḍī*, and so on.[77] Al-Khaṣṣāf affirms that the *kātib* should be a pious and honest Muslim, and that he should have adequate knowledge of the Sharī'a.[78]

The *a'wān* (ushers) were appointed directly by the *qāḍīs* They would give notice of the date of the hearing of the case, and would persuade the litigants to attend the court according to this notification, and to maintain law and order in the courtroom. This system originated during the period of Shurayḥ, as reported by 'Amr ibn Qays. He further reports that when the litigants were brought before the *qāḍī*, a court official would ask: 'Who is the claimant among you? Let him speak.'[79] The *ḥājib*, meanwhile, was the *qāḍī*'s bodyguard; he would stand close to the *qāḍī* and maintain law and order in the courtroom. Wakī' notes that the *qāḍī* Ibn Ḥazm was attended by a bodyguard who held a whip in his hand,[80] while the *qāḍī* Shurayḥ had two bodyguards.[81]

Al-Khaṣṣāf describes the post of *bawwāb* or *jilwāz* (doorkeeper) in a separate chapter of his *Adab al-Qāḍī*.[82] Umm Dāwūd relates the following: 'I saw a *shurṭī* (policeman) holding a whip in his hand, standing before [Qāḍī] Shurayḥ.' Ibn Māza identifies this *shurṭī* as the *jilwāz*. He was stationed at the door of the courtroom, and his role was to keep order among the litigants and the public.[83]

The duty of the *muzakkī* (secret investigator) was to investigate the character of ordinary witnesses. With the passage of time, the number of instances of false evidence increased, and *qāḍīs* sometimes felt the need to verify the authenticity of a testimony. Provisions, therefore, were made to examine a witness's character. The institution of the examination of a witness is first ascribed to Shurayḥ. When he was criticized for this innovation, his measured response was: '*idhā ḥaddathtum ḥaddathnā* (when you introduced innovations, so did we)'.[84] Ghayth ibn Salmān (d. 176/792) is recorded as having introduced this institution to Egypt.[85]

The institution of *al-ʿudūl* (accredited witnesses) involved a procedure by which the *qāḍīs*, after having ascertained the reliability of an individual, would recognize him as a truthful witness whose testimony could not, in principle, be doubted. This institution was introduced in 174/790 by the *qāḍī* al-Mufaḍḍal ibn Faḍāla.[86] The duty of the *ʿudūl* was to testify to the authenticity of legal documents such as trusts, wills, promissory notes, and so on.[87] This function was similar to the present-day function of 'Notary Public'.

The *mutarjim* (translator) was an official who was responsible for the translation of statements made by litigants who did not know Arabic. By definition, the *mutarjim* was a pious, honest and learned Muslim. The presence of two *mutarjims* at court was deemed preferable.[88] In cases of inheritance, *qāḍīs* were in need of experts who could divide property among the persons entitled to inherit in accordance with Sharīʿa laws of inheritance. Such an expert was known as a *qāsim* (distributor), and was paid from the public treasury.[89]

In the third century of the *hijra*, *qāḍīs* adopted the practice of entrusting to an *amīn al-ḥukm* (legal trustee), being a trustworthy person charged with the safekeeping of the assets of legally incompetent persons, such as orphans, absentees, and so on.[90] Lastly, according to al-Khaṣṣāf, the appointment of a *wakīl* (agent or solicitor) for the defence of the parties' interests before the court was also considered lawful. Indeed, this system has been in practice since the early Islamic period.

Court Proceedings and Procedure

This section discusses aspects of court proceedings and procedure as detailed in al-Khaṣṣāf's *Adab al-Qāḍī*, among them bail, summonses and other disciplinary actions.

Bail

In early criminal cases, bail was not generally accepted, although it was accepted in civil cases. Those accused who were well known to the public were exempted from undertaking bail. If the matter disputed was of little value, bail was not imposed on the accused. To act as surety, one had to be a person of integrity and honour, in possession of his own estate, business premises or the like. Therefore, a man residing in rented accommodation would not have been eligible to stand surety.[91] The tenure of bail varied from *qāḍī* to *qāḍī*; al-Khaṣṣāf allowed three days, while Abū Yūsuf extended it to the duration of the court session.[92] If the accused was unable to provide bail, the claimant was granted *mulāzama*, or close supervision of the daily affairs of the accused.[93]

Summonses and Other Disciplinary Actions

A summons took the form of a piece of paper or clay bearing the *qāḍī's* seal, and was delivered by a messenger.[94] Soon after a claim was lodged, the *qāḍī* had to ascertain whether the accused lived within the jurisdiction of the town. If the accused happened to be a town dweller, he received a summons to trial from the *qāḍī*. If he lived outside the jurisdiction of the town, then the claimant had to present evidence regarding his claim. Once this was done, the *qāḍī* would send a summons to the accused by means of a *rājil* (messenger).[95] As regards the demarcation of the area of jurisdiction, a most interesting method was practised. If the accused lived within a distance from where he could attend the law court by starting out on foot in early morning, and then get home after the trial by the end of the day, then he would be considered a resident of the town. If not, he would be considered beyond the jurisdiction of the court.[96]

Sick persons and *mukhaddarāt*, i.e. women who refrained from attending men's gatherings, were not forced to attend the law courts. Special provisions were made by the *qāḍīs* for the hearing of such persons, by sending a *khalīfa*, or authorized agent of the *qāḍī*, to them. In cases where the *khalīfa* was not *ma'dhūn* (authorized to judge), two trustworthy persons were sent with the *khalīfa*, to convey to the *qāḍī* the statements of the sick person or the *mukhaddara*.[97]

If the accused declined to attend the court to defend himself against the charges brought against him, the *qāḍī* would write to the governor requesting permission to use force. The defaulter would then be liable to punishment or imprisonment by the *qāḍī*.[98] If the accused deliberately hid himself in his home, and his presence in the town was attested to by at least two persons within three days of his concealment, the *qāḍī* could, at the request of the claimant, exercise his power to nail and seal the home of the accused, making it a prison for him. Al-Khaṣṣāf held, however, that if the period which had elapsed since the accused's appearance in the city exceeded three days, then the *qāḍī* should refrain from nailing the doors and sealing the home of the accused.[99]

If the claimant wished to expedite the case, the *qāḍī* was obliged to send a messenger and two witnesses to the home of the accused, and to proclaim these words: '*Qāḍī* So-and-So asks you or your authorized *wakīl* to attend the court; otherwise the proof of the claimant will be accepted against you.' The *qāḍī* would do this for three successive days, before pronouncing his judgement.[100]

Abū Yūsuf used to order court officials to raid the homes of defendants who continuously absented themselves from court hearings. Al-Khaṣṣāf, meanwhile, defined the term *hujūm*, whereby the *qāḍī* would send two trustworthy persons along with the court ushers, women and servants of the home of the accused, in order to make a surprise raid. The ushers would encircle the house, making it impossible for the accused to escape. With the house surrounded in this manner, the women would then be asked to enter it without permission, followed by a group of men, to find the accused. If the accused was not found in the men's quarter, a search would be made by the women of the ladies' quarter.[101]

Court Procedure

In early Islam, disputes brought to *qāḍīs* were few and, consequently, could be settled without delay. With the passing of time, however, disputes began to be filed in growing numbers, and *qāḍīs* had to decide cases in order of priority. Al-Khaṣṣāf introduced an organized lottery system for assigning dates to cases. According to this system, the *qāḍī* would send his *kātib* to the mosque, preferably accompanied by a trustworthy person. The *kātib* would accept notification and write the name of the claimants and defendants on a piece of paper, which he would then place in a box. If the number of cases was such that the *qāḍī* considered it possible to decide all of these cases in one day, then lots were drawn to determine the order in which the cases were presented.[102]

Should the number of cases be higher, the *kātib* took out as many papers from the box as the *qāḍī* could decide in one day. He put individual cases into separate files and wrote the name of a prominent person on each, since this name would be known to all of those whose cases were filed therein. Accordingly, several files were made. The clerk had to be careful in choosing the names for these files, as these names should not be similar. He then wrote the names on each file onto separate pieces of paper, which he placed in the box and then took out one after the other, assigning a date to each. He then informed the litigants that their names were in these files, and that such and such a date had been assigned for their hearing. The *qāḍī* then ordered the days for each case in the file to be announced, so that everyone might know the date of his case.[103] Each day, the *qāḍī* would take out the files for that date, and the pieces of paper on which the litigants' names had been written. Then, he would place these pieces of paper in the box, taking them out one after the other, and settling the cases in that order.[104]

Al-Khaṣṣāf states that, subject to certain genuine reasons, priority in hearing was given to witnesses, foreigners, travellers and women. Foreigners were required to prove their foreign status and, because they had to return to their native lands, they were not to be detained.[105] Women were given priority in hearing if the *qāḍī* considered it necessary; he could also fix a special day for the judgement of their disputes. In cases where one party consisted of both men and women, the latter could not be given priority. The *qāḍī* informed women litigants of the date of their cases through an elderly, female intermediary.[106] Having set all of the hearing dates, the *qāḍī* would write down the dates pertaining to each file in his register, which he would then set with a seal and store in his box.[107]

Court Proceedings

In his *Adab al-Qāḍī*, al-Khaṣṣāf gives the following vivid sketch of court proceedings: on a particular date, as the claimant and the defendant sat before him, the *qāḍī* opened his *qimaṭr* and took out a piece of paper on which the names of the claimants and defendants had been written. He then asked the claimant regarding his claim. Differences of opinion prevailed among jurists over the privilege of the *qāḍī* to question the claimant. Imām Muḥammad al-Shaybānī gave the choice to the *qāḍī* if the latter thought it necessary, otherwise, the *qāḍī* was to remain silent and let the claimant put his claim first. In the view of al-Shaybānī, the *qāḍī* had simply to look at the claimant.[108]

When the claimant put forward his claim, the *qāḍī* would immediately write it down in the claimant's exact words, adding nothing to the statement.[109] If the claim was inadmissible, he would tell the claimant: 'Your claim is inadmissible, go and correct it.' If the claim was admissible, the *qāḍī* would turn to the defendant and address him thus: 'He has put a claim against you. What do you have to say?' If the defendant agreed to the charge, the *qāḍī* would put this in writing, dating the agreement. He would record the defendant's agreement in the latter's own words, and could make neither additions nor omissions.[110] If the defendant denied the claim, the *qāḍī* would also record it with the same accuracy, and would put down the date of the denial.

Jurists also differ regarding the privilege of the *qāḍī* to question the claimant regarding evidence. According to al-Khaṣṣāf, the *qāḍī* would ask the claimant: 'Do you have any evidence?' If he replied in the affirmative, the *qāḍī* would hear the witness. If the evidence of the witnesses proved the claim, the *qāḍī* would put this down on his paper and send it to the *kātib*, who would in turn write down the case. When the claim before the claimant was, 'such and such is your claim', then the *qāḍī* would turn to the defendant and say, 'such and such is your statement'.[111]

Witnesses were not permitted to speak until the *qāḍī* requested them to do so, one after the other.[112] If the *qāḍī* was not acquainted with the witnesses, the *kātib* would take down their names, identity, residences, streets and places of worship. This information was recorded on a piece of paper, which was then attached to the front of the *maḥḍar* (register), to assist in any enquiry that might drive the court proceedings.[113]

If the evidence concerned an exhibit, the witness was required to point with his hand first to the claimant, second to the defendant, and third to the exhibit regarding which he was giving evidence. If the evidence was being given on behalf of a dead person, it was deemed necessary to present a *waṣīy* (authorized agent), and if it concerned an untraced person, a representative was called. In questions of immovable property, a full description of the item was given. Thereby, the *qāḍī* sought to avoid any ambiguity.[114]

Throughout, the *kātib* recorded the case in the register, giving details and names of the claimant and defendant, their fathers and grandfathers, and also the details of their professions, tribes and all other data deemed necessary for their full identification. In the cases of women, the *kātib* would either write down their description, or would leave a space for the *qāḍī* to do so. In the latter case, the *qāḍī* would simply look at the woman and record her description.[115]

Conclusion

In the Qur'an, the theme of justice is all embracing, free from any restriction, and universal. It is all embracing because it governs a person's life – both private and public – and insists that there should be no deviation from the path of justice in either the minor or major affairs of life. It is free from any restriction because it does not discriminate on the grounds of race, rank, colour, nationality, status or religion. All humans are the servants of God, and as such all should be treated equally in courts of law, and all are accountable for their deeds. It is universal because it is applicable to all who accept its authority.

The ethical code of judges and organized procedure of early Islamic courts of law, as reflected in al-Khaṣṣāf's *Adab al-Qāḍī*, is a reflection of human practice of the Qur'anic theme of justice. This theme is a governing force for the development of Islamic courts of law and related Muslim scholarship, and is a sublime goal which courts have attempted to attain in the course of their daily procedures. Failures and successes are inevitable for any human experience, and the Muslim experience in this regard is no exception. It should be noted, however, that glimpses of the Muslim experience may be seen in modern judicial systems, and especially in the system of western courts of law. Clearly, both systems share not one but several principles, elements and practices in their procedures for the promotion of justice and humanity in judgement.

Notes

[1] See also Q.5:8; Q.7:29; Q.16:90; Q.42:15; and Q.57:25
[2] Al-Khaṣṣāf's *Adab al-Qāḍī* itself is not extant. See my critical edition, *Sharḥ Adab al-Qāḍī*, 2 Vols, transmission and commentary by Ibn Māza (Minna, 1980), with an introduction on the administration of justice in early Islam. Unfortunately, this text remains confined to Northern Nigeria. It is referred to hereinafter as Al-Khaṣṣāf's *Adab al-Qāḍī*.
[3] Set out in my critical edition ofal-Khaṣṣāf's *Adab al-Qāḍī*, I, pp 81-5
[4] See Muḥyī Hilāl al-Sirḥān's critical edition of Ibn Abī Dam al-Shāfi'ī's, *Kitāb Adab al-Qaḍā'* (Baghdad, 1984), pp 52-62, hereinafter referred to as al-Shāfi'ī, *Kitāb Adab al-Qaḍā'*.
[5] See Ṣiddīqī ibn Muḥammad Yāsīn's critical edition of al-Imām Abū al-'Abbās Shams al-Dīn Aḥmad ibn Ibrāhīm ibn 'Abd al-Ghanī al-Surūjī's *Kitāb Adab al-Qaḍā'*, 2 Vols (Beirut, 1997), hereinafter referred to as al-Surūjī,*Kitāb Adab al-Qaḍā'*.
[6] Ḥajjī Khalīfa, *Kashf al-Ẓunūn*, I (Beirut, 1890), p 46;al-Khaṣṣāf: *Adab al-Qāḍī*, I, p 249
[7] These commentaries were: Ja'far Muḥammad ibn Ismā'īl ibn 'Abd Allāh al-Hindwānī (d. 362/973); Abū Bakr Muḥammad ibn Aḥmad al-Sarakhsī (d. *ca.* 483/1090); and Ibn Māza (d. *ca.* 570/1174). See also al-Surūjī: *Kitāb Adab al-Qaḍā'*, I, p 80, and al-Shāfi'ī: *Kitāb Adab al-Qaḍā'*, p 52
[8] Al-Khaṣṣāf's *Adab al-Qāḍī*, I, pp 52; 54; 58; 139; II, p 360
[9] Ibn al-Nadīm, *Kitāb al-Fihrist* (Beirut, n.d.), p 296
[10] Ibn al-Nadīm: *Fihrist*, p 288; al-Surūjī: *Kitāb Adab al-Qaḍā'*, I, p 158; II, p 743
[11] See al-Shāfi'ī: *Kitāb Adab al-Qaḍā'*, I, p 60
[12] Ibn al-Nadīm: *Fihrist*, p 289
[13] See, for details, Khalīfa: *Kashf al-Ẓunūn*, I, p 46, and al-Surūjī: *Kitāb Adab al-Qaḍā'*, I, pp 80-1
[14] Al-Khaṣṣāf's *Adab al-Qāḍī*, I, pp 60-90
[15] Muḥammad ibn Idrīs al-Shāfi'ī, *Kitāb al-Umm*, I (Cairo, 1321-25), p 204
[16] Al-Shāfi'ī: *Kitāb al-Umm*, IV, p 204
[17] Al-Nasā'ī, *Kitāb al-Sunan al-Kubrā*, (Bombay, 1972) s.v. *adab al-qaḍā'*
[18] Al-Bukhārī: *Kitāb al-Jāmi' al-Ṣaḥīḥ*, I (Leiden, 1862-1908), K. al-Maghāzī
[19] Ibn Qayyim al-Jawziyya, *Ṭuruq al-Ḥukmiyya fi'l-Siyāsa al-Shar'iyya* (Cairo, 1953), p 14
[20] Al-Khaṣṣāf's *Adab al-Qāḍī*, I, pp 36-7
[21] Al-Khaṣṣāf's *Adab al-Qāḍī*, I, p 100; Abū Dāwūd, *Sunan Abī Dāwūd*, trans Aḥmad Ḥasan (Lahore, 1984), K. al-'Aqdiyya
[22] Al-Khaṣṣāf's *Adab al-Qāḍī*, I, p 80
[23] Al-Khaṣṣāf's *Adab al-Qāḍī*, I, p 84
[24] Al-Khaṣṣāf's *Adab al-Qāḍī*, I, pp 67-104
[25] Al-Khaṣṣāf's *Adab al-Qāḍī*, I, p 84
[26] Al-Khaṣṣāf's *Adab al-Qāḍī*, I, p 103
[27] Al-Khaṣṣāf's *Adab al-Qāḍī*, I, p 103
[28] Al-Khaṣṣāf's *Adab al-Qāḍī*, I, p 338
[29] Al-Khaṣṣāf's *Adab al-Qāḍī*, I, chapters 11, 12
[30] Al-Khaṣṣāf's *Adab al-Qāḍī*, I, p 116; Wakī', *Akhbār al-Quḍāh*, I, ed A. M. al-Marāghī (Cairo, 1947-50), p 83
[31] Al-Khaṣṣāf's *Adab al-Qāḍī*, I, pp 121-35
[32] Al-Khaṣṣāf's *Adab al-Qāḍī*, I, p 100

[33] Al-Khaṣṣāf's *Adab al-Qāḍī*, I, p 116
[34] Al-Khaṣṣāf's *Adab al-Qāḍī*, I, p 101
[35] Al-Khaṣṣāf's *Adab al-Qāḍī*, I, p 150; for details, see chapter 20
[36] Al-Khaṣṣāf's *Adab al-Qāḍī*, I, p 150
[37] Al-Khaṣṣāf's *Adab al-Qāḍī*, I, pp 110-12
[38] Wakī': *Akhbār al-Quḍāh*, I, pp 79-80
[39] Al-Khaṣṣāf's *Adab al-Qāḍī*, I, p 60
[40] Wakī': *Akhbār al-Quḍāh*, I, p 79-80
[41] Al-Khaṣṣāf's *Adab al-Qāḍī*, I, p 104
[42] Wakī': *Akhbār al-Quḍāh*, I, p 183
[43] Al-Khaṣṣāf's *Adab al-Qāḍī*, I, p 61
[44] Ibn Qayyim: *al-Ṭuruq al-Ḥukmiyya*, p 25
[45] Al-Māwardī, *al-Aḥkām al-Sulṭāniyya*, (Beirut, n.d.), pp 65-75
[46] Al-Ṭabarī, *Tārīkh al-Ṭabarī*, VII, ed Muḥammad Abū al-Faḍl Ibrāhīm (Cairo, 1960-69), p 341
[47] Muḥammad ibn Yūsuf al-Kindī, *Kitāb al-Wulāh wa'l-Quḍāh* (London, 1912) pp 309; 311; 317; 322; 324; 325; 327
[48] In Majid Khadduri and H. J. Liebsny, *Law in the Middle East* (Washington, 1955), p 261
[49] See al-Khaṣṣāf's *Adab al-Qāḍī*, I, chapter 6
[50] Al-Khaṣṣāf's *Adab al-Qāḍī*, I, pp 67-84
[51] Al-Khaṣṣāf's *Adab al-Qāḍī*, I, p 119
[52] 'Ārif al-Nakadī, *al-Qaḍā'* (Damascus, 1922), p 5
[53] Wakī': *Akhbār al-Quḍāh*, II, p 227
[54] Al-Nakadī, *al-Qaḍā' fi'l-Islām*, p 9
[55] Al-Kindī: *Kitāb al-Wulāh*, p 317
[56] Al-Kindī: *Kitāb al-Wulāh*, pp 369; 377; 378
[57] Al-Nakadī, *al-Qaḍā'*, p 9
[58] Al-Khaṣṣāf's *Adab al-Qāḍī*, I, p 106
[59] Al-Kindī: *Kitāb al-Wulāh*, p 469
[60] Abū'l-Faraj al-Iṣfahānī, *Kitāb al-Aghānī*, V (Cairo, 1326), p 295; 'Alī ibn Ḥusayn al-Mas'ūdī, *Murūj al-Dhahab wa Ma'ādin al-Jawāhir* VIII (Paris, 1861-77), p 111
[61] Yāqūt al-Ḥamawī, *Irshād al-'Arīb ilā Ma'rifat al-Adīb*, II, ed Margoliouth (Leiden, 1907-25), p 257; al-Iṣfahānī: *Kitāb al-Aghānī*, V, pp 268; 295
[62] Al-Khaṣṣāf's *Adab al-Qāḍī*, I, p 89. For details, see chapter 7, pp 85-104
[63] Al-Khaṣṣāf's *Adab al-Qāḍī*, I, pp 144-8
[64] Al-Khaṣṣāf's *Adab al-Qāḍī*, I, pp 47-66
[65] Al-Khaṣṣāf's *Adab al-Qāḍī*, I, p 63
[66] Al-Khaṣṣāf's *Adab al-Qāḍī*, I, p 64
[67] Al-Khaṣṣāf's *Adab al-Qāḍī*, I, p 68
[68] Al-Kindī: *Kitāb al-Wulāh*, p 392
[69] Al-Kindī: *Kitāb al-Wulāh*, p 392
[70] Al-Kindī: *Kitāb al-Wulāh*, p 310
[71] Al-Khaṣṣāf's *Adab al-Qāḍī*, I, p 90
[72] Al-Kindī: *Kitāb al-Wulāh*, p 437
[73] Muḥammad 'Arnūs, *Tārīkh al-Qaḍā' fi'l-Islām* (Cairo, 1934), p 96
[74] 'Arnūs: *Tārīkh al-Qaḍā'*, p 98
[75] 'Arnūs: *Tārīkh al-Qaḍā'*, p 97
[76] 'Arnūs: *Tārīkh al-Qaḍā'*, p 98
[77] Al-Khaṣṣāf's *Adab al-Qāḍī*, I, pp 91-104

[78] Al-Khaṣṣāf's *Adab al-Qāḍī*, I, p 61
[79] Al-Khaṣṣāf's *Adab al-Qāḍī*, I, p 143
[80] Al-Khaṣṣāf's *Adab al-Qāḍī*, I, p 145
[81] Al-Khaṣṣāf's *Adab al-Qāḍī*, II, p 222
[82] Al-Khaṣṣāf's *Adab al-Qāḍī*, I, pp 142-3
[83] Al-Khaṣṣāf's *Adab al-Qāḍī*, I, p 142
[84] Al-Khaṣṣāf's *Adab al-Qāḍī*, I, pp 142-4
[85] Al-Khaṣṣāf's *Adab al-Qāḍī*, I, p 306
[86] Al-Kindī: *Kitāb al-Wulāh*, p 399
[87] Al-Kindī: *Kitāb al-Wulāh*, p 386
[88] 'Arnūs: *Tārīkh al-Qaḍā'*, p 132, quoting from Ibn Khaldūn's *al-Muqaddima*.
[89] Muḥammad ibn Aḥmad al-Sarakhsī, *al-Mabṣūṭ*, XVI (Cairo, 1906), p 89
[90] Al-Khaṣṣāf's *Adab al-Qāḍī*, I, p 597
[91] Al-Khaṣṣāf's *Adab al-Qāḍī*, I, p 80
[92] Al-Khaṣṣāf's *Adab al-Qāḍī*, I, p 239
[93] Al-Khaṣṣāf's *Adab al-Qāḍī*, I, p 234
[94] Al-Khaṣṣāf's *Adab al-Qāḍī*, I, pp 232-48
[95] Al-Khaṣṣāf's *Adab al-Qāḍī*, I, p 254
[96] Al-Khaṣṣāf's *Adab al-Qāḍī*, I, p 261
[97] Al-Khaṣṣāf's *Adab al-Qāḍī*, I, p 261
[98] Al-Khaṣṣāf's *Adab al-Qāḍī*, I, 254-5
[99] Al-Khaṣṣāf's *Adab al-Qāḍī*, I, p 254
[100] Al-Khaṣṣāf's *Adab al-Qāḍī*, I, p 259
[101] Al-Khaṣṣāf's *Adab al-Qāḍī*, I, p 260
[102] Al-Khaṣṣāf's *Adab al-Qāḍī*, I, pp 248-65
[103] Al-Khaṣṣāf's *Adab al-Qāḍī*, I, pp 61-2
[104] Al-Khaṣṣāf's *Adab al-Qāḍī*, I, pp 62-3
[105] Al-Khaṣṣāf's *Adab al-Qāḍī*, I, pp 66
[106] Al-Khaṣṣāf's *Adab al-Qāḍī*, I, pp 65-6
[107] Al-Khaṣṣāf's *Adab al-Qāḍī*, I, p 66
[108] Al-Khaṣṣāf's *Adab al-Qāḍī*, I, p 66
[109] Al-Khaṣṣāf's *Adab al-Qāḍī*, I, pp 91-2
[110] Al-Khaṣṣāf's *Adab al-Qāḍī*, I, p 92
[111] Al-Khaṣṣāf's *Adab al-Qāḍī*, I, p 92
[112] Al-Khaṣṣāf's *Adab al-Qāḍī*, I, p 92
[113] Al-Khaṣṣāf's *Adab al-Qāḍī*, I, p 95
[114] Al-Khaṣṣāf's *Adab al-Qāḍī*, I, p 101
[115] Al-Khaṣṣāf's *Adab al-Qāḍī*, I, pp 99-100

9

Judicial Training in Islamic Jurisprudence

Hassan Abdul Latif El-Shafei

The judiciary is one of the most important institutions in Muslim society; its concern is with the administration of justice, being the reason why prophets were dispatched and sacred texts revealed:

> *We verily sent Our messengers with clear proofs, and revealed with them the Scripture and the Balance, that mankind might observe right measure.* (Q.57:25)

Islamic law renders it imperative that any Muslim society should consciously support those who are suitably qualified to uphold the office of judge. The Shāfi'ī jurist, al-Qaffāl al-Shāshī (d. 336/948), remarks that the institution of the judiciary is one of the most authoritative religious obligations besides belief in the Almighty Himself. Moreover, it was in this very regard that God established Adam as his deputy (*khalīfa*), and also Dāwūd (David). Indeed, all prophets up to and including Muḥammad were commanded to uphold the office of the judiciary. As the Qur'an says:

> *Lo! We did reveal the Torah, wherein is guidance and a light, by which the Prophets [unto God] judged the Jews and the rabbis and the priests [judged] by such of God's Scripture as they were bidden to observe, and thereunto were they witnesses.* [...] *So judge between them by that which God hath revealed, and follow not their desires away from the truth which have come unto thee.* (Q.5:44-8)

Thus the act of governing righteously sustains the ethos of Islamic justice; moreover, in the Islamic tradition, the very heavens and earth were erected on the principle of justice.

Islamic law stipulates that the office of the judiciary is a collective obligation (*farḍ kifāya*); furthermore, the neglect of such an office places the body of Muslims in a state of sin, as they are enjoined to support this office, or to support those who endeavour to maintain it. In his *Nayl al-Awṭār*,[1] the jurist al-Shawkānī (d. 1255/1839) includes a chapter on 'The Necessity of Establishing the Office of the Judiciary and General Governance'. Moreover, he adduces two prophetic traditions which underline the importance of such an office, confirming that it is both valid and desirable, even within the context of small and brief gatherings. The first of these traditions, cited by Aḥmad ibn Ḥanbal, is transmitted on the authority of 'Abd Allāh ibn 'Amr, and recalls that the Prophet Muḥammad said: 'It is not permissible for a party of three men in open country to remain without a designated leader; they should elect from amongst themselves a figure to take charge of their affairs.'

The second tradition was narrated by Abū Dāwūd, on the authority of Abū Sa'īd, and reports that the Prophet said: 'If three men embark on a journey, then they should elect from themselves a leader.' A similar tradition is reported by Abū Hurayra. Al-Shawkānī comments that if such a state of affairs is pertinent to 'three men in open country' or 'on a journey', then it is so much more crucial for greater numbers of people who dwell in places such as villages and cities, where the populace requires assistance in dealing with injustices and disputes. The wisdom of these two traditions perhaps intimates the need to adjust and accept a measure of obedience within the system of Muslim society.[2] The Andalusian jurist al-Shāṭibī (d. 790/1388) reports in his *al-Muwāfaqāt fī Uṣūl al-Sharī'a*[3] that legislative responsibility is deemed a collective obligation, and that 'all are required to contribute in their own way to its maintenance; for there are those who are absolutely capable of establishing it, whilst those who are not in such a position are required to sustain those who are'.[4]

The appointment of a judge is based upon a distinct contract between the person possessing overall authority within the state (or his delegated representative), and the candidate aspiring to the position of judge. Furthermore, the contract's specific aim should be to protect the interests of the individual along with those of the collective, additionally upholding the objectives of Islamic law. The jurists call this form of contract the 'Pledge' or 'Oath of Office', and they insist that such a pledge be proclaimed before the general public. Indeed, a Prophetic precedent is cited in this respect: the Prophet dictated an extended letter to al-'Alā' ibn al-Hadramī, whom he had appointed as judge to the people of Bahrain, stating:

> This is the letter from Muḥammad ibn 'Abd Allāh, the illiterate Prophet of the Hāshimī clan of Quraysh, the Messenger of God and his Prophet for all of mankind, to al-'Alā' ibn al-Hadramī and those of the Muslims with him. This is an oath which I ask you to honour: fear the Almighty to the best of your ability. I have dispatched al-'Alā' ibn al-Hadramī and told him to fear the Almighty, He who has no partner, and to show grace towards you, and to be principled in his general conduct amongst you. Likewise, I have asked him to impose the legal code of the revealed Book of the Almighty God in respect of you and others whom he comes across.[5]

Similar instructions were issued to 'Amr ibn Ḥazm when the Prophet dispatched him as a judge to Yemen. The view expressed by a number of commentators – that it was in the "Abbasid period that judges were first appointed by the caliph, governor or his deputy, and that Abū Ja'far al-Manṣūr was the first to create the precedent of judicial appointments in the garrison towns – is a view which requires revision. This comes particularly in the light of the aforementioned texts and other documents emanating from the age of the Prophet, and from the age of the first four Rightly-Guided Caliphs.

The Precepts of Knowledge and Honesty

Knowledge and honesty are the foundations upon which the appointment of a judge rests, in accordance with the command of the Almighty. As the Qur'an states:

> *Lo! God commandeth you that ye restore deposits to their owners, and if ye judge between mankind that ye judge justly.* (Q.4:58)

Ibn Taymiyya remarks in respect of this verse:

> Those who are in charge of the affairs of the Muslims must strive to place in positions of responsibility persons able to fulfil such duties; moreover, no one person should be offered a position on the basis of his own desire to hold such a post, even if such a desire has been expressed previously; furthermore, such a desire should exclude him from being appointed.[6]

He also cites a tradition narrated by al-Ḥākim in his *Ṣaḥīḥ*:

> Whosoever is in a position of authority [regarding] the affairs of the Muslims, and uses this position to appoint an unsuitable person,

> knowing that there is someone more deserving of the position, indeed, he has betrayed the Almighty, his Prophet, and the believers.

Ibn Taymiyya then adds:

> ...being aware of this fact, it is imperative that he make use of the finest available in commissioning appointments. If one finds that those available are not suitable for certain positions, a process of elimination should follow, whereby the persons most suitable are nominated for the various positions. Indeed, nomination is based on two foundations: power and trust. Power is represented accordingly in the following: the conduct of war which emanates from bravery and an experience of waging war; whilst in relation to government, power stems from an understanding of justice and an ability to execute the rules of law. Trust stems from the fear of God.[7]

The precepts of knowledge and honesty are axiomatic in relation to all aspects of the executive of the Sharīʿa, including positions within the social sphere. However, the distinct and designated function of Sharīʿa is the protection of human life, honour, wealth, and so on. This predicates that it is essential to take into account suitability for office and, furthermore, to ensure that the level of competence necessary for the carrying out of this office is met by aspiring candidates. It is the opinion of both early and contemporary scholars that the aforementioned preliminaries relate to two factors: first, an understanding of the legal and judicial order; second, an appreciation of the pragmatics of circumstances to which the whole legal apparatus is applied. Let us consider the words of Jamīl al-Basyūnī, a veteran civil Egyptian judge, who said:

> The average level expected by jurists of a judge is that he should have an understanding of general law and similarly an understanding of peoples' circumstances. This is recognized by jurists of the conventional system of law with its two related components, precedents and law, moreover [it is recognized by] the actuality of case law and that of the actual executive of the judiciary. Ibn Qayyim [al-Jawziyya], in his *Iʿlām al-Muwaqqiʿīn,* states the following: 'In order to rule judiciously, a judge must possess two forms of understanding: a recondite understanding of the pragmatic situation, deduced from specific contexts, directives and general indicators, thereby providing him with an excellent grasp of the matter. Second, he requires a thorough knowledge of what is

obligated by the stipulated texts of the Qur'an or, indeed, Prophetic practice in respect of such matters; the two should be complementary. Therefore, the scholar should be able to attain, recognizing clearly the actualities of a given case, the appropriate ruling of the Almighty and his Prophet, in the same way that the witness reflecting upon the torn shirt of the Prophet Yūsuf [Joseph] was able to deduce that he was both innocent and telling the truth. Similarly, Sulaymān [Solomon] was able, by virtue of his statement "bring me a knife, that I may literally split the child between you", to discern the real mother.'[8]

Al-Basyūnī then moves on to show the importance of honesty and probity in the execution of judicial functions, owing to the highly precarious nature of the judge's position.[9]

On the subjects of knowledge and honesty, the Prophet Muḥammad is reported to have said:

> Judges are of three types: two in hell, and one in heaven. There is he who knows that which is right and judges accordingly: he is in heaven. Then there is .he who provides judgements based on ignorance for his fellow man: his abode is hell. Finally, there is he who knows what is right in relation to judgements but transgresses therein: his abode is hell.[10]

This *ḥadīth*, as observed by one commentator:

> ...takes into account competence on the level of knowledge and piety. Hence, the pious person who is seemingly ignorant is unsuitable for the positions associated with the judiciary: it is prohibited for him to either accept or seek an appointment. Similarly, the impious scholar is also unsuitable: he should neither accept nor seek such an appointment. Moreover, this is the reason why both are condemned to hell.[11]

Another tradition, related on the authority of Abū Hurayra, and transmitted by Aḥmad, Abū Dāwūd, Ibn Māja and al-Ḥākim, states that the Prophet said: 'He who has been assigned as a judge amongst people has been slaughtered without a knife.' Jurists have interpreted this tradition differently, though most have argued that it does not censure the service of the judiciary, but rather stresses the fact that the position is a burdensome one, and that he who takes on the service of such a function is faced with an arduous task analogous to that of a sacrifice. This demonstrates, therefore, that to judge correctly is a virtue, for it is akin to a sacrifice for something just.[12]

As Ibn Farḥūn asserts:

> Many of the scholars from our school and others seemingly exaggerated the consternation one should entertain in accepting judicial appointments; it created the perception amongst numerous jurists and men of piety that he who has accepted such a position has compromised his religion and delivered himself to impending devastation, favouring a state of affairs [i.e. accepting an appointment] to a preferable position [avoiding such a post]. Their view of such a person was negative; however, such a perception is a gross error which requires revision. It is essential to know that all the traditions which accentuate consternation and warning therein relate only to the commission of transgression in legal rulings by scholars or ignorant persons who occupy such positions of trust; it is to these groups that the warnings are addressed.[13]

The prerequisite of knowledge in both the Sharīʿa and actualities is one of the most important obligations in judicial appointments. Such qualities must be obtained through a judge's learning and training, and should also be subject to testing, as argued by al-Mawardī:

> If the aforementioned prerequisites are confirmed in respect of judiciary appointments, it is not permissible for such an appointment to proceed without first confirming that such qualities are possessed by the candidate. This can be achieved through both examination and questioning.[14]

The Shāfiʿīs were particularly stringent in the above respect, insisting that the criterion of *ijtihād* be attained by judicial appointees. The Ḥanafīs, meanwhile, deemed it sufficient for a would-be appointee to be well versed in jurisprudence, and that he should seek counsel on matters in which his knowledge was somewhat lacking. As al-Māwardī states:

> Abū Ḥanīfa permits a person who does not possess the qualities of a *mujtahid* to issue edicts and rulings, and to take up a judicial appointment. The majority of jurists take the view that the appointment of such a person is wrong and, indeed, his legal rulings are rejected.[15]

However, it is the case that later Shāfi'ī jurists took up the position adopted by the Ḥanafīs; they were also joined therein by some Ḥanbalīs, as the aforementioned statement of Ibn Taymiyya indicates. Having spoken at length about the lack of *mujtahids* in his era, the Shāfi'ī Ibn Abī Dam al-Ḥamawī said:

> Taking all this into consideration, it is my view that absolute levels of *ijtihād* or indeed partial levels are specific only to the early period [of Islam], when no province was devoid of groups of *mujtahids* and pious scholars able to issue edicts and proffer judgements. From a contemporary perspective, given the fact that the world is without them [*mujtahids*] and we do not find their kind in our time, it is imperative to state peremptorily that it is acceptable to appoint someone who is acquainted with the teachings of at least one of the prominent schools of jurisprudence, and who is aware of the methods of deduction and the analysis of proofs. Moreover, one has to accept as binding the applicability of his rulings and the validity of following him and taking his legal rulings into account.[16]

There is no disputing the fact that the position adopted by the Ḥanafīs and those in agreement with them is, in principle, more pragmatic. As the Ḥanafī Ibn 'Ābidīn (d. 649/1252) states in his commentary:

> If this jurist is faced with a perplexing legal matter concerning which he has no view, he should consult other scholars and reflect upon their opinions before proffering the ruling he deems to be correct – and nothing else.[17]

Indeed, *ijtihād* stems from the condition of priorities as opposed to that of qualification, as Ibn 'Ābidīn reiterates:

> There must be a bond of trust in relation to a judge's integrity, intellect and suitability. This also extends to his understanding and comprehension of the *sunna*, *āthār*, and the aspects of jurisprudence, for *ijtihād* is a condition of priorities.[18]

This is similar to what was narrated on the authority of Imām Mālik, and some of his companions:

> Ibn Ḥabīb said on the authority of Mālik: 'It is essential that the judge be both knowledgeable and intelligent.' Ibn Ḥabīb added: 'In the event that he is not a person of knowledge, then he should show

intelligence and piety, for the latter quality will restrain him and the former will allow him to query. If he truly seeks knowledge, then he will find it; but intelligence is not a quality that he can seek.'[19]

In general, Islamic law stipulates an appropriate level of experience in a given profession, and a sense of duty in performing the functions one associates with that profession. Accordingly, one finds extreme caution in the legal heritage of Islam towards the uneducated doctor or the jesting jurist, owing to the dangers they represent to the human anatomy and the realm of religion respectively.[20]

Qaḍā'* and *Ḥukm

Having concluded the above, let us now examine the related terms *qaḍā* (ruling), and *ḥukm* (judgement), both of which are functions of the judiciary, as they are found in the Holy Qur'an. This latter term appears frequently in the sources of Islamic law, and in the compilations on jurisprudence as a synonym of *qaḍā'* and its cognates. I have relied here upon 'Abd al-Bāqī's concordance of the words of the Qur'an, and have attempted to categorize the selected passages of the Qur'an relating to these forms.

Regarding the form *qaḍā'*: the root (*qāf / ḍād / yā'*) occurs 63 times in the Qur'an. Furthermore, its meaning generally centres around notions of notification, decreeing, completion, conclusion and culmination. These meanings occur in detail as follows: denoting culmination and completion, having concluded something; denoting notification and divulgence; denoting God's decree and ruling in respect of the world or his laws; and denoting decision and ruling not by God, but of a legal or related context.

Regarding the form *ḥukm*: the root (*ḥā' / kāf / mīm*) occurs 209 times in the Qur'an. It principally means 'the process of making decisions or rulings for mankind', and it can occasionally denote the following two meanings: mediation and arbitration. Its main meaning occurs in forms of address, such as the Almighty's determining the affairs of his bondsmen in the hereafter, or the Almighty's determining the affairs of his bondsmen in this world. It also describes the implementation of God's just rule of law in this world, and describes the implementation of God's rule of law by prophets and their followers. It is also used to refer to those who do not implement God's rule of law. It can denote fine conduct and eloquent speech, and can denote precision and perfection. It can simultaneously convey all three aspects: determining, fine conduct and eloquent speech, in which it is used to describe the Almighty, the authority of a wise one, or the Holy Qur'an.

In short, the words *qaḍā'* and *ḥukm* as they occur in the Qur'an denote 'ruling' and 'decision' amongst mankind. They describe the Almighty or his rule of law as sent down to messengers; those who implement this rule; the institution of rule amongst mankind; and a condensed set of semantic values (particularly in relation to testimony, proof, justice, breach, punishment, disobedience, obedience, rule of law and community). They distinctly confirm the genuine nature of the legal framework of Islamic law and its significance therein, according a distinguished status to its advocates, who should in turn possess an appropriate competence reflecting this distinguished status. This is something the Islamic community has safeguarded keenly since the days of the Prophet.

The Etiquette of Judges and the Qur'an

A particular branch of the Islamic legal heritage is *adab al-qāḍī* (the judge's etiquette, the protocol of the judiciary or, in today's terminology, the training of judges). *Adab al-qāḍī* arms the judge with an understanding of the specifics of jurisprudence, the practicalities of law and the formats for verification. It also relates to the conventions of office, which protect both the reverence and independence a judge should enjoy, and the requirements of administering the office in respect of support staff such as counsel; legal representatives; clerks; litigants; attendants; character witnesses; plaintiffs; litigants; accountants; police; lawyers; interlocutors; arbitrators; specialists in the division of inheritance; those holding trusts; translators; ushers; those responsible for guarding the rights of orphans; and other positions associated with the function of judges and the judiciary. Indeed, some researchers have suggested that there are approximately twenty separate professions designed to work alongside the judiciary, and which operate under its guidelines.

The majority of jurists relate *adab al-qāḍī* to the Qur'an itself, particularly in relation to the text's references to previous prophets, especially the Prophets Dāwūd and Sulaymān, who are noted for their prudent judgements between litigants and wise counsel, and, of course, its references to the Prophet Muḥammad. The most prominent example cited in this respect relates to the Qur'anic story of the angels who appeared before Dāwūd, as recounted in *Sūrat Ṣād*:[21]

> *And hath the story of the litigants come unto thee? How they climbed the wall into the royal chamber! How they burst in upon Dāwūd, and he was afraid of them! They said: Be not afraid!* [*We are*] *two litigants, one of whom hath wronged the other, therefore judge aright between us; be not unjust; and show us the fair way.*
>
> *Lo! This my brother hath ninety and nine ewes while I had one ewe, and he said: Entrust it to me, and he conquered me in speech.*
>
> [*Dāwūd*] *said: He hath wronged thee in demanding thine ewe in addition to his ewes, and lo! many partners oppress one another, save such as believe and do good works, and they are few.*

> *And Dāwūd guessed that we had tried him, and he sought forgiveness of his Lord, and he bowed himself and fell down prostrate and repented. So we forgave him that; and lo! he had access to Our presence and a happy journey's end.* [*And it was said unto him*]*: O Dāwūd! Lo! We have sent thee as a viceroy in the earth; therefore judge aright between mankind, and follow not desire that it beguile thee from the way of God. Lo! those who wander from the way of God have an awful doom, forasmuch as they forgot the Day of Reckoning.* (Q.38:21-6)

A number of commentators note that the incident which occurred between the angels and Dāwūd suggests a personal exhortation to this prophet, as he was allegedly inclined to take Uriah's wife, by dispatching him to war in the hope that he would not return. Moreover, this rendition shows the influence of some old reports, well known within the stock of Islamic heritage as *isrā'īliyyāt*. As many commentators have emphasized, when Dāwūd realized the significance of the angels' visitation, he 'fell down prostrate and repented'.

By contrast, a number of classical and contemporary exegetes have rejected this interpretation, historically and objectively. They believe that there is a general, rather than a specific, significance to this story: namely, it contains a warning against a procedural error which a judge might commit in a given case, when an equitable ruling appears obvious, and this obscures his taking into account other aspects of the case. From the above example, we see that Dāwūd failed to consider the testimony of the second brother, and the proofs or doubts therein that he might adduce. Thus, the lesson in this applies specifically to judges and rulers, who should not omit listening to both litigants, and should treat them equally in all respects.

It is true that Islamic jurisprudence determines that the precedents created by previous divine laws remain effective unless abrogated by our own legislature. This previous prophetic experience is an example, for our corpus of laws also affirms these precedents. This also pre-eminently confirms that the prophets are infallible, and are models of excellence for mankind; moreover, to taint their characters is like poisoning a well or a source of water: one might call this environmental pollution, but in the case of the former it is pollution on a spiritual and moral plane. Hence, one finds a report narrated on the authority of 'Alī, stating: 'Whosoever speaks of the affair of Dāwūd as told by story tellers, I will whip them 160 lashes', being the penalty imposed for besmirching prophets.

A second Qur'anic example is also cited regularly in the literature on *adab al-qāḍī*, and also relates to Dāwūd and his son, Sulaymān:

> *And David and Solomon, when they gave judgement concerning the field, when people's sheep had strayed and browsed therein by night; and We were witnesses to their judgement. And we made Solomon understand [the case]; and unto each of them We gave judgement and knowledge. And We subdued the hills and the birds to hymn [His] praise along with David. We were the doers [thereof]*. (Q.21:78-9)

Interpreters have said that this field was a vineyard or flourishing crop that had been spoiled by the sheep. Dāwūd ruled that the sheep should be awarded to the vineyard's owner, whereas Sulaymān said: 'It is something other than this, O Prophet of God.' Dāwūd asked: 'What is that?' So Sulaymān said: 'You should give the sheep to the owner of the vineyard, so that he might derive gain from [the sheep] until the vineyard has returned to its earlier state, whereupon the sheep should be returned to their owner.' Dāwūd sanctioned the judgement of Sulaymān and ruled accordingly, and the Almighty praised Sulaymān but did not censure Dāwūd. Thus, if a *mujtahid* applies himself to a case and is right therein, he has two rewards, whereas if he is wrong, then he has one reward.[22]

In relation to circumstantial proofs and contingencies, we have already mentioned Ibn Qayyim's reference to the story of how Sulaymān was able to determine the real mother of the child (see note 8 above). One can also mention *Sūrat Yūsuf* in this regard, and how, by virtue of Yūsuf's cloak, Ya'qūb (Jacob) was able to determine the spurious nature of the tale of the wolf:

> *And they came with false blood on his shirt. He said: Nay, but your minds have beguiled you into something. [My course] is comely patience.* (Q.12:18)

Furthermore, a relative of the wife of Azīz deduced that Yūsuf was innocent due to the tear in the rear of his shirt:

> *So when he saw his shirt torn from behind, he said: 'Lo! This is the guile of you women. Lo! The guile of you is very great.'* (Q.12:28)

Moreover, Yūsuf used the presence of the King's goblet in his brother's baggage as a pretext for detaining him:

> *He said: 'God forbid that we should seize save him with whom we found our property; then truly we should be wrong-doers.'* (Q.12:79)

Accordingly, Muslims believe that the stories of the prophets are a lesson and guidance for future generations, as is told at the end *of Sūrat Yūsuf*.

> *In their history verily there is a lesson for men of understanding. It is no invented story but a confirmation of the existing* [*Scripture*] *and a detailed explanation of everything, and a guidance and a mercy for folk who believe.* (Q.12.111)

Our last Qur'anic example here relates to the Prophet Muḥammad, and may be found in *Sūrat al-Nisā'*, wherein the Almighty revealed nine verses, beginning:

> *Lo! We reveal unto thee the Scripture with the truth, that thou mayst judge between mankind by that which God showeth thee. And be not thou a pleader for the treacherous; and seek forgiveness of God. Lo! God is ever Forgiving, Merciful.*
>
> *And plead not on behalf of* [*people*] *who deceive themselves. Lo! God loveth not one who is treacherous and sinful. They seek to hide from men and seek not to hide from God. He is with them when by night they hold discourse displeasing unto Him. God ever surroundeth what they do.*
>
> *Lo! ye are they who pleaded for them in the life of the world. But who will plead with God for them on the Day of Resurrection, or who will then be their defender?*
>
> *Yet whoso doth evil or wrongeth his own soul, then seeketh pardon of God, will find God Forgiving, Merciful. Whoso committeth sin committeth it only against himself. God is ever Knowing, Wise. And whoso commmitteth a delinquency or crime, then throweth* [*the blame*] *thereof upon the innocent, hath hardened himself with falsehood and a flagrant crime.*
>
> *But for the grace of God upon thee* [*Muḥammad*], *and His mercy, and a party of them had resolved to mislead thee, but they will mislead only themselves and they will hurt thee not at all. God revealeth unto thee the Scripture and wisdom, and teacheth thee that which thou knewest not. The grace of God towards thee hath been infinite.* (Q.4:105-13)

This reveals that, no matter how much human effort might be exerted in seeking the truth, it can often be concealed by conspirators; thus, a legitimate claim might almost be forfeited if a judge fails to be oblivious to those who insidiously seek to influence him. To give one example, it is reported that one of the hypocrites had stolen a rod and placed it with a Jew. Moreover, this hypocrite and his fellow tribesmen tried to falsely accuse this innocent Jew, who was seemingly implicated by circumstantial evidence. However, it was divine inspiration which absolved him of any blame, through the clear articulation of scripture.

The Judiciary in the Age of the Prophet

During this period, it was the Prophet himself who was responsible for legal affairs in Medina, at the heart of the Islamic state. He appointed judges and sent them to the Islamic provinces, in order that they may carry out this critical legal function.[23] Some of the Prophet's Companions were given the responsibility of issuing legal rulings and edicts in his presence, as a form of training, and there are many examples of this. As Ibn Qayyim mentions:

> Those on whose authority legal edicts are preserved amongst the Companions of the Prophet (peace be upon him) number around 130, including men and women, although there are seven prominent figures in this respect: ʿUmar ibn al-Khaṭṭāb, ʿAlī ibn Abī Ṭālib, ʿAbd Allāh ibn Masʿūd, ʿĀ'isha, Zayd ibn Thābit, ʿAbd Allāh ibn ʿAbbās, and ʿAbd Allāh ibn ʿUmar.[24]

Some of these mentioned, and others among the Prophet's Companions, performed judicial functions in Medina or in the provinces. Abū Dāwūd reports that ʿAlī ibn Abī Ṭālib said:

> The Prophet sent me as a judge to Yemen, and I said: 'O Prophet of God, you send me for this purpose, but I am inexperienced and young with no experience of the judiciary.' The Prophet said: 'Verily the Almighty will guide your heart and make your tongue firm; moreover, when two litigants sit before your presence, do not make a judgement until you listen to both of them; in that appropriate fashion the correct judgement will become obvious.'

Muʿādh was also sent by the Prophet as a judge and, in a well-known tradition, the Prophet asked him about the basis for his legal rulings. Muʿādh replied that the Book of the Almighty, the Prophetic *sunna*, and, failing these, personal opinion, would form the basis of his rulings. This was a form of training and teaching on the part of the Prophet, just as we find in his dialogue with ʿAlī in the previous example. In the case of Muʿādh, the issue was one of objectivity; however, in the case of ʿAlī, the issue was one of procedure.[25]

ʿAmr ibn Ḥazm was also sent by the Prophet to Yemen, as was Abū Mūsā al-Ashʿarī, who was subsequently employed by ʿUmar as Judge of Basra. Then there is al-ʿAlā' al-Hadramī who, as we have seen, received separate written dispatches counselling him and the people of Bahrain to espouse good conduct. Finally, there was ʿItāb ibn Asyad, who was sent by the Prophet to act as a judge for the people of Mecca following its conquest.

Despite the contrary views taken by some orientalists, a number of researchers have noted that those who were entrusted by the Prophet to carry out the office of judgeship, whether in his own presence or in the garrison towns, numbered around fifteen Companions. The following are additional examples:

> On the authority of 'Uqba ibn 'Âmir, who said: 'Two litigants came to the Prophet, whereupon he said to me: "'Uqba, rise and give judgement between them." I remarked: "The prerogative therein is surely yours." He said: "Indeed it is, but never mind, pass judgement between them, for if you apply your intellectual faculty therein and you are accurate, you will be rewarded ten times; however, if having applied your faculty therein, your judgement proves to be incorrect, then you will receive a single reward."'

> On the authority of Ma'qal ibn Yasār, who said: 'The Prophet ordered me to act as a judge between my people. I said: "What is the essence of ruling [*qaḍā*]?" He said: "Show resolve in your decree amongst them, for the Almighty (exalted and blessed is he) is on the side of the judge, as long as he does not deliberately commission an injustice."'

This is how the Prophet taught and instilled understanding into many of his Companions; furthermore, his tutelage did not stop there: he personally supervised their training in the etiquette of juridical practice.

The Judiciary in the Age of the Rightly-Guided Caliphs

The Caliph Abū Bakr appointed 'Umar al-Khaṭṭāb as judge, therefore he was the first judge to be appointed since the Prophet's time. For an entire year, however, not a single legal case was brought to 'Umar's attention in Medina. The articulated view that 'Umar was the first person to institute the nomination of judges in Islam should not be taken at face value, as we have noted that the Prophet nominated judges in his own lifetime, and this was also true of Abū Bakr. This probably suggests that, whilst in Medina, the Prophet and those after him did not appoint a permanent judge.

Abū Bakr used the explicit texts of the Qur'an and the *sunna* when forming his own legal judgements; otherwise, he would bring together the finest amongst his contemporaries and consult them. It is reported that he sent Anas as a judge to Bahrain and wrote a contract for that; he also sealed the contract with the seal of the Prophet Muḥammad.

As regards 'Umar, he appointed Abū Mūsā judge of Basra, sending his famous dispatch, which some consider to be the 'constitution of the judiciary' for ensuing periods. Moreover, Ibn Qayyim built upon this in his famous composition, *I'lām al-Muwaqqi'īn.* It is also narrated that Ḥāritha said: "Umar wrote to the people of Kufa, stating: "Verily, I have sent to you 'Ammār as a leader and Ibn Mas'ūd as your judge and adjutant; listen to them and obey them, for I have favoured you by appointing them.'"

Al-Khaṣṣāf narrates that 'Umar wrote to Mu'ādh ibn Jabal and to Abū 'Ubayda,[26] saying: 'Seek out the men of knowledge, those who are pious amongst you, and use them in the service of the judiciary, showing them generosity in respect of payments.' During the last years of his life, 'Umar appointed Yazīd ibn Ukht Numayr as a judge in Medina, and said to him: 'Take responsibility for some affairs for me: take care of those affairs of people which relate to the simple matter of one or two *dirhams*.' He also appointed the celebrated Shurayḥ as Judge of Kufa. The latter reportedly said: 'When 'Umar awarded me the office of judgeship, he stipulated that I should neither sell nor buy; nor should I accept bribes, nor submit a ruling whilst angry.' Thus, during the time of 'Umar, the office of judgeship acquired a greater sense of authority and independence, as well as financial and administrative organization. Furthermore, its office accumulated a wealth of experience, as the letter of 'Umar to Abū Mūsā indicates.

'Alī ibn Abī Tālib was one of the most prominent of the Prophet's judges; his statement 'the best-versed in *qaḍā'* is 'Alī', is testimony to that fact. 'Alī was known to have excelled in dealing with complex legal matters and citing juridical rulings. He also appointed Shurayḥ as judge, and awarded him a salary of five hundred *dirhams* per month. Furthermore, 'Alī was active in rising to the challenge of legislative issues, despite the fact that his era witnessed intense internal strife and instability.

In the ensuing periods, as a result of greater stability and advances in civilization and thought, the office of the judiciary enjoyed an increased level of systematisation, and accumulated wider experience and awareness. What is more, a real transformation occurred during the period of codification, which, as will be discussed below, was the period during which the training of judges and their preparing for office become an independent branch of learning within the family of the juristic sciences.

The Judiciary in the Age of Legal Codification

It was during this period that the schools and traditions of jurisprudence (*madhāhib*) crystallized. Furthermore, the codification of Islamic law took an enormous step forward, in all of its aspects, and from within this framework emerged the specific discipline of *adab al-qāḍī*.

It would appear that the Ḥanafīs were the first to produce treatises on this branch of the sciences of jurisprudence, in particular the companion of Abū Ḥanīfa, Abū Yūsuf (d. 182/798), the judge appointed by Caliph Harūn al-Rashīd. The science matured and was developed by many amongst the classes of jurists. It was also the case that the jurists excelled in establishing the field of legal maxims; indeed, it developed as a separate discipline particularly through the efforts of several Shāfiʿī scholars. Unfortunately, the work of Abū Yūsuf is no longer extant, nor is that of his pupil, Ibn Samāʿa (d. 233/848), a judge in Baghdād during the reign of al-Ma'mūn, and a distinguished scholar amongst the Ḥanafīs.

The oldest work on the subject of *adab al-qāḍī* that is known to have survived is that of Abū Bakr ibn al-Khaṣṣāf (d. 261/874), which was carefully drawn out from a commentary of the great Ḥanafī jurist Abū Bakr al-Jassās (d. 370/981).[27] This particular commentary by al-Jassās is one of ten on this text prepared by principal Ḥanafī jurists; the most outstanding of these is perhaps that of al-Ḥuṣām al-Shahīd (d. 536/1142). In addition to these commentaries, other Ḥanafīs also pursued scholarship in this area, hence the works of al-Ṭahāwī (d. 321/933) and al-Qudduri (d. 428/1042). One of the latest works on this topic was that of Badr al-Dīn ibn al-Fars (d. 932/1522), entitled *al-Fawākih al-Badriyya*.[28]

The Shāfiʿīs also made significant contributions to the development of the *adab al-qāḍī* genre, just as they had developed the field of legal maxims. Notably, in his appendix to al-Ḥamawī's *Adab al-Qāḍī*, Muṣṭafā al-Zuhaylī cites twenty-five works on this subject, produced by Shāfiʿī scholars. The most significant of these were those texts entitled *Adab al-Qāḍī* written by al-Imām al- Shāfiʿī (d. 204/820), al-Qāsim ibn Sallām (d. 224/839), Ibn al-Ḥaddād al-Miṣrī (d. 354/965), al-Māwardī (d. 450/1058), and al-Suyūṭī (d. 911/1505). But perhaps the most distinguished of these works is that of Ibn Abī Dam al-Ḥamāwī, mentioned above.

The first Mālikī scholars to write in this field included Aṣbagh ibn al-Farraj (d.225/840), followed by Ibn Shabtūn al-Lakhmī (d. 312/924); al-Qāḍī ʿIyāḍ (d. 554/1159); and Ibn Farḥūn (d. 799/1397), whose book *Tabṣirat al-Aḥkām*[29] is one of the most useful works in this field. Indeed, the Ḥanafī scholar al-Tarāblisī depended upon this earlier work in his own composition, *Muʿīn al-Ḥukkām*.[30] While the Mālikīs continued to produce useful works in this field, in comparison with the previous two schools, their works are fewer.

Ḥanbalī works in the field of *adab al-qāḍī* are rare. Al-Zuhaylī's appendix cites only one work, Ibn Qayyim al-Jawziyya's (d. 751/1350) *Ṭuruq al-Ḥukmiyya fi'l-Siyāsa al-Sharʿiyya*,[31] although Ḥanbalī works on jurisprudence do comprise important sections on claims, testimony, rulings and legal judgements. A possible explanation for this phenomenon might be that few Ḥanbalīs were appointed as judges; indeed, it is noted that the majority of those who produced works on the subject of *adab al-qāḍī* were judges, particularly the earlier works.

Scholarship in this field has continued through to this day, although it has evolved to take the name *al-murāfa'āt al-shar'iyya*. The most notable works include those of the Egyptian jurist Aḥmad Ibrāhīm, of whom his student Abū Zahra has said: 'He is the most well-versed of Ḥanafīs after Ibn 'Ābidīn, Muḥammad Ju'ayt al-Tūnisī, and Ḍiyā' al-Dīn al-'Irāqī.' We also find numerous university courses on the procedural aspects of Islamic law and the systems of the judiciary.

In summary, perhaps the most distinguished and invaluable of all the compilations in this field are those of al-Khaṣṣāf the Ḥanafī, Ibn Abī Dam the Shāfi'ī, Ibn Farḥūn the Mālikī, and Ibn Qayyim the Ḥanbalī. These scholarly compositions generally represent the essence of juridical thought in the four traditional schools of jurisprudence, although 'Ibādī, Imāmī and Zaydī jurists have also showed great interest in this discipline as part of their varied juristic endeavours. Furthermore, this also applies to the exponents of Ẓāhirī jurisprudence, whose founder, Dāwūd (d. 270/884) composed a treatise on *adab al-qāḍī* which, unfortunately, is not extant.

The Contemporary Training of Judges

To close, let us turn to the training of judges in the contemporary era. Modern Islamic societies have not neglected the conventions associated with the training of judges prior to their appointment, nor have they relinquished the conventions that follow the appointment of judges to their posts. Visitors to the district of al-'Abbasiyya in Cairo will find the National Institute for the Training of Judges, supervised by one of the assistants of the Egyptian Minister of Justice. In its entrance, one finds an inscription quoting the words of 'Umar ibn al-Khaṭṭāb to Abū Mūsā al-Ash'arī. Aspiring judges receive their training in this institute, along with representatives of the judiciary and the various legal organizations, studying both contemporary legal thought and Islam's ancient legal heritage.

Emulating this pattern, Pakistan has established the National Academy of the Legislature, for the training of judges in harmony with the laws and procedures used in the State of Pakistan. This so-called 'Sharī'a Academy' is a part of The International Islamic University in Islamabad, and is used for the training of Pakistani judges in the practical aspects of newly issued laws derived from Islamic Sharī'a. Similar institutions exist in other Islamic states, the most prominent of these being the Higher Institute of the Judiciary in Riyadh, Saudi Arabia. The emergence and proliferation of such institutions is yet another dimension to the field of *adab al-qāḍī*, which will also benefit from further study.

Notes

[1] Muḥammad ibn 'Alī al-Shawkānī, *Nayl al-Awṭār*, IX (Cairo, 1938), p 1157
[2] Al-Shawkānī: *Nayl al-Awṭār*, p 1157; Ibn Abı Dam al-Ḥamawī, *Adab al-Qāḍī*, ed Muṣṭafā al-Zuhaylī (Damascus, 1975), p 31
[3] Abū Isḥāq Ibrāhīm al-Shāṭibī, *al-Muwāfaqāt fī Uṣūl al-Sharī'a*, 4 Vols (Lebanon, 1991)
[4] Al-Shāṭibī, *al-Muwāfaqāt*, I, pp 128-9
[5] Shams al-Dīn ibn Shihāb al-Dīn al-Ramlī, *Nihāyat al-Muḥtāj ilā Sharḥ al-Minhāj*, III (Cairo, 1938), p 237
[6] Ibn Taymiyya, *al-Siyāsa al-Shar'iyya*(Cairo, nd), p 20
[7] Ibn Taymiyya: *al-Siyāsa al-Shar'iyya*, p 20
[8] Jamīl al-Basyūnī, *Uṣūl al-Ithbāt Shar'an wa Waḍ'an*(Cairo, 1980), p 44
[9] Al-Basyūnī: *Uṣūl al-Ithbāt*, pp 44-6
[10] This is a tradition narrated by the authors of the four *sunan* works and al-Ḥākim, cited in al-Shawkānī, *Nayl al-Awṭār*, IX, p 167
[11] Muḥammad Abū Fāris, *al-Qaḍā' fi'l-Islām* (Amman, 1980), p 19
[12] Abū Fāris, *al-Qaḍā'*, p 22; also al-Shawkānī: *Nayl al-Awṭār*, VIII, p 269
[13] Burhān al-Dīn Ibrāhīm ibn 'Alī ibn Farḥūn, *Tabṣirat al-Ḥukkām fī Uṣūl al-'Aqdiyya wa Manāhij al-Aḥkām*, XVI (Cairo, 1986), p 72
[14] Abu'l-Ḥasan al-Māwardī, *Kitāb al-Aḥkām al-Sulṭāniyya*(Cairo, 1966), p 67
[15] Al- Māwardī, *Kitāb al-Aḥkām*, p 67
[16] Al-Hamawī: *Adab al-Qāḍī*, p 33
[17] Ibn 'Ābidīn, *Ḥāshiyat Radd al-Muḥtār 'alā Durr al-Mukhtār*, IV (Damascus, 1421 AH), p 303
[18] Ibn 'Ābidīn: *Ḥāshiyat Radd*, p 305
[19] Al- Shawkānī: *Nayl al-Awṭār*, IX, p 169
[20] Muḥammad ibn 'Alī al-Tahānāwī, *Kashshāf Iṣṭilāhāt al-Funūn*, II (Lahore, 1993), p 1157
[21] See, for example, al-Hamawī:*Adab al-Qāḍī*, p 33
[22] Al-Hamawī: *Adab al-Qāḍī*, p 58
[23] Abū Fāris: *al-Qaḍā'*, p 192
[24] Ibn Qayyim al-Jawziyya, *I'lām al-Muwaqqi'īn 'an Rabb al-'Ālamīn*, I, ed Muḥammad 'Abd al-Ḥamīd (Beirut, 1987), p 12
[25] Ibn Qayyim: *I'lām al-Muwaqqi'īn*, I, p 202
[26] This may be the governor of Syria.
[27] Al-Khaṣṣāf, *Adab al-Qāḍī*, ed Farḥat Ziyāda (Cairo, 1978)
[28] This work was the subject of a commentary by Muḥammad ibn Ṣāliḥ al-Jārim in 1326 AH, entitled *al-Majānī al-Zahriyya*(Cairo, n.d.)
[29] Ibn Farḥūn, *Tabṣirat al-Ḥukkām fī Uṣūl al-'Aqdiyya wa Manāhij al-Aḥkām*, ed Ṭaha A. R. Sa'd (Cairo, 1986)
[30] Al-Tarāblisī, *Mu'īn al-Ḥukkām* (Cairo, 1300 AH)
[31] Ibn Qayyim al-Jawziyya, *al-Ṭuruq al-Ḥukmiyya fi'l-Siyāsa al-Shar'iyya*(Cairo, 1953)

Biographical Notes

Abdel Haleem, Muhammad
Professor M.A.S. Abdel Haleem, OBE, is King Fahd Professor of Islamic Studies at the University of London. He is the Director of the Centre of Islamic Studies at SOAS and editor of the *Journal of Qur'anic Studies.* He is also Member of the Academy of the Arabic Language, Cairo. His publications include *The Qur'an: A New Translation* (2004, 2005, 2010, 2015) and *Exploring the Qur'an: Context and Impact* (I.B.Tauris, 2017).

Sherif, Adel Omar
Judge Adel Omar Sherif is the Deputy Chief Justice of the Supreme Constitutional Court of Egypt, and Distinguished Visiting Professor of Law at the Dedman School of Law, Southern Methodist University Dallas, USA. He has lectured widely across different universities in Europe and North America. His recent work includes the chapter, 'The Relation between Constitution and Sharīʿa in Egypt', in *Constitutionalism in Islamic Countries: Between Upheaval and Continuity.*

Daniels, Kate
Dr Kate Daniels was Research Administrator at the Centre of Islamic Studies at SOAS. She then joined the Faculty of Asian and Middle Eastern Studies at the University of Cambridge, where she held the Mellon Fellowship in the Modern Middle East. She has held a visiting fellowship at Wolfson College and is a Senior Member of Newnham College, where she acts as Director of Studies in Asian and Middle Eastern Studies and is a Special Supervisor in Arabic.

El-'Awa, Mohamed Selim
Dr Muhammad Selim El-'Awa is an Attorney at Law, scholar and author in Egypt and the Arab countries.

Hussein, Gamil Muhammed

Dr Gamil Muhammad Hussein is an Attorney at Law and Professor and Head of the Public International Law Department. He is the form Former Dean at the School of Law at Banha University, Egypt. His spoke recently on the 'International Legal Implications of Urfi Marriages with Multinational Parties' at the International Symposium on 'The Urfi Marriage: Validity and Implications' Supreme Constitutional Court, Cairo Egypt.

Kamali, Mohammad Hashim

Professor Mohammad Hashim Kamali is the Founding CEO of the International Institute of Advanced Islamic Studies, Malaysia (2007 – continuing). He served as Professor of Islamic Law and Jurisprudence at the International Islamic University Malaysia (IIUM, 1985–2004) and was Dean of the International Institute of Islamic Thought and Civilisation (ISTAC, 2004–2006).

El-Dakkak, M. Shokry

Dr Muhammed Shokry El-Dakkak is Chief Judge of the Court of Appeals in Alexandria, Egypt.

El-Shafei, Hassan Abdul Latif

Professor Hassan Abdul Latif is Professor of Islamic Philosophy at the University of Cairo and President of The Academy of the Arabic Language, Cairo. He is also a member of the Organisation of Senior Ulama al-Azhar.

Ibrahim, Saeed Hasan

His Honour Saeed Hasan Ibrahim is a judge in the courts of the Kingdom of Saudi Arabia and a scholar of Islamic Law.

Mehemeed, Nasir bin Ibrahim

His Honour Nasir bin Ibrahim Mehemeed is a judge in the courts of the Kingdom of Saudi Arabia

Surty, Muhammad Ibrahim H.I.

Dr Muhammad Ibrahim H.I. Surty, now retired, was previously Senior Lecturer of Islamic Studies in the Department of Theology in the University of Birmingham. He is now Chairman of the Qur'anic Arabic Foundation Trust.

Index

abbreviated proceedings, 4
'Abd Allāh al-Zubayrī al-Shāfi'ī, 77
'Abd Allāh ibn 'Umar, 63
'Abd Allāh ibn Abī 'Āmir, 79
'Abd Allāh ibn Mas'ūd, 73
'Abd al-Bāqī, 174
'Abd al-Raḥmān ibn 'Awf, 137
'Abd al-Wahhāb Khallāf, 61, 70
abortion, forced, 133
Abū Bakr, 139, 180
Abū Ja'far al-Manṣūr, 169
Abū Mūsā al-Ash'arī, 179, 180
Abu Sufyān, 70
Abū 'Ubayda, 181
Abū Yūsuf, 63, 79, 113, 138, 181
Abū Zahra, 70
accusation. *See tuhma*
accused. *See* suspects
adab al-qāḍī, 175–78, 181–83
adultery, 37–38, 46–47, 120–22
aggression, 59
ahl al-kitāb, 138
Aḥmad ibn Abi Dāwūd, 155
'Ā'isha bint Abī Bakr, 85
alcohol, 39–40
'Alī ibn Abī Ṭālib, 64, 65, 140, 179, 181
Allah
  rights of, 5, 19, 97
  waging war against, 41
al-Alwani, Taha Jabir, 73, 86, 91
amnesty in *ḥudūd* crimes, 19
'Amr ibn al-'Āṣ, 62, 70
'Amr ibn Ḥazm, 169, 179
'Amr ibn Qays, 158
Anas bin Malik, 180
apostasy, 42
'āqila, 68, 101
Arab states
  criminal procedure in, 11–12
  unjust legal practices, 91
Armenia, 132
arrest, 63, 76-81
Asad, Muhammad, 73
Aṣbagh ibn al-Farraj, 81, 150, 182
'Attāb ibn Asad, 155
attorneys, 50
average accusations, 75
a'wān, 158
'Awda, 'Abd al-Qādir, 69, 104
al-Awza'ī, 68, 139
Badr al-Dīn ibn al-Fars, 182
bail, 159
al-Bājī, 86

al-Balādhurī, 138
banquets, 152
barā'a al-dhimma al-aṣliyya, 65
Barīra, 85, 87
Basil, Emperor of Byzantium, 141
bawwāb, 158
beating the accused, 81
Bilāl, 137
blood money, 68
Bosnia and Herzegovina, 135
boycotting the offender, 105
Bulgaria, 132
burden of proof, 66

caliphate
  judiciary during early era of, 180–81
  role of caliph in judicial system, 13
  role of caliph in *ta'zīr* crimes, 6
capital punishment
  adultery, 38
  for *ta'zīr* crimes, 21
Chief Justice, 157
Christians, 138
circumstantial evidence, 22, 122–27
civil proceedings, 125
claimants, questioning, 162
clerks, 158
community, crimes against, 19
companions, judiciary during era of, 180–81
compensation, 5, 19. *See also diya*
  amount of *diya* for murder, 102–3
  burden of paying *diya*, 101
  for homicide, 100
  for manslaughter, 100
  for miscarriages of justice, 51
confession, 22
  conditions of validity, 66
  as evidence, 112
  level of detail necessary for validity, 114
  limited role of, 117
  obtaining through coercion, 50, 63, 82, 116–17
  retracting, 66, 114–16
confiscation of property, 105
Convention on the Prevention and Punishment of the Crime of Genocide, 131
corporal punishment, 105
Coulson, N. J., 104, 111
counsel, right to, 89-91
courts
  emergence of, 150
  holidays, 156
  hours, 156
  location of, 156
  officials, 157
  organization and function, 153
  procedure, 161–62
  proceedings, 159, 162–63
  registers, 157
  summonses, 160
crime
  against humanity (*See* genocide).
  boycotting the offender, 105
  categories of, 5–6, 18–19
  defined, 5, 17, 29
  defined by legal texts, 69
  forms of, 30
crime (cont.)
  of *ta'zīr*, 20
  proving non-perpetration of, 29
  retracting, ix, 8
criminal justice, 29
criminal proceedings
  initiation and termination of, 4–7

powers of the judge, 18–20
right to counsel, 89-91
role of the victim, 9
under Islamic *Sharīʿa*, 12
cross-examination of witnesses, 9

al-ḍarūriyyāt al-khamsa, 62
Dāwūd, 175–77
Dāwūd al-Ẓāhirī, 68
de Taube, Baron Michel, 141
defence rights, 50
detention, 9, 76–81
analogy with the responsibility of a trustee, 87
deterrents, 30, 115
Deuteronomy, 140
dhimmīs, 138
dignity of the human being, 48, 59
discretionary penalties, 5
dīwān, registers, 157
diya crimes, 43–44
amount of *diya* for murder, 102–3
ʿāqila, 68, 101
awarding *diya*, 19
burden of paying *diya*, 101
defined, 6
fixed punishment, 5
homicide, 100
manslaughter, 100–101
documentation, 157
doorkeepers, 158
doubt, 25–26, 45

Egypt
criminal procedure in, 11
training of judges in, 183
equality before the law, 65
espionage, 35, 49, 91
Ethiopia, 132
ethnic conflict, 135
ethnic minorities, 137–38
European influence on Arab legislation, 11
evidence
access to, 8
circumstantial, 122–27
confession, 112
doubtful, 25
establishing, 22–23
evaluating, 23–24
obtaining illegally, 8
principal forms of, 111
questioning, 162
examination of witnesses, 9
execution, 135
expiation for manslaughter, 100
extremism, 92

fair trial, 49
al-Faraj, Abū ʿAbd Allāh Aṣbagh, 150
Farewell Pilgrimage, 82
fines, 105
flogging, 30-31
foreigners, 161
frisking, 73

genocide
Bosnia and Herzegovina, 135
compared to homicide, 134–35
in the Bible, 140
in the Qur'an and Sunna, 138–41
international element of, 133
material element of, 132–33
mental element of, 133
under international law, 131
under Islamic law, 137–38
Ghāmidī, 122
Ghayth ibn Salmān, 158
al-Ghazālī, 81–83
government. *See also* state
accountability of, 65

justice as foundation of, 49
violating a Muslim ruler, 41–42
guilty plea, 4, 63

ḥadd punishment, 18
ḥājib, 158
ḥajj al-wadā', 82
hajr, 105
ḥakam, 149
Ḥamza, 70
Ḥanafī school
adab al-qāḍī, 181–83
on confession of adultery, 113
on definition of an honest witness, 118
on death penalty for *ta'zīr* crimes, 106
on expiation for murder, 101
on forced confession, 116
on imposition of fines, 105
on knowledge of the judge, 128–29
on limits of *ta'zīr* penalties, 72
on preventative detention, 79
on qualifications of a judge, 172–74
on use of destructive weapons, 140
on *wakāla*, 89–91
Ḥanbalī school
adab al-qāḍī, 182
on beating a suspect, 78
on confession of adultery, 113
on definition of an honest witness, 118
on forced confession, 116
on knowledge of the judge, 128-29
on limits of *ta'zīr* penalties, 72
on number of witnesses required, 117
on qualifications of a judge, 172
on *wakāla*, 89
Hārūn al-Rashīd, 63, 157
al-ḥaqq al-ādamī, 89
ḥaqq al-amn, defined, 58
harshness in punishment, 32
Ḥāṭib ibn Abī Balta'a, 84
Herzegovina, 135
highway robbery, viii, 41
ḥirāba, viii, 41
ḥisba, 74
homicide
'āqila, 68
compared to genocide, 134–35
as crime against an individual, 19
manslaughter, 100–101
obligation of the murderer to surrender, 99
pardoning the murderer, 99
penalties for, 98
as a *qiṣāṣ* crime, 44
rights of the heirs of the deceased, 99
homicide (cont.)
sanctity of life, 97
honesty, 169–74
honour, ix, 61
ḥudūd crimes, 37–43
ḥirāba, viii, 41
adultery, 37–38
apostasy, 42
defined, 5, 18
doubt about guilt, 25–26
drinking alcohol, 39–40
meaning of *ḥudūd*, 103
powers of the judge, 19–20
retracting a confession, 114–16
slander, 38–39
theft, 40
violent disobedience, 41–42
ḥukm, 174
human being, dignity of, 48, 59

Ibn Abī Dam al-Ḥamawī, 173
Ibn ʿĀbidīn, 86, 173
Ibn Farḥūn, 66, 85, 86, 172
Ibn Ḥabīb, 173
Ibn Ḥazm al-Ẓāhirī
 on beating the accused, 81
 on confession under coercion, 116
 definition of an honest witness, 118
 on knowledge of the judge, 127-29
 officials in the court of, 158
 on principle of non-liability, 79
Ibn al-Hujayra, 155
Ibn Khaldūn, 65
Ibn Masrūq, Muḥammad, 157
Ibn Masʿūd, 180
Ibn Māza, 157
Ibn al-Qayyim al-Jawziyya
 on beating the accused, 85
 on detaining the accused, 76
 on evaluation evidence, 23
 on imposition of fines, 105
 on judging with direct knowledge of a crime, 27
 on knowledge of the judge, 128
 on proof of guilt, 66
 on qualification of a judge, 170
 on validity of circumstantial evidence, 123–25
Ibn Samāʿa, Muḥammad, 150, 181
Ibn Taymiyya, 23, 66, 126, 169
Ibn Ubayraq, 68
Ibrāhīm, Aḥmad, 182
ijtihād, 22, 172-74
illegally obtained evidence, 8
impartiality, 67
imprisonment, 63–64
 preventative detention, 78–81
 prisoners of war, 140
 without trial, 74
individuals, right of, 98
inheritance, 159
initiating criminal proceedings, 4–7
injury, 19
innocence, presumption of, 45, 48, 65, 115
intention, 139
inter alia, 3
international law, genocide, 131
intimidation, 61
intoxicants, 39–40
ʿĪsā ibn Munkadir, 157
Islamic law. *See Sharīʿa*
Islamic State, 11
 judiciary in the age of the Prophet, 178–80
 position of ethnic minorities in, 137–38
Israel, 140
ʿItāb ibn Asyad, 179

Jews, 138
jilwāz, 158
jināya. *See* crime
judgement, 174–75
judges
 avoiding inculcating witnesses, 67
 direct knowledge of a crime, 26–29, 127–29
 contemporary training of, 183
 criterion of ijtihād, 172–74
 establishing criminal evidence, 22–23
 etiquettes of, 175–78
 evaluating evidence, 23–24
 impartiality, 67
 insignia and dress, 155
 institution of the judiciary, 167
 interpreting penal texts, 24–26

knowledge and honesty, 169–74
miscarriages of justice, 51
office of the *qāḍī*, 153–54
powers in *ḥudūd* and *qiṣāṣ* crimes, 19–20
powers in *ta'zīr* crimes, 21–22, 104
powers of, 18–20
professionalism, 174
qualities of, 151–53, 169–74
questioning claimants, 162
questioning the evidence, 162
reasons for dismissal, 154
role of in criminal proceedings, 4, 7, 9
ruling and judgement, 174
salaries, 155
judiciary
in age of legal codification, 181–83
in the time of the Prophet, 178–80
in the time of the rightly-guided caliphs, 180–81
separation from other state powers, 13
justice
as foundation of governance, 49
impartiality, 67
institution of the judiciary, 167
and punishment, 32
in *ta'zīr* offences, 105

kaffāra, 100
kāhin, 149
Kashmir, 132
kātib, 158
Khālid ibn al-Walīd, 140
al-Khaṣṣāf, Abū Bakr, 150
court arrangements, 156
court hours, 156
court procedure, 161–62
ethical code, 151–53
organization and function of the court, 153
Khaṭīb Faqīh, 155
khazz, 155
kidnapping, viii
knowledge, 169–74

lawyers, 50
Le Bon, Gustave, 141
legal aid, 7
legal codification, 181–83
legal systems compared with *Sharī'a*, 11–12
legal texts, 69
legal trustees, 159
legality, principle of, 35–37, 64–72, 70
legislation in Arab states, 11–12
leniency, 60
life
as an essential value, 62
sanctity of, 61, 97
al-Lu'lu'ī, al-Ḥasan ibn Ziyād, 150

Macedonia, 135
madhāhib, 181-83
maḥāḍir, 157, 162
Mahmassānī, 65
Mā'iz, 113, 122
Mālikī school
adab al-qāḍī, 182
on accusation, 76
on beating a suspect, 78
on beating the accused, 81, 86
on confession obtained under duress, 83
on confession of adultery, 113
on death penalty for *ta'zīr* crimes, 106
on definition of an honest witness, 118

on knowledge of the judge, 128–29
on limits of *ta'zīr* penalties, 72
on number of witnesses required, 117
on qualifications of a judge, 173
on *wakāla*, 89
al-Ma'mūn, 155, 157
manslaughter, 100-101
ma'ṣiya, 71
maṣlaḥa, 88
al-maṣlaḥa al-'āmma, 71
mass killing, 135, 139
Medina, judiciary in, 178–80, 181
minorities, 137-38
miscarriages of justice, 51
Māwardī, 64, 65, 77
mental competence, 69
modern legal systems
compared with *Sharī'a*, 11–12, 104
in present-day Muslim countries, 91
Mu'ādh ibn Jabal, 179, 181
al-Mufaḍḍal ibn Faḍāla, 159
muḥtasib, 4, 7
Mujāhid, 73
mukhaddarāt, 160
Murder. See homicide
Muslim rulers, violating, 42
mutarjim, 159
mutilation, 140
muzakkī, 158

nafaqāt, 154
Nazis, 132
Nigeria, 132
non-combatants, 139
non-liability, principle of, 79
non-retroactivity, principle of, 45
al-Nu'mān ibn Bashīr, 80, 82

oath of condemnation, 123
officials
initiating criminal proceedings, 7

pardon, 99
Pakistan, 183
penal texts, interpreting, 24–26
permissibility as basis of actions, 69
personal safety. *See ḥaqq al-amn*
plea bargaining, 5
Police Commissioners. *See ṣāḥib al-shurṭa*
pre-Islamic Arabia
'āqila, 68
homicide laws, 99
legal procedure in, 149
presumed proof, 23
presumption of innocence, 45, 48, 65, 115
pre-trial procedures, 63
preventive custody, 76, 78–81
principle of legality, 35–37, 64–72, 70
principle of non-liability, 79
principle of non-retroactivity, 45
prisoners, 63–64
prisoners of war, 140
private accusation, 74
professionalism, 174
property, 61
prophets, 176
prosecutors, 4
public accusation, 74
public interest, 71
public trials, 8
punishment
averting, 126
avoiding mistakes, 26
beating the accused, 81
corporal punishment, 106
defined, 29

enforcement of, 32–33
fines and confiscation, 105
forms of, 30
ḥadd, 18
for homicide, 98
ḥudūd crimes, 5
interpreting penal texts, 24–26
and justice, 32
leniency, 60
limits of *ta'zīr* penalties, 72
not applied retroactively, 70
pardoning, 20
perceived harshness of, viii
powers of the judge, 19–20
purpose of, 31
qiṣāṣ crimes, 6
retracting a confession during, 114
ta'zīr crimes, 20–21, 71–72
when there is doubt over guilt, 25–26, 45
without proof of guilt, 66

qaḍā', 174
qadhf, 30, 38–39
qāḍī. *See* judges
qāḍī al-quḍāh, 157
qalansuwa, 155
Al-Qarāfi, 66
qimaṭr, 157
qiṣāṣ crimes, 43–44
amnesty, 19
defined, 6
fixed punishments, 5
homicide, 99
powers of the judge, 19–20
quḍāh. *See* Judges
Qur'an
etiquettes of the judge, 175–78
personal safety, 59
principle of legality in, 36–37
prohibition of genocide, 138–41
style of regarding legal rulings, 98
al-Qurṭubī, 73
Quṭb, Sayyid, 73

Religious Police. *See muḥtasib*
renegades, 42
repentance, 5
responsibility, 70
retaliation, 5, 19. *See also qiṣāṣ*
in pre-Islamic Arabia, 68
for murder, 102
Richard, King, 141
ridda, 42
rights
categories of, 5
to counsel, 89–91
fair trial, 49
of God, 97
of heirs of a murdered person, 99
importance of distinguishing between, 6
of man, 89
personal safety, 59
of prisoners, 63–64
of suspects, 7, 50
of worshippers, 18
rightly-guided caliphs, 180–81
rulings, 174–75
finality of, 10

safety. *See ḥaqq al-amn*
ṣāḥib al-shurṭa, 4, 7
Ṣalāḥ al-Dīn, 141
al-Saleh, 66
sanctity of life, 97
al-Sarakhsī, 83, 152
Saudi Arabia, 12, 102, 183
sawadā', 155

schools of thought, 181–83
secret investigators, 158
secret police, 74
self-defence, 59
Serbs, 135
Shāfi'ī school
  adab al-qāḍī, 182
  on confession of adultery, 113
  on definition of an honest witness, 118
  on expiation for murder, 101
  on limits of *ta'zīr* penalties, 72
  on knowledge of the judge, 128–29
  on qualifications of a judge, 172–74
  on use of destructive weapons, 140
  on *wakāla*, 89
Shāfi'ī, Imam, 27
Shaltūt, Maḥmūd, 68
al-Sha'rānī, 67
Sharī'a
  compared with modern legal systems, 11–12, 104
  crime defined by legal texts, 69
  criminal justice, 29
  emergence of Islamic courts, 150
  equality before the law, 65
  leniency, 60
  life as an essential value, 62
  objectives of, 20
  perceived harshness of punishment, viii
  personal safety, 59
  principle of equality, 137-38
  prohibition of genocide, 138-41
  purpose of criminal punishment, 31
  protection of minorities, 138
  scope of, 4
  spying, 73
Al-Shāṭibī, 81, 87
Shawkānī, 25
al-Shaybānī, Muḥammad ibn al-Ḥasan, 150
Shurayḥ, 155, 158, 181
sijillāt, 157
silent, right to remain, 8, 50
al-Sirḥān, Muḥyī Hilāl, 150
al-siyāsa al-shar'iyya, 22, 77
slander, 38–39
Somalia, 132
spying, 35, 49, 91
state
  limiting power of, 64
  role of in criminal proceedings, 6–7
sterilization, 133
strong accusations, 75
ṣukūk, 154, 157
Sulaym ibn 'Aṭr, 157
Sulaymān, 175–77
sulṭat al-ikhtiyār, 71
sulṭat al-taḥakkum, 71
summonses, 160
suspects, 7
  access to evidence, 8
  accusation (*tuhma*), 72
  beating, 78, 81
  confession under coercion, 63, 116–17
  declining to appear in court, 160–61
  imprisonment of, 63–64, 78–81
  presence of doubt, 25–26
  retracting a confession, 114–16
  rights of, 50
  trial in the absence of, 10, 65
suspicion, 73–76
al-Suwaylim, Fahd, 81
taklīf, 70

tawba, 5
ta'zīr, 5
ta'zīr crimes, 6, 20–21, 44–45
in cases where there is doubt, 26
corporal punishment for, 106
meaning of *ta'zīr*, 104
objectives of, 104
powers of the judge, 21–22 , 71–72, 104
types of punishment, 20
quantitative limits of, 72
violating public interest, 71
tashhīr, 105
ṭaylasān, 155
terminating criminal proceedings, 4–7
terrorism, 41
testimony
as method of establishing evidence, 22
in cases of adultery, 120–22
definition of an honest witness, 117–20
secret investigation of witnesses, 158
theft, viii, 40
Torah, 140
torture, 81
translators, 159
trial, in the absence of the accused, 10, 65
tuhma, 72–76
Tynan, Emile, 153

'udūl, 159
'Umar ibn 'Abd al-'Azīz, 64
'Umar ibn al-Khaṭṭāb
appointment as judge, 180
attitude to punishment without proof, 82-83
on circumstantial evidence for adultery, 124
on confession under fear, 63
fairness of, viii
meeting with officials, 62
payment of judges, 155
unintentional homicide, 68
United Nations, 134, 137
unlawful detention, 9
'Uqba ibn 'Āmir, 180
'Uqūba. See Punishment
'urf, 149
ushers, 158
'Uthmān ibn 'Affān, 155

validity of accusation, 75
victims of crime
heirs of a murdered person, 99
retaliation, 102
right to pardon criminal, 20
role in criminal proceedings, 9
self-defence, 60
victim impact statements, ix
Vietnam, 132
violent disobedience, 41–42
void accusations, 75

wadā'ī', 154
wafiq, 105
wakāla, 89–91, 159
waqfs, 154
war
genocide, 139
prisoners of war, 140
waṣīy, 163
weak accusations, 75
witnesses
in cases of adultery, 120–22
examination of, 9
inculcating, 67
judge as a witness, 26–29
proving inaccuracy of, 29

reviewing probity of, 120
secret investigation of, 158
value of witness statements, 117–20
worshippers
crimes against, 19
non-combatants, 139
wulāh, 13

Yaḥyā ibn Aktham, 155, 158
Ya'qūb, 177
Yāsīn, Ṣiddīqī ibn Muḥammad, 150
Yazīd ibn Ukht Numayr, 181
Yugoslavia, 135
Yūsuf, 123, 177

Ẓāhirī school
on confession of adultery, 113
on definition of an honest witness, 118
on forced confession, 116
on judge's direct knowledge of a case, 27
on testimony of women, 120
on the judge's direct knowledge of a crime, 127–29
ẓann, 73–74
ẓannī proof, 23
Zayd ibn 'Alī, 140
Zaydī school on confession of adultery, 113
ẓulm, 59